GUITAR ARMY

Rock & Revolution with MC5 and The White Panther Party

BY JOHN SINCLAIR

INTRODUCTION BY MICHAEL SIMMONS

PROCESS

Leni, Celia and Sunny Sinclair

GUITAR ARMY *IS DEDICATED*

To my spiritual fathers & brothers:
John Coltrane, Charles Olson, Jack Kerouac,
Malcolm X, Eric Dolphy, Lenny Bruce,
Frantz Fanon, Albert Ayler, Ho Chi Minh,
Che Guevara, Fred Hampton, George Jackson

To our people's martyrs:
Dean Johnson, James Rector, Meredith Hunter,
Diana Oughton, Ted Gold, Terry Robbins,
Sandra Lee Scheuer, Allison Krause, Bill Schroeder,
Jeff Miller, Scott Kabran, Sandy Garland,
Greg Walls, Tony Brown, Alan Wilson,
Jimi Hendrix, Janis Joplin, Sam Melville

To my comrades & their guards
who were murdered by the State of New York
at Attica Prison September 13, 1971

To all the electronic aborigines of the
Rainbow Nation

And more than anything, to my powerful
Rainbow sisters:
Celia-Sanchez Mao, Leni & Marion Sunny Sinclair

with all the love there is in the world

The May 14, 1970 Pulitzer Prize-winning photo by John Paul Filo of 14-year-old runaway Mary Ann Vecchio kneeling over the body of Jeffrey Miller, one of the victims of the Kent State shootings.

you got to
live it not just
say it or

play it that's what this
all
about

—John Sinclair,
Bridgework IV: 1965

Pun and Genie Plamondon, photo by John R. Fulton Jr.

9

TABLE OF CONTENTS

Dennis Thompson of MC5, photo by Leni Sinclair

JOHN SINCLAIR IS FREE

By Michael Simmons

"John Sinclair is a huge lover with masses of curly black hair flowing all over his head and shoulders. John is a mountain of a man. He can fuck twenty times a day and fight like a bear. He and his White Panther brothers and sisters from Ann Arbor, Michigan, are the most alive force in the whole Midwest. They turn on thousands of kids each week to their own beauty and build them into warriors and artists of the new Nation. For this John Sinclair was entrapped into giving two joints of grass to two undercover Pigs. For this some bald-headed judge named Columbo sentenced John Sinclair to nine-and-a-half to ten years in the penitentiary at Jackson, Michigan."
—Abbie Hoffman, *Woodstock Nation*, 1969

In 1969, John Sinclair began serving a sentence of a decade in prison for *giving* a nark two joints. TEN FOR TWO. Sinclair had become a threat to the ruling class because he was exhorting young people to reject the system that had murdered, enslaved and colonized tens of millions of non-Caucasians. He openly called for Revolution to fight greed and bosses and squares. He publicly dreamed of a Utopia where, after the act of profiting from the blood and sweat of others was relegated to the status of antiquated servitude, the human race would evolve beyond the hamster wheel of WORK, KILL, DIE.

Sinclair championed ROCK & ROLL, DOPE AND FUCKING IN THE STREETS. He insisted it was within our power to create a life that celebrated freedom by means of TOTAL ASSAULT ON THE CULTURE. For this, The Man took his freedom away.

"FREE JOHN SINCLAIR!" we screamed in the streets. Abbie screamed it onstage at Woodstock and Pete Townshend of the Who, unaware of who he was or why he was there, booted Abs off the stage. Years later, Pete said he thought Abbie was correct in reminding the hordes that one of ours was rotting in prison.

I was a teenager in 1969 and already a hairy and feral Yippie wombat kicking over NYPD sawhorses at demos to end the war in Vietnam. Surrounded by a society that bred young people for the human being lawnmower of war to support the economy of profit, millions of us were inspired by visionary hipsters like Sinclair and chose to revolt.

Nobody ever walked on the moon until we sent a human there to do it in 1969. Just because we don't all live in space, doesn't mean that the Space Program was foolhardy "idealism." To dig that era is to dig that it was a time WHEN HUMANS FIRST WALKED THE MOON. Everything was possible! Fuck the rules! DEMAND THE IMPOSSIBLE!

But if you desire to walk on the moon, first you gotta get a spaceship.

John Sinclair was a poet who had courage, vision and verve. Among his accomplishments was the co-founding of an Artists Collective (Detroit Artists Workshop); then a Commune (Trans-Love Energies) in Detroit and later Ann Arbor, Michigan; a Revolutionary Political Party (The White Panthers); and ultimately a working Political Party (Rainbow People's Party); the latter in a far-reaching attempt to empower lowly hippies and people of color to work within the system and affect democratic electoral change. He managed Rock & Roll Bands (MC5, The Up, The Rockets, Mitch Ryder & the Detroit Wheels) and wrote for Underground Newspapers (*Fifth Estate, The Sun, The Argus, East Village Other, San Francisco Oracle*). He didn't merely mouth slogans—he did the work.

The Beatles had exposed us to the idea of the rock band as a model for family. If you've seen their second film *Help!* you'll recall the Fab Four's mythical co-living quarters. Myth is important because it allows us to dream beyond the confines of enforced reality and see the possibilities. Sinclair dug. The MC5—a band that's finally achieved the respect they deserve after 35 years—really did live communally (unlike the Beatles) with their sisters and brothers in Trans-Love Energies. The MC5 was Trans-Love was White Panther was Guitar Army.

Not only did John accomplish all of the above, he wrote the manual: *Guitar Army*.

Sinclair was (and remains) a prodigious scribe. Astonishing ideas and poesy flow from the man on a daily basis. Sinclair had a Unified Field Theory of Freakdom. *Guitar Army* is the result of approximately eight years of John's unique synthesis of Black Culture, the improvisation and spontaneity of Jazz, Marxism (Karl and Mao, as well as Groucho, Chico, and Harpo), the Beat Generation, the Total Energy of Rock & Roll, sundry influences such as scribes Charles Olson ("A Foot Is To Kick With"), William S. Burroughs, Ed Sanders and Amiri Baraka, and John's perspective of Prison as Politi-

"It ain't fair / John Sinclair / In the stir for breathin' air."
—John Lennon, "John Sinclair," 1971

cal Prisoner, mad-to-talk fellow freaks (particularly Abbie Hoffman and the Yippies), and the pervasive psychic and spiritual obliteration of psychedelics. OBLITO IN TOTO.

The very phrase *Guitar Army* describes the same phenomenon Abbie dubbed *Woodstock Nation*. We not only had our own culture—music, books, art (including comics and posters), film and video, press, radio—but we had our own look, our own language, and we organized communally. It's difficult to fully relate to contemporary youth how young hippies would trust each other purely on sight. I recall sitting at the Port Authority Bus Terminal/NYC in 1971 and befriending a fellow freak. I asked him to watch my guitar while I took a leak. I knew both he and my Fender Telecaster would still be there when I returned. They were.

In its day, *Guitar Army* fit into our cloth school backpacks with our stash (10 to 20 bucks a lid!), vinyl copies of *Exile On Main Street, Kick Out The Jams*, and *A Love Supreme*, and paperback editions of *Revolution For The Hell Of It, Soul On Ice* and *The Communist Manifesto*. Sometimes we'd remember to pack our schoolbooks as well. Those were different times than young people have experienced since the mid-1970s or so. Shitloads of us kids thought we were in the midst of The Revolution. Not some "brought to you by Hot Topic" fantasy, but the real deal: an irreversible planetary transformation that would bring Peace, Justice, Art, Love and Fun for the rest of eternity.

We were wrong, but one has to recall the circumstances. In our lifetime, we'd witnessed the end of legal racial segregation in our own country. We stood up to the government and demanded that they stop slaughtering Southeast Asians. While they didn't acquiesce quickly or easily, we forced their hand, and even Richard Nixon dubbed himself a "Peace Candidate." We proclaimed our consciousness Our Fucking Business—off-limits to our parents, teachers, cops and politicians. In this spirit and on certain plants and chemicals, we collectively traveled through space and time and were awed by the limitlessness of everything.

We, too, could walk on the moon.

Again, we were wrong, so shoot us (which the authorities did at Kent State and Jackson State in 1970, killing six). The biggest limitation turned out to be ourselves. It was too easy for those of us from white, privileged backgrounds— that is to say, most of us—to hang a hard right on easy street and become our parents. John's thesis of YOUTH AS A CLASS was brilliant but illusory. However, his theory that CYBERNETICS WILL LIBERATE was prescient and is still being played out. The true believers amongst us kept The Dream lit in the underground through the remaining 1970s, up through today. "It ain't over till it's over," said Yogi Berra, a smarter man than neo-conservative Frances Fukuyama, who proclaimed THE END OF HISTORY *before* September 11, 2001.

One of the self-defeating factors amongst post-hippie bohemian movements was the rise of the too-hip. The jaded and ironic and sarcastic and smug and selfish attitude that all that '60s stuff was yesterday's papers and there was no point in challenging anything, much less creating a Revolution. The *fait accompli* of this deadly torpor is that Evil Incarnate is currently in power.

It's more urgent than ever that we fight back, as Malcolm X speechified over 40 years ago, *by any means necessary*. Hopefully, we'll be more savvy this time. Our analysis needs to be more realistic. Just as importantly, we must never, ever surrender. But *Guitar Army* is not about realism per se. It's about THE SINGULAR VALUE OF IDEALISM. We dream of a man walking on the moon, and then we walk.

John Lennon and Yoko Ono joined many rockers, jazz daddies, poets and radicals and played the historic John Sinclair Freedom Rally on Friday, December 10, 1971. Lennon sang a song he'd written for the event called "John Sinclair." The following Monday the Michigan Supreme Court ordered Sinclair released from prison on appeal bond and ruled in favor of John's appeal in March of 1972.

Certainly the Beatle's help was immeasurable, but it was Sinclair's staunch legal challenges and public support that encouraged the Michigan State Legislature to change the marijuana laws one day BEFORE the concert. Sinclair presented the facts that: "1) marijuana is not a narcotic, 2) marijuana was improperly and without foundation classified as a narcotic absent due process of law and 3) 10 years for possession of marijuana is cruel and unusual punishment no matter the amount possessed but particularly with respect to two joints." The legis-

lature bought the arguments, reclassified cannabis from a narcotic to a controlled substance, and reduced the penalty for possession from a 10-year maximum to one year (with a possible 90-day misdemeanor charge for "simple possession") and the penalty for sales or dispensing from a 20-year mandatory minimum and maximum of life to four years maximum. It was a stunning victory thanks to Sinclair's perseverance.

Ultimately John Sinclair is a classic American hero who stood up for what he believed in. He insisted on *practicing* democracy and that's why so much trouble befell him. Thanks to him, marijuana decriminalization subsequently swept the nation like a prairie fire until a senile actor was elected President in 1980, the same year John Lennon was killed. Time thereafter proceeded to move backwards.

After serving two and a half years of the 10-year sentence, Sinclair thereafter proceeded *to live freely*. He organized arts and music festivals. He wrote poetry and performed it live with musicians. He became a revered disc jockey and musicologist. He traveled from Michigan to New Orleans to Amsterdam, where he spends much of his time today. Most importantly, John Sinclair is free and he wants you to know that you are too.

—Michael Simmons,
December 7, 2006
Los Angeles, CA

Kick Out the Jams LP photo session, photo by Emil Bacilla

"Only barbarians are able to rejuvenate a world in the
throes of collapsing civilization"
—Frederick Engels, *The Origin of the Family,
Private Property, and the State*

PREVIEW

"The characteristics of the white rebels which most alarm their elders—the long hair, the new dances, their love for Negro music, their use of marijuana, their mystical attitude toward sex—are also tools of their rebellion. They have turned these tools against the totalitarian fabric of American society—and they mean to change it."

—Eldridge Cleaver, *Soul on Ice*

This book talks about a lot of different things, but mostly it's a book about rock & roll music and the new life-form that's grown up around the music—the rainbow culture is what we call it, and if it is a rainbow then rock & roll is the sun that shines through it and gives it its definition, the energy source that moves the rainbow people and makes them glow and vibrate with new life.

But I shouldn't say "them" because what I mean is "us"—this book was written from inside the rainbow colony, it's a record of that life, and if these writings have any use it's because my own experience is one with that of my rainbow brothers and sisters as we all struggle to survive and grow here inside the belly of the dying Beast of the West.

A guitar army is what we are—a raggedy horde of holy barbarians marching into the future, pushed forward by a powerful blast of sound. "The roaring harmony of need" is what I read once, and it goes beyond even that now. A roaring harmony of being, this song is, rocking & rolling us straight out of our heads and thus out of the West forever, into what I can only call the post-western future. A wholly (holy) new harmony based on post-scarcity economics, communalism, sharing, the international image flash and depth of electronic technology, all crystallized and brought into focus by the magic eye of LSD and the pounding heartbeat of our music, re-sensified at last and ready to move on, as far into the future of humanity as we can go.

So this book is given to the task of defining who we are and what we might be able to do with ourselves as we stumble through the world—and it's also a record of my own progress and the progress of the people I work with toward finding these things out for ourselves. We started out like anyone else does, with very little idea of what we were doing here or what our possibilities might be, and we learned what we learned by making all the mistakes you have to make in order to learn anything. Whatever ideology or theory we've got now we came by the hard way.

I. ROOTS

Individual experience,
because it is national
and because it is a link
in the chain of national existence,

ceases to be individual,
limited
and shrunken
and is enabled

to open out
into the truth
of the nation
and of the world.

　　　　　　　—Franz Fanon
　　　The Wretched of the Earth

I was born in Flint, Michigan on October 2, 1941, and I grew up in the small Amerikan town of Davison, Michigan, where I spent the first 17 years of my life. My father, Jack Sinclair, worked for Buick Motors in Flint for 43 years—he had grown up on a soybean farm in Kinde, Michigan, "The Bean Center of the World," left home hitchhiking for California three days after he finished high school, stopped overnight in Flint on the way and heard they were hiring at Chevrolet, got himself a job carrying water to the men on the assembly line, switched to Buick, worked on the line and attended General Motors Institute at night, worked his way up over the years to a position in the Buick Main Office and retired in 1971 as assistant director of distribution for Opel in the USA.

My mother was born Elsie Dudley Newberry in 1912 in Detroit. Her father, Clyde Newberry, worked in the Dodge Motors factory (his father had been a lumberjack in northern Michigan) until the Depression put him out of work, and he finished out his life as a janitor in the Berkley school system in Berkley, Michigan.

My mother was the first person on both sides of my family to go to college, and she met my father in Flint in 1935 while she was teaching at Fenton High School, and he was working on the line at Buick. They got married in 1936 and five years later, just before I was born, they made a down payment on a small house near Potter's Lake, between Davison and Lapeer, about 13 miles east of Flint, and my mother quit teaching school to raise a family.

I was born in 1941, my sister Kathy in 1943, and my brother David in 1945, at which time my parents moved us all into a little bigger house in Davison, which at the time had a population of maybe 1000 people. I grew up there on Lapeer Street, the last street in town going east, and there were fields and woods out beyond our back yard where all the kids on the block spent a lot of time. They've got subdivisions out there now, of course, but then they've got a big "marijuana problem" in Davison now too, which just goes to show you.

There wasn't anything like that back in the '40s and '50s, though, and I grew up just like everybody else in those places—I had a dog, rode my bike all over town, read plenty comic books, listened to Sky King and the Lone Ranger and the Fat Man and the Shadow and the Green Hornet on the radio every week, went on automobile trips to relatives' houses in Detroit on Sundays with my parents, played cowboys and Indians, cops and robbers, war, doctor and "house" with the other kids on my street, and went to school every day at the only school in town (besides the Catholic school, of course, which my parents, although my father was a Catholic and brought us up in the church, refused to send us to because they didn't believe in segregated schooling of any kind). I made my first communion at seven, went to confession on Saturday nights, to mass on Sunday, ate fish every Friday, and did all the things everybody else did according to the directions in the script.

OK. That would seem to be it, right? I should have grown up and married the girl next door after graduating from college (which my parents saved up for from the day I was born) and then settled down to the mortgage and the car payments and mass every Sunday and a happy little family, if not in Davison, Michigan then in some similarly satisfying Amerikan town in this best of all possible worlds. Except a lot of things I didn't even know about at the time were happening in the world, and things would never be like that again. Harry S. Truman had the atomic bomb dropped on a few million yellow people in Hiroshima and Nagasaki just before I turned four, for example. The People's

Republic of China was established the day before my eighth birthday, two years after the U.S. government authorized the creation of the CIA; and the next year Amerikan troops were sent into Korea to combat the people's forces of the Democratic People's Republic of Korea in a struggle to determine the future of Amerikan imperialism in Asia. Television began to replace the Jack Benny radio and the Vaughn Monroe record player in millions of Amerikan homes (we got our first set in 1952 but I never could get into it too much), the 45 rpm record disc was developed and marketed, and a whole lot of strange shit was starting to go down everywhere you looked.

But I didn't know anything about these strange new forces which were changing the whole course of western civilization, except maybe the spread of the 45 rpm record and the effect it had on the development of a whole new class of people in the USA—the postwar Amerikan rock & roll teenager—and I certainly didn't understand any of it the way I do now. I just turned the radio dial one day sitting in my little bedroom in Davison, Michigan and BOOM! There it was—the music that would turn my whole life around and shoot all of us into a totally new future which is now just beginning to take shape before our eyes.

"We are living proof that life can be different"
—Tom Hayden, *Trial*

"The only way to support a revolution is to make your own."
—Abbie Hoffman, *Woodstock Nation*

Up!, photo by David Fenton

II. First Generation Rock & Roll

"The turning point in the history of western civilization was reached with the invention of the electric guitar."
—Leni Sinclair, 1971

There's no way really for me to describe or do justice to the impact of rock & roll music on the West, except to say that it made all the difference in the world, and don't let anyone try to tell you differently! Rock & roll emerged as a reflection and as an expression of the economic and technological changes taking place in western civilization. It was no accident, it was the precisely perfect manifestation of the tremendous changes going down throughout the western world, and for you to listen right now to "Maybelline" by Chuck Berry, or "Tutti Frutti" by Little Richard would explain what I'm trying to say much better than I ever could—especially when you consider that there had never been any music like that on earth before. I mean the music says it all, it's a precise metaphor for the whole situation and just to hear Richard Penniman scream "Womp-bob-a-loo-momp-a-wompan-bam-boom!" into the face of Dwight D. Eisenhower and John Foster Dulles and the New York Yankees is enough to get the whole rest of the picture.

It was incredible! These dudes opened their mouths to sing and a whole new race of mutants leaped out dancing and screaming into the future, driving fast cars and drinking beer and bouncing around half-naked in the back seats, getting ready to march through the '60s and soar into the '70s like nothing else had ever existed before.

Rock & roll kicked off the 21st century almost 50 years ahead of time—it made the leap from the mechanical to the electronic age in the space of three minutes, 45 revolutions per minute, crystallizing all the new energy generated by the clash between these two monstrous technologies and squeezing it into the most compact possible form, the most explosive (and implosive!) form possible, and then shot that energy out through the radio into every corner of Amerika to retribalize its children and transform them into something essentially and substantially different from the race which had brought them into the world.

Whew! Yeah, it did all this and even more—rock & roll not only reflected but it also created a whole new lifeform on this planet, it was marked but it also created the line of debarkation from the old world to the New, and if you don't understand what I'm getting at just take a listen to, say, Patti Page singing "Mockingbird Hill" or Julius LaRosa or Snooky Lanson, the "popular" western singers pre-rock & roll, and then flip on Elvis Presley wailing "Jailhouse Rock" or "Blue Suede Shoes" or even "Heartbreak Hotel"—it's a whole new world, it's all right there in the music, and Elvis Presley wasn't nothin' compared to Chuck Berry or Little Richard, it was a whole new world which was as different from the old world of our parents as Elvis Presley was from Ed Sullivan, or even Steve Allen, or Richard Nixon and Adlai Stevenson, say, as extremes, or alternatives to each other, and then all of a sudden there was Screamin' Jay Hawkins, Fidel Castro, Billy Riley and his Little Green Men, spreading the spectrum of possibilities all the way over to where we had never been told it could go, and it was just too much for us to believe.

What was even stranger was that it was an outlaw world from the beginning—we could see Elvis on Ed Sullivan, right, but they wouldn't let the camera show him shaking his ass and wriggling his legs. Far out! We were outlaws from the very start, and we knew it and loved it too, even though we didn't understand at the time why it had to be that way. After Elvis made the mass breakthrough we started to find out that it was black people who were making all that beautiful music, and there was definitely supposed to be something wrong with black people, too, although it got increasingly harder for us to figure it out—there couldn't be too much wrong with people who made music like that, especially if it was such absolute genius music and musicians like Little Richard, Fats Domino, Chuck Berry, the Moonglows, Frankie Lyman and the Teenagers, Clyde McPhatter & the Drifters, LaVerne Baker, Ruth Brown, Shep & the Limelites, Little Anthony & the Imperials, Ivory Joe Hunter, what incredible poetry! Otis Willimas & the Charms, Hank Ballard & the Midnighters. The Chord Cats, the Crows, the Ravens, the Flamingoes, the Spaniels, the El Dorados and the Cadillacs, Bo Diddley, Muddy Waters, Howlin' Wolf, Little Walter, Big Maybelle, the Jive Bombers, the Royal Jokers, even such familiar sounding names as Ray Charles and Chuck Willis and Jimmy Reed made such incredible music that we wanted to scream. Tony Allen & the Champs singing "Here comes the night owl, whoo, whoo, walkin' through my front do-oo-or," Larry Williams with "Short Fat Fanny" and "Bony Maroney," the Heartbeats, the Devotions, the Cufflinks with "Guided Missiles," hundred and hundreds of beautiful weird records by unheard-of spaced-out spooks, and we were supposed to ignore all this and do what the principal told us to do?? Are you crazy?? Mickey Mantle was never like this!

These black singers and magic music-makers were the real "freedom riders" of Amerika, but nobody even knew it. They walked right into the bedrooms of middle-class Euro-Amerika and took over, whispering their super-sensual maniac drivel into the ears and orifices of the daughters of Amerika, turning its sons into lust-crazed madmen and fools, breaking down generations and generations of self-denial and desensitivity and completely destroying the sanctity of the Euro-Amerikan home forever—and nobody even knew what was happening! Kids spouted their parents' rehashed racist dogma between verses of "Long Tall Sally" or "Ain't That Loving You Baby" and started to figure out which made the most sense, the Ku Klux Klan or the Cleftones? It was no contest, even though the game went on and on before we realized that it had been over a long time ago. We had been given a spectrum from white to gray, from the Minutemen to Richard P. Nixon, or from Jake La-Motta to Yogi Berra, from Kate Smith to Kay Starr, and all of a sudden there was this whole new world of color our parents had never told us about, there

was a whole new range of possibilities that they didn't even know about, and just because they were so dumb wasn't going to keep us from checking it out, no matter how weird or how silly it sounded to people who thought playing golf, for chrissakes, was the most exciting thing on earth.

Rock & roll was just that, a possibility, a whole new way to go, and we jumped into it like there was nothing else for us to do—and there really wasn't, except to do all the bullshit the old people told us we had to do, and we could see with our own eyes how stupid and jive their plastic trip was. We had seen our parents turned into robots on the job and robots at home, stuck in front of meaningless television sets and bashed over the head with the hard sell hour after hour, day after day, year in and year out, desensitized and eggreaded without even known what was happening to them. We could see this happening, and we could sense what it meant, but all we could do was reject it out of hand with no way of putting into words what we felt at all—we just knew that we didn't want that to happen to us, and we took the first alternative to present itself to us, which was rock & roll music and the whole new world it spoke of.

Because from the beginning rock & roll was also about a whole way of life and not just the music, although the music was certainly the core of that new life in 1954 just as it is today. The music was precise to the feeling we had, just as precise as "Rock Around the Clock" was to the first movie about our culture, Blackboard Jungle, which was about high school kids telling the teachers to fuck off and leave us alone. Daddio! You dig? Leave us alone! We got Billy Haley and the Comets kickin' out the jams, and that's all we need! and that's all we need!

And we had James Dean in *Rebel Without a Cause*, too, in his bad leather and his long hair and his car shooting over the cliff with the door handle caught in the strap on his sleeve and his comb between his teeth—we could dig all that but we knew somehow that they were just trying to scare us with that shit. And we knew that the "without a cause" trip was just a ruse, too, because we knew what the cause was even if the old people couldn't understand it, or wanted to pretend that we were just "going through a stage."

We knew what James Dean was into the movie because we felt the same way, and we had just as much trouble as he did trying to articulate what it was we felt. Our parents wanted us to "straighten up" and go back to the way things were in their day, "as if" nothing had changed (they were always throwing those "ifs" in there), and we knew that was impossible—everything is different now, we kept saying, but they just wouldn't believe us, even though nothing could've been plainer to see. We were living in this new world in which we were the natives (as Margaret Mead had pointed out) and our parents the aliens, although that wasn't how we said it then.

I always have to go back to the music, because the music is finally the cutting edge between the old culture and the new. To our parents music was simply "entertainment," a commodity thrown to them like a scrap or used like aspirin to dull the throbbing pain of their mechanized lives—muzak in the elevator, the dentist's office, the shopping center—Dorothy Collins and Snooky Lanson on "Your Hit Parade" on Saturday night playing out some ridiculous fantasies in the name of Lucky Strikes or some other shit—Hugo Winterhalter and Vaughn Monroe and Matovani oozing out some disastrously innocuous noise and calling it "music," as if they were made out of cotton candy or plastic apple pie—this is what the old people called music and held up to us as something to be taken in and revered, this is what they wanted us to become, this is what they offered us as balm for our jangled nerves, as food for our supersonic appetites and it just didn't make it.

Because we didn't want to be calmed down at all—we wanted to go faster and faster, harder and harder all the time. We were looking for that "anciently heavenly connection to the starry dynamo of night" which Allen Ginsberg was hooked into right then without even knowing he existed, and and the closest we could get to it was Chuck Berry and Little Richard and Billy Riley and his Little Green Men singing the songs of our lives. Fats Domino and Jerry Lee Lewis, and if we wanted anything slower than that it had to be deeper too, Little Anthony & the Imperials, it had to be the Platters or the Flamingoes, and if it had to be the old people's songs they had translated into the language we knew. "Smoke Gets in Your Eyes" by the Platters, "I Only Have Eyes for You" by the Flamingoes, Clyde McPhatter & the Drifters humanizing "White Christmas" and making it ours, because if we weren't a whole new people by then we were sure a whole lot closer to the forbidden niggers of our parents' nightmares than we were to them.

And it worked the other way around too—when they wanted to get next to us they had to translate our music into their language, and if they thought they could fool themselves that way they sure weren't fooling us. We knew what we had to have, and if they thought they could lure us back into Amerika by sticking Pat Boone up there to sing "Tutti Frutti" or "Two Hearts" (really!) and pretend it was all the same they were just whistling a new chorus of "Dixie" and we didn't wanna hear it at all. We had to have that energy, that primal push and thrust in the music which connected up with the drive in our guts and the power under the hoods of our cars crusing up and down the drive-in highways where we did our living in those days—"gotta be rock roll music" is the way Chuck Berry put it, and we couldn't've agreed with him more.

We wanted to do something, we wanted some action, everything was moving faster and faster all the time and we just wanted to keep up with it, and the music would do that for us. We moved as the music moved, and even if it was only back and forth from one drive-in hangout to another and back even, even that was better than sitting at home watching TV, and at least we could be with our own people, our own crazy teenage comrades and not with the old people who thought there was something wrong with us because we listened to Jimmy Reed all the time and never wanted to come home.

Rock & roll was just what we had been waiting for, all right, and we didn't even know it like that. Rock & roll hit us right at the right time, right when we were ready for it, and it was so perfect we didn't even give it a second thought. Rock & roll destroyed history. It caught us coming out of grade school and we thought everything had always been like that. We couldn't get the old people to understand that we were different from them, that we had a life of our own and we were determined to live the way we wanted to, and the same time we couldn't ever understand why they were so uptight either. They kept talking about the past and wanted to drag us back into it, but we didn't have any idea of what they were talking about beyond the certain knowledge in our cells that we couldn't live like them, we had to follow our own way, and if we couldn't articulate what it was we wanted we sure could sense it.

The problem was that there wasn't anything ready for us to move into except the music—we didn't want to live the way they told us we had to live, but there wasn't any alternative available, or at least any alternative which we knew about. The music was driving us, and driving us, and pushing us further and further from the given, but it didn't give us any place to go to, and when the music ended we always had to go back home to our parents' house. We could dance to the music all day and all night, we could drink beer and wine until we were out of our minds, we could drive and drive and talk all that jive—but we always had to go back home, because there was no place for us to go.

That was the deadly part of it, that there wasn't any alternative, but what that meant was that we had to make one for ourselves, and we had to make it out of whole cloth without any pattern except the beat of the music which drove us further and further out of the terminal stasis Amerikan life had become. The higher we got off the music the higher the contradiction between the new culture and the old became until it finally exploded us right out of the '50s into the future we've been shaping for ourselves the past ten years.

You have to understand it that way because that's the way it happened, and it couldn't've been any different. Our culture has developed dialectically, as all living things do, starting from the given and moving step by step into the unknown, making it known and alive and more and more clearly defined.

We didn't know what we were doing, we had no idea of where were going, we had no plan or path to follow—all we knew was that we had to have something different or else we'd go crazy, which is precisely what happened to the rest of the first generation rock & roll people who gave up along the way—they're even crazier than their parents and they've even more convinced that we're the ones who are nuts. But they can't feel any other way—they have to believe in what they settled for or else they flip out right on the spot.

In the beginning—that is, at the end of the '50s, when we started graduating from high school and were thrust out into the "real world" to go it on our own—it was easier than it is now to settle for something less than what was needed, easier to settle for a kind of hybrid existence which sent kids into the factories or the "service" or the kitchen and the supermarket, pretending to be "grown up" but really just extending that peculiar '50s adolescence into one's twenties and thirties, slipping into a new kind of plastic "adulthood" which was different from their parents' but not that different either, because the parents too were becoming increasingly plasticized with the neon times.

What became the norm was like a compromise between rock & roll and Lawrence Welk which was precisely reflected in the popular music of that particular period—Frankie Avalon and Fabian and Bobby Vee. Ricky Nelson and the post-Army Elvis, even Ray Charles and the Drifters started putting strings and shit on their records. Phil Spector creeped onto the scene with his half-assed extravaganzas, and if you went to college it was the Kingston Trio and Dave Brubeck and Peter, Paul and Mary, that is, the westernization of rock & roll into something distinctly less than actual music, into a new muzak that drained all the life out of rock & roll and replaced it with—well, with nothing.

People who had been around earlier—our real ancestors, the flipped-out beatniks and dharma bums of the '40s and '50s—had seen the same thing happen to jazz in the earlier '50s, when the driving new energy of bebop was transmogrified into what they called "west coast jazz," meaning Gerry Mulligan, Chet Baker, Shorty Rogers and other sufficiently weak shit suitable to be spewed out as popular muzak, that is, capable of serving as background music for hip pigs like Peter Gunn and other wimpy television fantasies selling more products and sinking people's lives deeper into the plastic foam of Burger Chef milkshakes and ridiculous furniture kept covered with plastic sheets so it'd always look "new." Because the people who literally control culture in this country always have to suck the life out of any music that threatens to stir people up and turn them against the thrust of profit and manipulation which is the real Amerikan grain—they have to drain out the energy before it informs people totally and moves them to rebel finally and decisively against the creeps who keep them where they want them, that is, keep them in line. And the line is always the one leading to the box-office or the checkout counter, to the time-clock or the teller's cage, where they are always under control.

Rock & roll was driving us out of control, so the control addicts subverted the music and turned it against us before we could get too far out of line—gleaming new white stars replaced the dangerous black rock & roll maniacs of two years back who had been exiled to simple starvation, insanity or jail (Chuck Berry in the penitentiary, Little Richard preaching in a church somewhere in the South, even Jerry Lee Lewis locked up for a while and turned back out "rehabilitated," singing hillbilly songs and not bothering anybody at all), and the music industry moguls could reap the praise of their cronies in the other sectors of the newly-named "military industrial complex" with western civilization saved once more. It might have looked like a close call there for a while, but the barbarian invasion had been safely repelled and it was time for another return to normalcy where profits could be neatly turned and Amerika kept pure and clean for capitalism again.

That's the way it looked anyway, as the first generation rock & roll teenagers lurched out of high school and into the adult world of factories and supermarkets and drudgery with no alternative in sight. We either had to go for that or plunge off into the totally unknown, and there weren't very many of us who managed to get through the next few years without giving up completely on the vision which had come to us through the radio and the record player, pounding into our bodies and our brains and turning us into mutants, strange new carriers of a strange new culture which seemed to lay dormant for five or six years before it finally exploded full-blown onto the stage of history.

Slowly, torturously, cell by cell we were transformed, almost person by person our new peoplehood evolved—the seeds had been planted, the first shoots had bloomed and then been cut back down to the ground, but the kernel of life was there waiting for the sun to burst through again and bring our culture to fruition. We were the natives of the electronic age, and it didn't take much to set us off—a new sound over the radio, new voices from across the sea, new electric chemicals, new syntheses of cultural experience brought into a new focus—any kind of catalyst would do us, because we were ready for

Wayne Kramer of MC5, photo by Leni Sinclair

whatever spark would leap through the gloom to light up the world again, and when it finally came a few years later all hell broke loose.

III. Rock & Roll Revolution

"Rock music must give birth to orgasm and revolution!"
—Jerry Rubin, *Do It!*

It sure did look dark for a while, through those first years of the '60s, but that was only on the surface—an irrepressible ferment was working in the very bowels of the West, and the control addicts in power could keep the lid on only so long before everything exploded in their faces. They had stomped out rock & roll in the land of its origin, sapping it of its power and strength and forcing its followers back into the model that had been created for them before they were born, but there was no way to destroy the rebellious energy it had generated, and the attempted repression only intensified the incredible thrust for total liberation which the music had first given voice to. Within five years from the suppression of Chuck Berry and Little Richard their music was back in power again, carried back into Babylon by the Beatles and the Stones, only this time it was even more dangerous than before—it was really our music now, it was being made by people who were just like us, and it spoke even more clearly of everything that was on our minds.

We are a people which has never existed before in human history, we are a product of historical forces which most of us aren't even aware of, we have been thrust forward onto the stage of history with nothing but our sense to guide us, and it took the music to give definition to what we in fact are, but once we could hear our lives being played back for us by these long-haired missionaries from England ("I Want To Hold Your Hand," "I Can't Get No Satisfaction") we could see that we had only one way to go—and more than that, we could see that some of us were already going that way, and that they wanted to bring us along with them.

That was what the Beatles and the Rolling Stones did—they stood up there in front of the world with their long hair and their guitars and their prototypical alienated stance and said Come on people, we don't haveta stand for these old creeps' shit no more, look how far out we are and we're getting away with it! They told us we had to go to college or get a job, but we ain't goin' for it—we're gonna get high and we're gonna fuck any time we want to and we ain't gonna work on Maggie's farm no more! It's just like we heard Gene & Eunice tell us a long time ago—

"You can do what you wanna do, I don't care,
I dug your conversation and it ain't nowhere!"

Far out! For years kids had been stumbling around in the dark muttering things like this to themselves, scared they were going crazy because it went against everything they'd always been taught, and now there were these maniacs on the radio shouting it out for everyone to hear—I CAN'T GET NO SATIFACTION! I FEEL JUST LIKE JESSE JAMES! HELP! THE KIDS ARE ALRIGHT! TALKIN' 'BOUT MY GENERATION! THE PUMP DON'T WORK CUZ THE VANDALS TOOK THE HANDLE!

All of a sudden we had a voice of our own, and the effect was incredible—the dam that had been holding everything back burst right open, and there was no way the flood could be stopped. It was time to move. The music sounded the call to arms for the second time in our brief history, only this time the troops had not only the inspiration but the direction they needed to get started, and they began pouring out of the suburban concentration camps where they'd been held all their lives to take their place in the ranks of the guitar army which was just beginning to take shape.

The direction, like the music itself, came from the heart of the black nation which had been held in captivity in Babylon for four hundred years. Stirred into action by the same forces that had created our people—the bankruptcy of industrialism as a viable means of providing for the needs of the people, the emergence of electronic technology with its retribalizing influence and its push towards a post-industrial social order, and the accelerating nation had begun to move for its freedom from the "white power structure," and although we still thought we were "white," too, we could see that the same people and the same system that were oppressing black people were keeping us down at the same time, and even wanted us to help them put these uppity black folks "in their place."

But we couldn't go for that any more than we could go for the rest of the old people's tricks, and instead of being turned against the people who had brought us our music we started to pick up on their social energy, too. Black people taught us that we didn't have to take the shit that was thrown at us, and their determination to win their freedom for themselves—which we could see every time we watched the news on TV—gave us the inspiration to begin our own struggle against the same monstrous "white power structure."

That wasn't all of it, either—we learned our music from black people, we learned that we could resist the established order, but we also learned how to live from black people, we learned about the sense of community, of brother and sisterhood, that black people had developed as a powerful survival technique during their generations of oppression. And we learned how music can be a first term in people's lives from them, too, how a whole culture can be built up on a strong musical foundation, and how the music can sustain a whole people and keep the together even under the most oppressive conditions, as the blues and its later variations had sustained black people all those years.

We learned that a people's culture can help them to withstand the most vicious assaults on their very existence, that it can help them not only to preserve their humanity but also raise it to higher and higher levels, and that it can express their hopes and aspirations in a way that will inspire them not only to resist their oppressors but to strike out against them when conditions demand it. We learned all of that by digging on

black people's music and assimilating it into our own embryonic culture, letting it interact with the other terms of our lives and mixing it with the elements of other people's cultures we picked up during our journey through the darkness of the first half of the '60s, until we had a rainbow culture of our very own which reflected all its sources but also transcended them to become something absolutely unique in the history of civilization.

It was the black experience that was echoed in the first wave of the new rock & roll—Bob Dylan, the Beatles, the Stones, the Animals, the Yardbirds, the Who—and it was black rebellion which was most prominently evident in that music, having been translated into terms that related directly to our own situation as the outcasts of Euro-Amerikan society. Frank Zappa said it best a year later in a song about the Watts uprising of 1965: "I'm not black, but there's a whole lot of times I wish I could say I'm not white." ("Trouble Comin' Every Day") The new rock & roll was about that kind of alienation, that kind of utter rejection of the world we'd been born into, and the music gave us more than anything a powerful sense of being a people, of being united in our alienation and rejection of "white society" where we'd though we were alone and isolated as single individuals before we heard the Beatles and the Stones come blasting into our lives to tell us otherwise.

That was the start, but it wasn't until the next wave reached its first crest, in 1966, that our music, and the culture it precisely reflected, came to speak of something essentially positive, to move

32

beyond simple alienation and rejection to propose a real alternative to the world we were determined to reject. And this time it was native American bands who took us this one huge step closer to the future we had always been headed for—it was the Jefferson Airplane, and the Grateful Dead, Big Brother & the Holding Company, Country Joe & the Fish, Quicksilver Messenger Service, the Great Society, the Fugs, the Mothers of Invention, Captain Beefheart & His Magic Band, all these great weirdo conglomerations of native-born maniacs who seemed to rise up out of nowhere to sing the new truths which we had already begun to live. The Airplane was the first to record, or at least to get our music out there where it could be heard, and they laid it out like a banner to the wind:

"Hey people now smile on your brother
Everybody get together and love one another right now!"

The focus had jumped from one end of the spectrum to the other, from alienation to the total embrace of humankind, and it was LSD that had brought about the change—because the music was only half of it, the music was what gave us our energy and our ideology which could direct that energy. Marijuana, which had come to us directly from black people and black musicians in particular, had given us our start in this direction, but LSD opened the road into the future as wide as the sky and we were soaring! Acid blasted all the negativism and fear out of our bodies and mind and

gave us a vision we needed to go ahead, the rainbow vision which showed us how all people could live together in harmony and peace just as we were beginning to live with each other like that. Rock & roll had been the form—and even in its 1965 incarnation it was still more a form than anything else, because the words only articulated the message of rebellion which was carried in the rhythm and the sound—but LSD supplied that form with its revolutionary content, and the synthesis created by the wedding of these two expose elements of our culture became the foundation for the New World which has already begun to rise out of the ruins of Babylon.

LSD was the catalyst that transformed rock & roll from a music of simple rebellion to a revolutionary music with a program for living in the New Age of post-industrial, post-scarcity abundance which will come to flower with the final collapse of western civilization. It has to be understood like that, or else it's impossible to comprehend everything that's going on now.

LSD brought everything into focus for the first time in our mixed-up lives, but it was more than just a subjective phenomenon too—acid appeared on the scene at the precise moment in history when it was needed, and the ideology it gave rise to in our minds and bodies made perfect sense of all the previously confusing objective developments which had taken place in the West since the emergence of electronic technology and the isolation of the atom. Electronic technology made industrialism obsolete, the atomic bomb made war even more obsolete, and LSD brought us into full consciousness of these simple facts and more than that, it enabled us to see exactly what the New World would be like once these obsolete forces were allowed to fade into history. That was the farthest out thing of all, because until we started eating all that acid we couldn't figure out what was happening—we knew things were all wrong the way they were, but we didn't know how they could be different, which meant we really didn't know which way to move.

LSD cleared all that up, and the musicians who rose up to put their LSD visions into the cosmic amplifier of rock & roll projected the post-western ideology out over the face of the West, illuminating the darkest corners of Babylon and providing millions of electronic aborigines with the direction they had been aching for. The music was theirs, it was the music of their lives, and it laid down the alternative to the death-life they had been chained to in their parents' suburban cemeteries.

The music spoke of living together with the people you loved, of sharing what you had, of loving all your brothers and sisters on the planet equally, of getting high and merging with the universe, of communalism and peace and harmony and no more wars, of touching and feeling and loving and being together—it spoke of freedom above and beyond everything else, and what made the music so powerful in its effect was the fact that the musicians who made it were living that way themselves. They weren't talking about any kind of abstract dogma or made-up fantasies, they were singing about their own lives, and they made it clear that everybody who listened to them could live like that, too. The alternative which had been missing in the past was now available for everybody to pick up on, and the kids who listened to the music followed it back to its source in the musicians to see how they could actually do the things the music told them about.

The most obvious advance on the rock & roll of the past was the communal or group character of the new music, and the way the new groups (particularly the American bands) came directly out of the communities in which they lived. They were people's bands, and their music was an integral part of the life of their communities as it had never been before. The English bands still came up through the entertainment industry, the top ten / pop star sector of the society and represented it themselves, they were still removed from the people they spoke for. The San Francisco bands, on the other hand, were hippies off the street who happened to play dynamite music as part of their lives, and when they first emerged out of the west coast rainbow community to take their place on the stage of history they brought all the elements of that new community with them.

They sang about being together, and they were together—they repudiated the whole separation ruse that makes western entertainment such a poisonous thing, and their example inspired thousands and thousands of new people to drop out of the death culture

altogether to find their place in the new world the musicians advertised every time they sang and played their incredible electronic rock & roll music.

The bands sang about getting high, and the kids tracked down all the grass and acid they could find; the bands sang about dancing in the streets, and the kids jumped up off their asses and started flailing the air in a holy frenzy; the bands sang about taking off your clothes and getting down, and the kids couldn't wait to do it just like that; the bands sang about getting together and living together in the music and the colors and the flesh, and thousands of communes sprang up all over the land. The music spoke of energy and vitality and freedom, and as soon as it was heard the whole country was flooded with a wave of new energy like the world had never seen before.

It was just too much—as soon as the words were out of the musicians' mouths the people responded to them like they'd been waiting for them all their lives—and they had been! DO YOU BELIEVE IN MAGIC? YES! Yes, we do, we do, we believe in everything! We want it all! Well then, come on out to San Francisco and wear some flowers in your hair. Wham! The pilgrimage started as soon as the schools let out for the summer, and the hip community was choked with wandering mendicants who had to see for themselves what this beautiful thing was all about. They had been questioning everything they'd been told ever since they were born, and they had to know if the musicians really meant what they were saying. They wanted to be free, and they were ready to do anything to get that way. The music was the only thing they could trust, and they trusted it and believed in it even harder than the musicians did themselves, which turned out in the end to be the whole problem.

Because the music misled people finally—it turned on all these people to the vision of a new life in Babylon, but it made everything sound too easy without meaning to at all. The people who were involved in advertising and propagandizing this new culture had the most beautiful intentions imaginable, but we couldn't know when we started pushing it how many kids would respond to our call, or that they wouldn't be able to understand or even relate to all the changes we'd had to go through to get to where we were. And we left most of that out, too, in our frantic rush to get the news of what we'd discovered out to the kids who were waiting for it.

It wasn't just the bands either, it was the whole spectrum of our public activity which projected a simplistic picture of what the "revolution" was all about—because that's what we were calling it, a revolution, and we said that all you had to do was "tune in, turn on, and drop out," as if that would solve all the problems of humankind. We had more than our bands to push this message—we had our own newspapers, we invaded the straight newspapers and magazines with our charismatic visions, we went on TV and prophesied the immediate and total rebirth of Amerika, we spread the word every way we could and we believed everything we were saying, which only made it worse because we were just as surprised as all the kids who had believed us when we told them there wasn't anything to it.

What happened was that it didn't work that way at all—we were challenging the biggest death machine in the history of the world, and what we didn't understand, spaced out as we were behind all that acid, was that the machine was determined to keep things the way they were. We had fallen for the biggest trick of all—although we knew enough to reject all the basic premises of western civilization because we could see that the whole thing was completely phony, we still believed the people in power when they said that they were just as unhappy as we were with the way things are, and that they wanted to make a better world for all the people who lived in it. We believed them when they said the war was a "mistake," that poverty and oppression was a "mistake" that they were trying to correct, that all the bad things which existed under their system were just "mistakes" which they were racking their brains to find solutions to. We believe all that, and we came forward with our beatific visions and said, look, people, we've got the solution! We've just found what you've been looking for, here it is, we've got it all figure out—isn't it beautiful? All we have to do is get together and love one another right now—here, take this LSD, smoke this joint, listen to the music, put your arms around the person sitting next to you, now get up and dance around—doesn't it make you feel good? Isn't this what you've always wanted? Well, let's do it!

We really thought it was going to be that easy, despite all the evidence to the contrary, and we were ecstatic when we saw thousands and then millions of kids pouring into our alternative communities in response to the music and the other messages we had sent out to them.

It was all too perfect to believe, but we wanted to believe it so bad that we managed to overlook the contradictions that had been developing all along until it was almost too late to do anything about them. We just kept urging people to "drop out" in greater and greater numbers until we looked up one day to see kids sleeping in doorways and begging on street corners, shooting speed to stay awake because they didn't have any place to sleep, getting busted by the police for getting high like we'd told them to, falling for all kinds of exploitative tricks just so they could hear some music and be with each other somewhere like we'd told them was so hip, and generally tripping around in utter confusion because there wasn't anything else for them to do. We had told them that the world was ready for them, and it wasn't ready at all, and they were stuck out in the middle of it with nothing to do but try to make it on their own, fighting off the police and the hucksters and the psychedelic exploitation experts with no help from the people who'd lured them out there in the first place.

Because by this time there was a full-scale suppression campaign underway, and the control addicts who were running it were determined to put an end to this madness by any means necessary. They knew what they were up against even if we didn't understand it ourselves, and they knew that our

"revolution," if it were to succeed, would put an end to their rule once and for all, which was something they just could not relate to at all. They had no interest in changing things except to bring everybody under even tighter control so they could increase their profits and pave over the rest of the world, and when they saw that we were going in exactly the opposite direction, towards a world where all the people in it would share in the collective control of the planet's resources and wealth, their reaction was immediate and intense. Stomp 'em! Stop 'em! Get 'em under control! Shut 'em up however you have to, but we can't wait any longer—they're out of control and it's all because of that goddamn rock & roll!

Well, it wasn't as simple as all that, of course, but we've got to work from what we can see, that is, from the effect, back to the cause, and the effect of the suppression campaign was and is precisely reflected in what's happened to our music since the repression started. Because we were so naïve, we had so much faith in our visions, we were so sure that the huge wave of love and energy we had generated would wash out all the fear and hatred and greed in the world that we left ourselves wide open to attack, and it happened so fast that the whole scene had changed before we even knew what hit us.

We had created an alternative culture which was a free and open and unorganized as we were, that was what we considered its strength, and all we wanted was to give it all away to everybody who wanted to share it with us so they could be free, too, just like we were. We thought they were ready for it, but we didn't understand, and couldn't understand how what we were doing would destroy the whole of western civilization if it were allowed to spread itself unchecked. What happened after that gave us our first taste of political education and brought us closer to the genuinely revolutionary stance which we are just now beginning to assume.

The attack on the rainbow culture took two distinct forms, subversion and outright repression, and while both of them have managed to slow us down they've also brought us to a new stage of our development by making us aware of what we're up against and teach us what we have to do to get through to the other side of the great Amerikan desert. Neither of them could work finally, because there's no way we can be stopped and that fact has given rise to a number of contradictions which have progressively undermined the position of the greedheads who are so frantic to wipe us out. They try as hard as they can to drive us back, and it looks sometimes like they've been successful, but even when things seem to be getting worse every day the irreversible drive for freedom which was first felt in our bodies and then in our incredible rock & roll music is still pushing us forward and breaking down all the barriers thrown up in our faces by the forces of capitalism and control.

Dig it—they saw that our music was the lifeblood of the alternative culture, the thing that held us together and showed us how to live with each other outside the system, so they moved in and took it over by buying off the musicians and turning the music into a simple Amerikan commodity which could be bought and sold like anything else. They cut the bands off from their roots in the rainbow community and made them into big P*O*P S*T*A*R*S who could be manipulated any way the owners wanted to use them, which was generally against the people who loved the music and wanted to believe it. The bands didn't really understand what was happening, none of us did at first, because the recording industry just seemed like a better way to get the music out to more and more people, you know? And the performance circuit likewise, especially at first when the bands were really like missionaries carrying their message into the darkest corners of Amerika for all the kids to see and her and feel, and besides, they were actually getting paid for doing what they would've been doing anyway. It was like we were putting something over on the old people, and in a way we were, but at the same time they were taking over our forms and subverting them without us being aware of it until it was too late.

When we started to wake up it looked like it was all over—the music was no longer wholly ours, it was no longer completely integrated into the life of our communities, it had been turned into an entertainment form instead of a life form and it was out of our hands. It still sounded good, it still spoke of freedom and life, but the thing that had made it truly revolutionary before—the self-determination aspect of the whole rainbow rock & roll scene, and the total integration of the music and the musicians into the community—no longer existed, at

least not in the way it had started out to be. The music and the musicians were commodities, their audience had been turned into consumers, and the western separation ruse was wreaking havoc on everything we'd created for ourselves as an alternative to it.

But even that wasn't enough to stop what was happening, because the music still carried enough weight, enough of a message, despite the way it had been ripped out of its organic context and pressed into plastic, it still managed through the surge of its rhythms and the thrust of its lyrics to heighten the contradictions between the old order and the new, to continue to speak of love and freedom and harmony and even of revolution, and it could no longer provide a place for people to go to it kept on making them wonder why it was so hard to make a place for themselves.

The music still posits the solution, it still points the way to the future, it still gives us our essential definition as a people, it continues to bring us closer and closer together all the time, and every attempt to suppress it just makes people who live the music (even if the musicians themselves don't live it any more, having been separated from the people like they are now) more aware of the problems they face I they want to be free.

The greedheads might be able to buy off the musicians, but they can't buy off the people who live the music, and that's where the repression comes in. The music tells kids to smoke dope and get high, but when they actually do that they come up against the organized police power of the capitalist-industrial state, and they start to figure out that

MC5 crowd at West Park, Ann Arbor, 1968, photo by Leni Sinclair

"Any image around which any people concentrate and
commit themselves is a usable one just because it is theirs"
—Charles Olson, *Apollonius of Tyana*

if they really wanna get high, they have to fight that state and eventually put it out of commission.

The music draws thousands of kids to big pop festivals and indoor rock & roll concerts, but when they get there they find out that the state doesn't want them to get together like that, or if they can get together they have to pay through the nose for it, and either way they get so pissed off that they move closer and closer to the point where they are ready to fight for what they need so they can have it when they need it, and for free, too.

The music tells them to drop out of the plastic nightmare and live together in communes and communities of their own people, but when they do that they run up against weird industrial housing regulations and police raids and all kinds of other shit, and they start to understand that they simply can't live the way they want to as long as the present system maintains its control.

They begin to understand what we couldn't understand before, in all our naivete, that it's going to take a real revolution, a total revolution which has as its conscious purpose the overthrow of the established order in all its manifestations—economic, political and cultural—in order for the rainbow culture to be able to grow and flower into the thing the music tells us it can be.

The music keeps drawing more and more people into its spaced-out orbit, and the deeper they get into it the clearer all these contradictions become. The music draws them out into the world and starts them moving, it gives them the initial push they need to get started, and once they get moving they

begin to find out for themselves what they have to do to stay on their feet, and they do it. They definitely stumble around for a while, and they don't get much direction from the people they look to for that, they don't much help at all, but the thing is that they're moving, they're on their way, and that once they get moving they begin to create their own organizational forms which will help them survive and keep their energy alive until another massive wave of new energy rolls over the horizon to push them further into the future.

The music provides that impetus then, and it keeps us together, it defines us as a part of each other, as a people, once we've started to move. Rock & roll is the one thing that has been capable of doing that, the one thing which has done that, the one thing which even now continues to do that for our people despite the concentrated efforts of the mother-country imperialists to drain the music and the musicians of their revolutionary content and turn all of us back into simple consumers. Rock & roll still does what it did back in the '50s, what it did in 1965 and 1966 and 1967 and 1968, it still pours out into the wilds of Babylon to turn more and more kids on to their revolutionary possibilities, and as more and more bands and other cultural workers begin to realize our own possibilities as conscious agents of change we will make the essential, the absolutely necessary next move and start to seize control over our own music so we can use it consciously and precisely in the service of the people's revolutionary struggle. We will begin to use the music not only to turn people on, not only to get them moving, but also to give our people very specific directions, or ways, in which to move—we will fill the revolutionary form of rock & roll music with a definite, very concrete, unmistakably revolutionary content, and we will increasingly come to understand and use ourselves and our music as weapons of revolutionary change. We will reintegrate our music and our bands with the people, and we will move with the people to create the kind of world all of us need to live in—which means that we will use the music as it was intended to be used, as a force which can help blow the obsolete dinosaur order and all its institutions off the face of the earth forever, and which can help lay the foundation for the New World of our dreams.

I would like to say at this time that it is the opinion of myself and that of my department that the White Panther Party is working toward obtaining control of large masses of young people for the primary purpose of causing revolution in this country.

"The methods used to recruit these people is based upon a complete dropout of our society and the adoption of a system involving 'rock' music and the free use of drugs and sex in a setting of commune living.

"It is apparent that every attempt is being made to break down the moral relationship between the youth and his or her parents along with a complete disregard for law and order.

"It is also apparent that much of the material used in the writings published by this organization came directly from the 'Red Book' of quotations by Mao Tse-Tung. While Mao relates to the 'masses' as young people...

"Gentlemen, based on the information we have obtained through other normal police functions, we would have to consider the White Panther Party as an organization bent on total destruction of the present Government of the United States and detrimental to the welfare of this country.

"Thank you."

—Sgt. Clifford A. Murray,
special investigation unit,
Intelligence Section,
Michigan State Police,
testifying before the U.S. Senate
Internal Securities Subcommittee,
September 25, 1970

IV. Liner Notes

When I started writing this Preview sitting in the maximum security block at Jackson Prison, I meant to talk about the specifics of my own experience a lot more, but most of that experience is written into the pieces in this book one way or another, and the only thing I would add is that I graduated from high school in Davison, Michigan, in 1959, went to Albion College for two years where I hung up my rock & roll shoes (the ones with the long pointed toes) and got turned on to the beatnik scene for next few years, dropped out of school and wandered the streets of the north side black ghetto in Flint, Michigan, trying to be black, worked in record shops and jazz clubs, started writing poetry in 1961, got turned on

44

"Who's to say that the cops of America and the Republicans and Democrats are going to tell everybody what to do?"
—Jack Kerouac, *The Dharma Bums*

"All of my work is directed against those who are bent, through stupidity or design, on blowing up the planet or rendering it uninhabitable. Like the advertising people we talked about, I'm concerned with the precise manipulation of word and image to create an action, not to go out and buy a Coca-Cola, but to create an alteration in the reader's consciousness."
—William Burroughs, in an interview, 1965

to weed later that year, ate peyote in 1963, finished school at the Flint College of the University of Michigan in January 1964 and moved to Detroit, attended graduate school in American literature at Wayne State University, got busted for weed in October 1964, hooked up with my powerful partner Leni and helped organize the Artists' Workshop as a neo-beatnik self-determination center for musicians, poets, photographers, painters, filmmakers, dope fiends and lovers of all kinds, published a poetry magazine (*Work*) and an avant-jazz magazine (*Change*) out of the Artists' Workshop Press, served as the Detroit correspondent for *Downbeat* magazine and wrote jazz reviews for *Jazz, Coda, Sounds & Fury*, and a number of other magazines, wrote and published three books of poems (*This is Our Music, Fire Music: A Record*, and *Meditations: A Suite for John Coltrane*) got busted for weed again in 1965 and served six months in the Detroit House of Corrections, got turned on to rock & roll again and put together a band for a while (the Down-Home Tyrannosaurus of Despair, also known as the Detroit Edison White Light Company) in the fall of 1966, wrote about Detroit rock & roll and jazz for the *San Francisco Oracle*, co-edited *Guerrilla: A Magazine of Cultural Revolution* with Allen Van Newkirk, ran a book shop/record store for the *Fifth Estate*, got busted for weed the third time on January 24th, 1967, helped organize Trans-Love Energies as a hip community service organization that spring, wrote a column ("The Coatpuller" and later "Rock & Roll Dope") for the *Fifth Estate* on and off for almost four years (1965–'69), edited and published the *Warren-Forest Sun*, and later, the *Ann Arbor Sun* ("free newspaper of rock & roll, dope, and fucking in the streets") with Gary Grimshaw, Leni and Pun & Genie Plamondon, managed the MC5 for two years (1967–'69), moved to Ann Arbor with my people in 1968, helped organize the White Panther Party that fall and served as Minister of Information during its first year, traveled around with the MC5, did a radio show on WABX-FM in Detroit with Jerry Lubin until I got banned from the air, produced the first Detroit Rock & Roll Revival in the spring of 1969, and did a lot of other stuff until I got locked up in July 1969 on this 9 ½ - 10 year sentence for possession of two joints of weed. Since then I've been in Jackson Prison, Marquette Prison (September 1969–September 1970), Jackson again, the Wayne County Jail (January–April 1971), and back in Jackson Prison where I am right now. Also since I've been locked up I have been charged with "conspiracy to destroy government property," to wit, the Ann Arbor CIA office, which was blown up in September 1968. My rap partners, Pun Plamondon and Jack Forrest, are both in the federal penitentiary right now on other charges, along with our comrade Skip Taube. My sixth application for appeal bond on the marijuana sentence was denied last month.

The writings in this book are basically the newspaper columns I wrote for the *Fifth Estate*, the *Ann Arbor Argus*, and the *Ann Arbor Sun*, along with some longer pieces published in Sun/Dance and Green during 1970.

The Street Writings have been edited only to cut out esoteric references to local events and to eliminate the sexist language that was characteristic of much of my writing at that time. The Prison Writings start with the transcript of the sentencing proceedings from the day I got sentenced, July 28, 1969, Judge Robert J. Colombo presiding. The letter to Leni is from my first day in the penitentiary and is really the only document (outside of a few statements in the interview with Peter Steinberger) that refers to my prison experience at all.

The two major writings from Marquette Prison were composed in the summer of 1970. "We Are A People!" was originally titled "Message to the People of Woodstock Nation" and was printed under that title in *Sun/Dance* Nos. 1 & 2; *Sun/Dance* was the national organ of the White Panther Party. "Bringin' It All Back Home" appeared in *Creem* magazine later in 1970 as "Liberation Music."

The interview with Peter Steinberger, titled "The Penitentiary Ain't Shit To Be Afraid Of," was published in *Big Fat* magazine in the summer of 1970. It has been expanded considerably to get in most of what we would've talked about that day if we'd had enough time to talk. Since we had only two hours in the visiting room without a tape recorder and under the pretense of discussing legal business (I have been forbidden to talk to reporters of any kind since October of 1969, so Steinberger was there in his guise as an attorney), a lot of things were left out that I've tried to write into the text for publication here.

In September of 1970 I was transferred from Marquette to the "world's largest walled prison" at Jackson and composed "The Lesson of Goose Lake" and "Slaughter at Stonehead Manor" in the segregation block here during the fall of 1970. "The Greening of America" was written in the Wayne County jail, where I spent five months in 1971 waiting to go to trial on the CIA conspiracy charge. It was published in the *Michigan Daily* and later in *University Review*.

"Vietnam Parking Lot Blues," "Operation Jones" and "Rainbow Power" were composed in Jackson Prison in the summer and fall of 1971 and printed in the *Ann Arbor Sun* as part of a series of columns titled *Dragon's Teeth*. "Long Live the Black Panther Party" was published in the *Ann Arbor Sun* in June 1971 as the statement of the Central Committee of the Rainbow People's Party.

"Free At Last" was written upon my release from prison on December 13, 1971 and printed in the *Ann Arbor Sun* for December 17-31, 1971.

I wish we could just bind together all the newspapers these writings first appeared in so you could read them like that, but this is the best I can do—the only other thing I can suggest is that you get your hands on a copy of *Kick Out the Jams* by the old MC5, put it on the record machine, turn up the volume, light up a joint, maybe take all your clothes off, roll around on the floor for a minute, and return with us now to those thrilling days of yesterday.

—*Jackson Prison, October 1971*

STREET WRITINGS

Photo by David Fenton

"When 'the man' becomes more oppressive he only heightens revolutionary fervor.... The oppressors, by their brutal actions, cause resistance by the people."
—Huey P. Newton, *To Die For the People*

TOTAL ASSAULT
ON THE CULTURE!

*"Revolutionary culture is a powerful revolutionary
weapon for the broad masses of the people. It prepares
the ground ideologically before the revolution comes,
and is an important, indeed essential, fighting front in
the general revolutionary front during the revolution."*
—Mao Tse-tung, *Culture & Art*

"Revolutions are festivals of the oppressed and exploited."
—V. I. Lenin, *Two Tactics*

MARCH 1, 1968

The SUN represents a growing body of people who live and work together in the city. It doesn't follow any "line" except the line that goes straight from us to you, and we're trying to make that line straighter all the time, not crooked. The SUN brings you the news of our lives, that we are alive and well and that *all* of us can be well too. We *have* found that there are three essential human activities of the greatest importance to all persons, and that people are well and healthy in proportion to their involvement in these activities: rock & roll, dope, and fucking in the streets!

Rock & roll music is the great liberating force of our time and place here in the West. Its most beautiful aspect is that it gets to millions of people every day, telling them that they can dance and sing and holler and scream and *feel good* even when they have to listen to all those jive commercials and death news reports all around the music, everything's gonna be all right as soon as everybody *gives it up!* Rock & roll—and we mean John Coltrane and Pharoah Sanders and Archie Shepp and Albert Ayler and Sun Ra and all *those* people as much as the Beatles and Jimi and the MC5 and Canned Heat and the Cream and the Grateful Dead and Big Brother & the Holding Company and the Up—rock & roll is the music of *right now,* every minute, pounding and screaming at your head, twisting inside your

51

belly, pulling you up off your ass to *give it up* and let the energy flow through your cells and back out into the universe so you can be *free* again. Wave your freek flag high! HIGH! YAAAAA! *Stone free*—do what you wanna!

And now, a message from our sponsor. . . . But first, let me take a toke on that joint. Yeah, that sure is good. Good *for* you, too. Makes you *feel good*. Don't let old people fool you, there's nothing wrong with feeling good, you don't have to sacrifice anything for it, you don't have to hurt anybody, you don't have to feel brought down and nasty all the time just because people tell you that's reality, kid, and you'd better face up to it. GET FUCKED, thousands of freeks scream at them, and mean every word of it. But that's getting a head of things a little.

Dope is marijuana, LSD, peyote, mescaline, psilocybin, sacred mushrooms, hashish, DMT, nitrous oxide, and other beautiful chemical substances that make you *feel good* without *hurting* you. The other kind of dope hurts—heroin, alcohol, morphine, amphetamine crystal and other forms of speed, barbiturates and downers, television programming, schools, jails, police, control, power, greed—the people who are addicted to these heavy narcotics try to tell us that we are the dope fiends. Well, okay, mister, but what does that make *you?* You know you're really *people* under all that fear and thought! Come out in the open and smoke some dope with us. Pass the joint around to your friends. That's it. Now smile. Doesn't it make you *feel good?* Doesn't it make you want to *fuck?* Well then, go right ahead!

Last but certainly not least is *fucking in the streets,* the most important and the most misunderstood aspect of our program. We believe that fucking, or "sexual intercourse" (as if any form of human intercourse, or any form of human activity, wasn't "sexual" to begin with!), is the highest and most basic form of human communication. Everything else is *about* fucking; fucking is fucking. You can't get closer to another person than inside her, or around him, or vice versa for our spaced out gay brothers and sisters as the case may be, and even rock & roll and dope, heavy as they are, don't get down to the nitty gritty like fucking does. We suggest the three in combination, all the time.

Fucking is very valuable—it creates children if you're into that, it opens you up and frees all your body energy by letting it flow freely out of your body and into the cosmos, it gives you the grace to move and walk and dance and speak freely when you've given it all up from way back inside you, it keeps you giving it up so you don't have to hold on to it no more, and most of all, when two people (or more!) can get together in their purest human form and *merge* with each other outside of all the stereotypes and hangups that are drilled into us in this weirdo country, it *feels good* like nothing else on earth.

Our position is that all people must be free to fuck freely, whenever and wherever they want to, or not to fuck if they don't wanna—in bed, on the floor, in the chair, on the streets, in the parks and fields, "back seat boogie for the high school kids" sing the Fugs who brought it all out in the open on stage

52

From Wayne Kramer's letterhead

"The social consciousness displayed in that music. Which is more radical than sit-ins. We get to Feel-Ins, Know-Ins, Be-Ins."
—LeRoi Jones, "The Changing Same"

"The passion with which native intellectuals defend the existence of their national culture may be a source of amazement, but those who condemn this exaggerated passion are strangely apt to forget that their own psyche and their own selves are consistently sheltered behind a French or German culture which has given full proof of its existence and which is uncontested."
—Frantz Fanon, *The Wretched of the Earth*

"One of the first tasks of those creating a new society is that of creating a new and distinct identity. This identity cannot be fully conscious at first, but as a movement grows, through years or generations, it contains its own body of experience, its styles and habits, and a common language becomes part of the new identity.... Music and dance are forms of communication partly because they are directly expressive of feelings for which there is as yet no language.... Our language thus becomes evidence of our criminality because it shows us to be outside the system. Perhaps our language would be acceptable if it were divorced from practice. ... It is the fact that our language is part of our action that is criminal."
—Tom Hayden, *Trial*

"It is good if we are attacked by the enemy, since it proves that we have drawn a clear line of demarcation between the enemy and ourselves. It is still better if the enemy attacks us wildly and paints us as utterly black and without a single virtue; it demonstrates that we have not only drawn a clear line.... But achieved a great deal in our work."
—Mao Tse-tung, "Classes and Class Struggle"

Gary Grimshaw, photo by Leni Sinclair

and on records, fuck whoever wants to fuck you and everybody else do the same. America's silly sexual "mores" are the end-product of thousands of years of deprivation and sickness, of marriage and companionship based on the ridiculous misconception that one person can "belong" to another person, that "love" is something that has to do with being "hurt," sacrificing, holding out, "teardrops on your pillow," and all that shit. BROTHERS AND SISTERS! LOVE IS FOR EVERY BODY! WHO GAVE YOU YOUR BODY? IS IT "YOURS"? *GIVE IT UP!* NOW!!!

We know we're gonna get yelled at for saying all this right out in the open like this, but we *know* it and we have to tell what we know or be as dead to the world as everyone else who's holding it back and trying to fool people. This is our responsibility to ourselves and to the planet, that we have to *tell the truth* as long as we live and breathe, because when you stop telling the truth you're dead. That's one of the reasons why the American "system" is dead, because it's based on lies and on the practice of lying to people. It doesn't *work* anymore, you can see that and feel that for yourselves, and somebody's got to say it because it's *true.* Government officials tell reporters they're crazy if they they don't think they can get away with anything else. We're here to tell you with this newspaper—and this *is* the news!—that we all *can* get away with whatever we dare to do. ALL YOU HAVE TO DO IS DO IT! *GIVE IT UP!* Everything is Everything. Can you dig it? You'd better—it's all true!

STATEMENT OF RESPONSIBILITY: The SUN is a product of the lives of, and a reflection of the lives of a hard core of a community of total freeks. We are not afraid anymore! Many of us are fighting in the city's courts and on the streets of Detroit to change the laws that supposedly control marijuana and other holy agents, that supposedly control and choke off freedom of speech, religion, assembly, of expression in any human form. We love our nation and we want to make it free again as it was before the European robbers got here and ripped it off from our heroes the Aboriginal red tribes and confederations. We will not be stopped. Since October 6, 1966, the day the federal government Narcotics Squad tried to break up our community here in the Warren-Forest by arresting 56 people and charging 13 of us with sales and/or possession of marijuana. Instead of stomping out the scene, the police action united us and brought us all closer together than ever before. WE ARE NOT AFRAID! We will warn those who may try to stomp out our newspaper the SUN that we will be free and *stay free.* This newspaper is fully and equally the responsibility of each one of us. We are *all* "leaders." You can't go to Sinclair or Grimshaw or any one of us separately and talk about "individual responsibility" for the SUN or anything else we might do. WE ARE ALL RESPONSIBLE! We have no "private lives." We are all part of the total universal energy scene and can't be separated from it! GIVE IT UP! Turn on to yourself! Tune in on the energy flow! *Take over* your bodies and your lives from the control addicts *NOW!* The world is yours—BE FREE! *FREE!!* FREEEEEEEEE!!!

Wayne Kramer and Michael Davis of MC5

KICK OUT THE JAMS, MOTHERFUCKER!

The "Total Assault on the Culture!" issue of the *Warren-Forest Sun* was one of our last formal actions in Detroit—a few weeks later we packed up everything and moved en masse to Ann Arbor after the Board of Zoning Appeals and the Detroit Police Department combined to run us out of town. We couldn't get any printers in the state to touch our paper, but the *Sun* continued as a mimeographed free street paper and our total assault program intensified with the crazed rock & roll guerrilla warfare we were waging with the MC5 and the Up. In Ann Arbor we copped two big houses next door to each other and had everybody in one place for once—both the bands were right there with us, our operation tightened up, and we had the added advantage of a greatly increased base in the mushrooming freek community as well as a much smaller and much less dangerous police presence to deal with. We suffered a serious setback in June with the arrest and incarceration (under a $20,000 bond!) of brother Pun Plamondon by narcotics officers from Traverse City, who snatched up Pun on a charge of giving away one roach three months earlier and held him until the middle of September. They came with a warrant for Gary Grimshaw too, but Grim beat it out of town before they could get to him and remained underground until the summer of 1970, when we finally got him back.

During the summer of 1968 we started running into more and more hassles with the police and other mother-country authorities as we refined our total assault campaign and struck deep into the heart of honkie-land with the MC5 night after night. We followed the principle of relying on the people and using the police assaults on our activities to expose the repressive nature of the mother-country system while building up our base of support among the people and constantly increasing the scope of our operation. Every two weeks I would write up what had happened for the *Fifth Estate* and try to interpret it so our people could understand what was going down. What follows is a series of "Rock & Roll Dope" columns, *Sun* stories and press releases from that period, which culminated in the band's ill-fated recording contract with Elektra Records and the founding of the White Panther Party after Pun was finally released from jail in September. We didn't understand exactly what was happening when all this shit was going down, because there'd never been anything like it before, but the increasing harassment and repression we were encountering in Michigan coupled with the massive police stomp scene we experienced in Chicago at the "Festival of Life" in August (where the 5 was the only band to show up for the opening of the celebration) pushed us out of our hippie drop-out peace-love consciousness and into an explicitly political-radical stance which grew directly out of our experience that summer.

More than anything else we learned that our culture itself represented a political threat to the established order, and that any action which has a political consequence is finally a political action. The result was that we became consciously political, and the White Panther Party became the formal expression of our new consciousness. But the documents tell the story better than I can do it now . . .

1. ROCK & ROLL DOPE #2

A strange polarization (or maybe it's a natural one) seems to be happening with rock & roll fans right now, with white teenage audiences turning toward either total freek scenes or greasy reactionary hostility when confronted with the revolutionary guerrilla tactics of the MC5. Three incidents in the last three weeks illustrate the current scene:

Friday, May 31st, the MC5 was booked into the Grosse Pointe Hideout, an eastside teen dance joint. We produced our own handbill for the gig, a Grimshaw design featuring a picture of the band naked against a backwards American flag and the legend, "Break through American stasis with the MC5!" Four hundred kids jammed into the tiny hall to dig the 5— the Hideout's biggest crowd in months— and were first treated to two fine sets by a new Detroit trio, the 3rd Power. MC5 drummer Dennis Thompson and I stepped outside during the second set for a smoke and met some young brothers in the parking lot next to the building. The young rock & roll addicts produced some grass, and while the sacrament was being ingested two rent-a-cops strolled onto the scene,

Wayne Kramer and Dennis Thompson get cast by Cynthia Plaster Caster

surprising one brother with a joint in his hand.

The two associate pigs called their big brothers, the Harper Woods police, who appeared on the scene some 30 minutes later to see ten freeks lounging against some cars under the watchful eye of the hired guards. Questioning followed, and the ten were told that we'd be taken into the station and booked on marijuana charges. I asked that the rest of the band be informed of this revolting development, which was done, and band members Wayne Kramer, Fred Smith, Rob Tyner and Michael Davis, along with equipment manager Ron Levine, immediately burst upon the scene woofing at the cops and demanding an explanation, causing enough confusion that those in the assembled company who were holding the sacrament could get rid of it. Then the real shit went down.

Levine hassled the pigs until he was sure that subtle persuasion wouldn't work (resulting in one cop pushing Fred Smith in the chest and threatening him with a whupping) and then returned to the club, turned on the PA, and informed the eager MC5 fans that me and Dennis were getting popped in the parking lot and that the only way they'd get to hear the band would be to surround the cops outside and *make* them give us up. While Levine was rapping, the club's manager had a cop drag him off the stage and then closed the doors, trapping the kids inside. He was sufficiently shook up, however, to persuade the police to release the suspects, except the one who was caught with the weed and the two under-17 "juveniles" who were taken

in and released later to the custody of their parents. By this time Kramer was on the phone contacting LEMAR attorney Bill Segesta, and Dennis and I were threatening the clumsy suburban police with false-arrest suits and extra-legal retaliation.

When the band, intact once again, returned inside to play their first set, the crowd went into a spontaneous scream scene to welcome them back to reality. And when Tyner kicked off the first tune with "KICK OUT THE JAMS, MOTHERFUCKER!" it was madness all the way, with wild applause and jubilation before and after every jam.

The Hideout's manager was furious by this time, but he was caught in a simple capitalist contradiction: he couldn't move to censure the band because the paying customers were behind us all the way, and they were a lot more than "paying customers" by that time too—they were *ready!* When the chomp shut off the electricity during the closing energy-orgy "Black to Comm" to get the band off the stage, the crowd joined Fred Smith in chanting *"Power! Power! Power!"* until the juice came back on and the music soared to its natural climax.

The next Friday the MC5 joined the Cream for the Grande Ballroom show. Excited by the success of the previous week's guerrilla theatre event, the band planned to burn an American flag on stage during "Comm" to make their feelings about this shit clear once and for all. Ballroom owner Russ Gibb got wind of the scheme through the underground grapevine and left word for us that if any burning went on, he would have the police sent in to capture the ragged symbol and take appropriate action against the traitors, so we came up with a last-minute alternative plan and went ahead as scheduled.

When the 5 danced on stage for the second set of the evening, the temperature in the Grande was over 100 degrees on Detroit's first boiling weekend and there were close to 2000 sweating rock & roll fiends packed onto the floor, lured into action by the promise of the Cream *and* the dangerous home-town favorites the Motor City 5. Again a huge cheer erupted from the crowd when Tyner announced his purpose, and the people carried on like that all through the explosive hour-and-fifteen-minute set in the sweltering heat.

As "Black to Comm" built to a screaming frenzy, equipment manager Steve "the Hawk" Harnadek introduced a tattered plastic-nylon American flag onto the stage, and he and Tyner ripped it to shreds while the audience freeked and cheered. The symbol of imperialism and oppression demolished, Tyner then struggled back to his feet and raised his freek flag high: a 4' x 5' red banner inscribed with a rampant marijuana leaf, green in a yellow circle, in the upper-left-hand corner, and the word FREEK scrawled across the body of the banner. Again the freeks in the crowd—most everybody—screamed and cheered in a burst of patriotic frenzy. Simultaneously, the spectre of madman Jerry Younkins (of the Magic Veil Light Company) materialized on stage with the band, fully naked, and the cheers turned to gasps of disbelief as Younkins settled cross-legged on the lip of the stage and began chanting "OM" into a microphone, merging his spectral voice with the distant humming "OM" of the amplifiers as the music faded into history and the band stumbled off stage leaving the people stretched out on the floor in exhausted awe.

Repercussions followed immediately: Ballroom manager Larry Feldmann was called on the carpet by building owner Gabe Glantz and was summarily discharged from his duties. Glantz also started ranting at Tyner and me about "committing crimes" and *"obscenity"* and "is that what you think of your country?" threatening us with eternal expulsion from the Grande, which was pretty comical all in all. The next day Feldmann reported scores of phone calls from irate parents, we were lectured by our booking agent, and everyone involved in this heinous caper was met with frosty silence from "Uncle Russ" Gibb, who carried on as usual about freedom, dope, police brutality, and rock & roll music on his radio show. Only the Cream, it seemed, were unaffected by the whole scene, as they didn't bother to show up at the Ballroom until the beginning of their set, which began half an hour after the 5 had left the stage and continued until they collapsed from the heat an hour later.

The following Wednesday, June 12th, we traveled to Lansing for a gig at the (yes!) Lansing Hullabaloo. Our audience seemed at first to be 90% grease and maybe 10% freeks, and there was a lot of hostility generated throughout the three sets by young short-haired anti-freek forces in front of the stage.

Wayne Kramer of MC5, photo by Leni Sinclair

Warned by our booking agent against any unAmerican and/or obscene acts, the 5 merely kicked out the jams throughout the evening and into the last set, holding their rap down to their usual blasphemous cant and raunchy music. Kramer periodically swept the front row of the audience with his guitar held like a gatling gun to cool the greasers out a little bit, the band worked its magic on the rest of the kids to warm them up, and by "Comm" time the polarization was down to maybe 50-50. As "Comm" climbed to its howling climax, the freeks in the crowd began howling with the music and waving their arms in the air, flashing a two-handed "V" and jumping up and down with glee.

The converted short-hairs joined them, while the most hostile elements raised their middle fingers in the traditional gesture of rejection and disgust. The Tommy James fans made menacing gestures toward the stage, and one of their number responded to direct musical attacks by Wayne and me (I was playing saxophone) by climbing up on the stage and shaking his fist in our faces. He was pulled back down by his friends in the audience before anything physical could jump off, and it seemed that a lot more Vs went up, starting with those on the bandstand, as the music decrescendoed into the everlasting cosmic drone of the assembled Sunns. Rumors of toughs waiting outside filled the dressing room as the freeks rushed to join the band backstage, but the purity and accuracy of the music as usual equalized the bad vibes and we rolled home unscathed.

As everyone wonders what will happen next, the MC5 is girding its loins and readying some new tactics. Our itinerary for the rest of June includes dates at the Sarnia (Ontario) Arena, the Birmingham-Bloomfield Teen Center, the Michigan State Fair grounds, the Benton Harbor Scene, the Grande again with Blue Cheer and the Psychedelic Stooges, a return to the Grosse Pointe Hideout, the Jackson Hullabaloo, and the Greenlawn Grove in Romulus. The MC5 will also headline the first Saugatuck Pop Festival on the 4th of July, with the Amboy Dukes, the Rationals, the Up and the Flock. See you on the street!

2. ROCK & ROLL DOPE #3

I promised you when I started this column that I'd take you behind the scenes in the rock & roll industry so you can see what your bands have to go through just to be able to do their thing on stage, and ever since I said that so many weird things have been going on that I hardly know where to start. But the Grande Ballroom scene last Sunday was probably the weirdest of all, and if you just paid your money and sat and waited for the MC5 that night, you deserve to know that it wasn't the band that kept you waiting in all that heat—it was the creeps who took your money. Be advised.

The MC5's freek scene at the Grande June 7th (as reported in the last issue of the *Fifth Estate*) has touched off a string of creep scenes with clubowners around Michigan, starting at—you guessed it—the Grande itself. So far only two major incidents have gone down, but if they're any indication you can look for a lot more shit to hit before the fan is shut off.

There was a long line of rock & roll fiends waiting outside the Grande last Sunday night (June 23rd) when the 5 arrived at 6:45 to play the evening concert with Blue Cheer and the Psychedelic Stooges. The band was ready to kick 'em out like never before, but we were accosted by greedhead Glantz before we could even get to the dressing room and warned not to use any "dirty words," no nakedness on stage, and no incidents with the American flag, "real or simulated," during the band's performance.

We told him that we just wanted to do our show and make the people happy, but he didn't seem to be too convinced and ended up threatening to turn off the power onstage (I guess he meant the electricity) at the first sign of any obscene language or any other tom-foolery. At this point I overheard the conversation and told Glantz to go away and count his money and leave us alone, whereupon he ordered us not to play the evening's performance and stomped off to the ticket office.

I had been talking with reinstated Ballroom manager Larry Feldmann about the order of performance when the business with Glantz went down, and Feldmann immediately got on the phone to Russ Gibb, who made it down to the Ballroom with his attorney to see what was going on.

Meanwhile the Stooges were forced into starting the first set—by this time it was maybe 8 o'clock and getting hotter all the time, and the Grande was still filling up with easily-recognized MC5 addicts who began to wonder what the fuck was going on when the Stooges finished and the record player went back on.

No MC5. The band was in the downstairs office with Gibb and his attorney, talking it out. Management contended that for the band to go on stage and kick out the jams would result in an immediate bust—if not of the band then of the Ballroom itself. The band maintained that Glantz had created the whole affair (there were supposed to be three detectives there ready to snatch the Grande's license if any more unAmerican shit went down) because he wanted to get rid of us, and that if we couldn't do our show at the Grande without being submitted to prior censorship then the place might as well be closed, because we didn't even want to play there anyway if we couldn't play what the people wanted to hear.

This argument went back and forth for more than an hour, with us trying to get Gibb to understand the significance of what he was trying to do—to see that the Grande had been created by the people as a place where they could get down and do what they wanted to do, and that he was actually destroying the beautiful thing that has been built up in that place over a period of two whole years—but nothing was happening toward a resolution until a brother named Gut, one of Blue Cheer's managers and a righteous freek himself, came into the office and told Russ that his band couldn't go on unless the MC5 went on, "because the audience wants to hear the MC5 and won't settle for anything less."

Upstairs the people were chanting

"MC5! MC5!" and getting madder and madder by the minute. By this time it was way after 9 o'clock and Russ was still wondering what to do. He had to be reminded that the MC5 had opened the Ballroom with him, had worked there for free to get it off the ground, was still working for peanuts ($125.00 a night!), our light show (Trans-Love Lights) was getting $25.00 a night for 6 people working 5 hours, Grimshaw still gets $25.00 a poster, the Ballroom is packed every weekend now and it's bad enough that the people who were supposed to share in the profits don't share in them. But now if people can't talk like they want and do what they want there, then the whole thing just ain't worth it. He had to be reminded that we hadn't started the bullshit about the "dirty words"—we *always* used them—but Glantz had, and that all we wanted to do was play our music or else go home—forever. And take the light show, the Trans-Love store, and everything else we'd brought—including the Ballroom's *mojo*—with us.

The act of worker's solidarity by Blue Cheer seemed to've been the decisive factor in the whole thing—after all, *they* were the "big band from out of town" and we were just the local chumps—and at 9:30 Russ decided that the MC5 had better go on, even though his attorney advised him that the police could easily lift his license if they wanted to. (We had tried to tell him that they could lift his license anytime *anyway,* if they really wanted to, but that only scared him even more.) Actually, the final decision was made when Glantz appeared in the office and told Russ that the alleged defectives

were no longer upstairs. That was all he needed to get out of this mess.

When the MC5 charged on stage the crowd exploded. The audience, estimated at some 1500 on a Sunday evening (the biggest Sunday night crowd in the Grande's history), knew something funny was going on, but they'd waited for the 5 through a whole hour of silence as the heat level in the place mounted, and when Wayne Kramer kicked off the show with Ted Taylor's old smoker "Ramblin' Rose" they were really ready for it. And when Tyner leaped out and hollered "KICK OUT THE JAMS, *MOTHERFUCKER!*" everything broke loose. Hands shot up in the air and never came down as the band truly kicked out the motherfucking *jams.*

Our original plan had called for an hour-and-a-half set of new and established material which the band had been working on all week so the people would get as much music as they deserved for being so far out, but four songs into the set Gibb sent word to the stage that his attorney (who had been "monitoring" the show) had to leave, and that the band would have only one more piece to play.

I relayed the message to Tyner in between tunes, and Tyner *blew up.* He ran the whole thing down to the people, telling them it was "another bullshit Grande Ballroom scene" and that they were being cheated out of what they were supposed to get because of the creeps who ran the place. The freeks in the audience started hollering for Gibb's ass. "Kick out Uncle Russ, motherfucker!" someone shouted from the middle of the room. Tyner was furious, looking around the place for Gibb and, finally spotting him, screamed into the microphone: "One of these days / and it won't be long / you'll look for *me* mister / and down the road I'll go. . . . cuz I *believe,* to my *soul,* "and everybody knew exactly what was being said. Tyner directed all his energy at that one spot and made Gibb leave the room, only to send his flunkies back to shut off the electricity to the stage before the music could be fully realized. But things won't be the same there for quite some time now, and the people are getting hip to what the real deal is.

On Tuesday (June 25) our booking agent called to report that the job at the Jackson Hullabaloo for that night had been cancelled when the local police read about the flag scene in the *Fifth Estate* and took the Hullabaloo manager to the City Council, which threatened to rip up his license if he allowed the MC5 to play his club. The club owner was pissed off because he knew he would've made some money, but he was so thoroughly convinced that the police would pull a stomp scene that he broke his contract with the band and cancelled.

Other club owners around the state are beginning to realize that it would be in their best interest to hire the MC5, no matter what they think of our show. The people who have to have the music are the ones who control the scene anyway, once you let these club owners know what they have to do to keep you coming back. Let them know, and we'll see you then. Kick out the jams!

3. ROCK & ROLL DOPE #4

In the past two weeks since the last issue of this paper a bunch of new developments have taken place. Almost every job for the MC5 brings a new and different creep scene into being.

At a Wednesday night job in Tecumseh, Michigan, at the local teen center, Wayne Kramer ripped a pair of pants early in the second set and went off to change them. Later in the same set he ripped the second pair, this time accidentally exposing his genitals to the tender crowd. Everybody just laughed, Wayne changed pants again, and the music went on to its natural conclusion with no untoward incidents.

We didn't think anything about it until the musicians' union and our booking agent both sounded us about it, claiming that some insane Tecumseh woman had written them a letter describing the accidents in lurid detail, among other claims asserting that Kramer had purposefully "exposed his personal self" to the shame and dismay of the teenage audience. The union made vague threats about "expelling" the band, etc., but so far nothing has been done about the matter. Honk on!

The 4th of July brought the Saugatuck Pop Festival on the west coast of Michigan, and it showed how beautiful things can be if you keep the police off the grounds and out of the people's way. There wasn't any creep scene at all, but there *was* a huge freek scene that warmed the hearts of everyone there.

The festival was presented by a Detroit promoter as an attempt at a local version of last summer's incredible

Wayne Kramer and Fred "Sonic" Smith of MC5, photo by Leni Sinclair

Monterey Pop Festival, and it featured among other things, a totally pig-less performance area. With no police on hand and a cooled-out promoter the band's natural chemistry was free to work its magic on the crowd without interruption, and we were surprised to see a whole raft of MC5 addicts from around Detroit out there in the sun waiting to get down with us. They called for the MC5 all throughout the afternoon, and their chant spread through the whole crowd—over 3000 people, a mixture of stoned-out freeks and drunken frats—until the 5 took over the stage from the mighty UP around 9 o'clock.

It was the 4th of July and everybody was ready to get down. The people cheered their asses off all the way through the show, and when Rob Tyner called out "Kick Out the Jams, Motherfucker!" so many arms shot into the air that it looked like the end of World War II. By the time "I Believe To My Soul" surged into "Black to Comm" the whole crowd was on its feet screaming and waving their arms in the free night air for the 5 to bring it all back home NOW!

The band was ready for them. Kramer had had his Stratocaster decorated for the Independence Day festivities: red-and-white striped body, blue pickguard with white stars, and tiny flags hanging from the tuning pegs: truly an All-American guitar, and fit to be freed. The energy built up and up and up until people couldn't stand it any longer, and finally Kramer stepped back, unstrapped his star-spangled Fender, and began smashing the motherfucker against the top of the stage, on

his speaker cabinets, on the floor and every solid object in sight, smashing it to smithereens. Dennis kicked his drums over and they sprawled across the stage. Fred Smith lunged for his speakers and leaped on them, kicking over everything in his path. The people hollered and screamed and surged at the stage as the band staggered off, and the energy level in that field got so high it was almost unbelievable. That's rock & roll, people, the way it's supposed to be!

On Monday night we returned to the Grosse Pointe Hideout, where the weird shit had started the 1st of June, and it just got weirder. The fire marshal was there, the Harper Woods pigs were there, the same rent-a-cops were there, the owner was running around in circles from all the hassles he was getting, our booking agent was there trying to cool him out, and the kids were there too—in full force. The fire marshal made the Hideout management turn people away and keep all the lights on during the band's two shows. The police lined up outside the doors complete with riot helmets and grim pig faces, the heat mounted, and the manager kept breaking in with announcements all during the show: "Please stop smoking grass in the girl's toilet," "You'll all have to fold your chairs up and sit on the floor," "No dancing," "No obscenity or they'll take our license away," "You've got to turn down, it's too loud for the fire marshal," etc. Warnings and threats cluttered up the air, but the kids were right there and they didn't wanna hear no shit—they wanted the 5 and nobody was gonna stop them from getting it.

Kramer kicked off the second set with "Ramblin' Rose," and when it came time for the magic moment Tyner strolled onstage and told the kids he needed some help. Everybody knows what comes next, he said, and we need your help in calling off the tune because we've been hearing all kinds of weird stuff about it. Everybody knows it's all right, don't you now (YEAH!!), so I'll just count three and then we can get this old tune started. But everybody's gotta do it together, or else it won't be any good.

Tyner counted to three—the whole band counted—and then the place exploded: "KICK OUT THE JAMS, MOTHERFUCKER!!" 400 deranged teenage freeks screamed in unison, and the band *got down.* The pigs were infuriated, but they would've had to've arrested everybody in the place on the phony rap to get *anyone.* And after that it was freedom all the way

Tuesday night we rested. Wednesday night we drove down the street to the new Ann Arbor Hullabaloo for a scheduled gig, our first in Ann Arbor. Everything was cool while the first band, the Sugar Cube from Dearborn, did their thing, although we noticed that there were a lot more rent-a-cops than you would expect in such a small place. The shit hit the fan when the MC5 started playing: by the time "Borderline" was over, at the start of the first set, the squad cars had started to turn into the parking lot, and before 5 tunes had been played there were 7 squad cars, at least two cars full of detectives, Lt. Staudemire of the Narcotics Bureau, and other assorted officials hassling the club owners about the

"noise." When the band refused to alter their amplifier settings and protested what we saw as an attempt at artistic censorship (something to be expected since Staudemire's seizure of the flick "Flaming Creatures" the year before), the police moved inside and shut off the power to the stage.

The enraged audience started yelling with the band: "Power! Power!! Power!!!" But the electricity stayed shut off. Tyner started running it to the people, without benefit of a microphone, about the pigs and how they're trying to cut off our power on all levels, and how we have to go ahead for ourselves and do it however we can, *together.* The saxophones and gongs and bells and drums came out as Tyner was rapping, and then everyone merged in a non-electric orgy of music and feeling, chanting and dancing around and jumping up and down with glee in the face of the outraged police bandits. A police official in a white shirt with gold trim—obviously a lieutenant or an inspector or something—came up to the stand where I was playing my saxophone and handed me . . . a ticket! A ticket! For having "a noisy band"! I took one look at it and then tore it up in his face and went on playing like everybody else. We kept on until everybody was tired out, for another hour at least, and then packed up and went home, grinning.

We matched our magic against the pigs' brute tactics and it worked—any respect any of the people there might have had for "law and order" as represented by the Ann Arbor police just disappeared, and their futile tricks were exposed to the light. All this

Photo by Leni Sinclair

bullshit was totally unnecessary—we just wanted to do our thing and let the people do their thing with us, but the police just won't let that happen without trying to stomp us out one way or the other. The old people seem to want to pretend that the world is just the way it is on television, and that other peoples' lives have no validity. They don't want people to know—or if they know they don't want it acknowledged—that men have cocks in their pants, that women have tits and cunts under their clothes, that people can say and do whatever they want as long as it doesn't *hurt* anyone else, that their guns and orders and phony laws and honkie power are all bullshit, that there's no way any common words can "shock" and "corrupt" kids who are really hip to the whole deal and who are instead shocked and hurt by the insane disregard for human freedom that the police and other authorities practice as a matter of course.

People are getting hip to all of the old people's lies and perversions, and they aren't gonna stand for it much longer. *We* sure aren't!

4. ROCK & ROLL DOPE #5

Poet-MC5 manager John Sinclair and MC5 guitarist Fred Smith were brutally assaulted, beaten, Maced, and arrested by members of the National Security Police, the Oakland County Sheriff's Department, and the Michigan State Police while performing at a teen-club in Oakland County last Tuesday, July 23rd. The two victims of police terrorism were charged with "assault and battery on a police officer" and are presently free on $2500 bond pending their pre-trial examination September 12th. The charge is a high misdemeanor and carries a maximum two-year sentence.

The scene took place at the Loft, a converted barn in Leonard, Michigan, where the MC5 had been contracted to play a dance job. What follows is Sinclair's account of the incident:

We had worked at the Loft twice before in the past month or so and never had any trouble out there, just great crowds of high-energy kids, you know? But the club owner had bounced two checks on us for a total of almost $400, and we were going to take him to court and also try to get his place closed down by the musicians' union, because he had beat a bunch of other bands around here too. This dude, Harold Boumer his name is, called our booking agent and told him that he wanted to settle everything with the bands he had ripped off, and he set up this date for us to go out there the 23rd and play again in exchange for all the money he owed us plus 40% of the gate for that night. We didn't want to hang him up anyway—we just wanted to get our money, and we dug playing out there because the kids are so far out. So we agreed to the deal and drove out there the night of the 23rd.

When we arrived, and before we could even get out of the van, we were confronted by this rent-a-pig named Capt. Kenneth Osborne and told that he didn't want us to play "that song with motherfucker in it." I told him that he didn't have anything to do with our show, and that if he wanted to say anything to us he could say it through the manager, because we worked for him and not for some rent-a-cop, right? This pig had given me some shit the last time we were there anyway, about moving the equipment out faster or something, and I didn't wanna talk to him at all.

When we went inside Boumer ran up to me and apologized for Osborne's actions. I told him that we would just as soon turn around and go back home if there was gonna be any funny shit, because we were giving this dude a break in the first place and we didn't haveta stand for any of his pig's madness. Boumer said never mind Osborne, just play the gig and I'll pay you your money afterwards. Well, we were supposed to get it all in front, but he only had $100 and he said he'd give us all the money that came in that night, because he had a full house and he knew he'd have all the money by the end of the night.

So I took the $100 and the band went on stage to kick 'em out. The 5 smoked through the first 3 tunes and were really flyin', but this chomp Osborne had the house announcer stop the show "because of obscenity." We asked the people if we should stop, explaining that we had come to play for them and we'd let *them* decide what we should do. They told us to keep on playing, but we decided to play one more thing and then go right into "Comm" so we could get out of there in case this pig started any shit. We didn't wanna stop right there because we didn't wanna leave the people with nothing, you know, but on the other hand we knew this fool was crazy and

we wanted to get outa there as soon as we could.

Meanwhile the rent-a-pigs apparently called the Oakland County Sheriff's Department and told them there was a "riot" going on because we wouldn't stop playing and were "inciting the kids to violence." That was a bunch of bullshit, because what we actually told them was that there were a bunch of crooks running this place and they should never come back because the owners were cheating the bands and pulling funny shit all the time, right? Anyway, Osborne and his flunkies blockaded all the exits to the place so nobody could get out—evidently they figured they'd better *have* a riot situation when the real pigs got there or else they wouldn't look so good, you know?

I had the equipment dudes pack up all the shit and take it out to the van, and got the band changed and all the guitars and shit packed up and sent them downstairs to wait for me. I didn't know that the doors were shut off or anything, I was up there checking the stage area to make sure all the equipment was taken care of and checking the dressing room and all the stuff you have to do before you leave, so you won't leave anything behind, you dig? I'm standing by the stage when this dude Boumer comes up to talk to me. We sit down on the edge of the stage, and he apologizes again for the police and asks me to bring the equipment back up so we can play another set and he won't have to give the kids their money back! *What?* I couldn't believe what I was hearing! I told Boumer he was stone crazy if he thought we'd stick around that madhouse for another

Yet more pigs talk to John Sinclair, photo by Leni Sinclair

minute—we wanted our money and if he didn't want to pay it right there we'd see his ass in court. I also told him that we were going to put the word out on him to all the bands in the area, and that I was going to get the musicians' union to shut him down for good—not just because he beat us out of the money, but because he couldn't control his police and he was cheating all the people who went there.

Boumer kept talking, mumbling on about a second set and dodging the money issue, when all of a sudden the rent-a-pigs and a bunch of uniformed police in riot gear appeared at the top of the stairs and started marching over to where we were sitting. Osborne was in the lead, and he came up to me and started oinking in my face.

"Sinclair, get out of here!" Osborne grunted. I asked him what the fuck he was talking about, looking at Boumer expecting him to explain what was happening. Osborne oinked again: "I told you to get out of here—*now!*" I told him I couldn't possibly leave until I got the money. Osborne and his partner snatched me by the arms and yanked me up, but I broke free for a minute and smashed him in the face. Then the whole force jumped on me and beat me down to the ground. Osborne squatted on top of me and kept hitting me in the face while the other porkers were smashing me with nightsticks, blackjacks, fists and booted feet while I tried to cover up my head and genitals. During the melee an Oakland County pig, Donald Gilbert, badge number 81, squirted me in the face with Mace, and another pig handcuffed me.

There were still about 100-150 kids on the dance floor standing around in horror as this bloody scene flashed into action in front of their eyes. They were just as dumbfounded as I was, and it all happened so fast that it must've been hard to believe that it was really happening. Girls were screaming and crying, everybody was trying to figure out what was happening, and by this time the pigs were beating on Fred Smith, who had run up from downstairs to help me when he heard all the noise. Fred leaped into the pile of pigs who were beating on me, but two of them pulled him off and beat his ass with clubs. They subdued both of us, got us handcuffed and dragged us over into the corner before they started clearing the room. A bunch of sisters, righteous MC5 addicts who came to all our gigs, came over and started wiping the blood off of us, but the pigs grabbed them and pushed them down the stairs. One sister had a camera and I told her to get pictures of this shit, but the pigs spotted her and grabbed her camera and broke it before they pushed her down the stairs too. They beat up quite a few kids and shoved everybody else out of the place, finally letting the doors be opened so people could leave.

They took me & Fred and put us in the car and started for the county jail in Pontiac, with about 15 cars full of kids following them all the way. One kid tried to set the place on fire he was so mad! When we got to the jail they booked us on charges of assault and battery on a police officer, but when Osborne tried to sign the arrest warrant the desk sergeant told him that he wasn't a police officer and couldn't legally arrest us. So one of the Oakland County pigs stepped up and said he'd sign it—that was Gilbert, the one who Maced me, right? All these kids were milling around outside, but the deputies all went outside and started threatening them, so they yelled up to us one more time and then pulled up. When we got in court to be arraigned the next morning some other pig's name was on one of the warrants too. We pleaded not guilty and our people posted $2500 bond for each of us, which was the highest bond the judge could set, you dig? We're gonna fight this as hard as we can, and then we're gonna sue all these creeps. These fascist dogs are trying to stomp *all* of us out—DON'T LET THEM DO IT!

5. FLASH! MC5 ARRESTED IN ANN ARBOR FOR PLAYING FREE MUSIC IN THE PARKS— CHARGED WITH DISTURBING THE PEACE!

Rob Tyner, Wayne Kramer, Fred Smith, Michael Davis and Dennis Thompson—the MC5— were arrested by Ann Arbor police Friday, July 26th, and charged with "disturbing the peace" and "disorderly person" as a result of a free concert they played in West Park last Sunday (July 21). The band posted $125 apiece in bond money and will face the charges in Ann Arbor Municipal Court next Monday.

The warrants stem from complaints by neighbors of the park about the alleged "noise" created by the band last Sunday. The principal complainant, Johannah Lemble, whose name appears on the warrant, charges the brothers individually with "creating an unreasonable and disturbing noise" and with "disturbing the peace" by being "loud and boisterous" in violation of city ordinances. Mrs. Lemble and her husband are active in the local chapter of the John Birch Society.

What went down is this: Last summer free rock & roll concerts were held in West Park every Sunday through the middle of September. Ron Miller, bassist for the now-defunct Seventh Seal (who is presently in Europe with his new band, the Pigfuckers), would pay the city the $10.00 permit fee every week, and the Seal as well as bands like the Prime Movers, Charles Moore's avant jazz group, Billy C. and the Sunshine, the Up, the Roscoe Mitchell Unit from Chicago, and the Grateful Dead when they were in town, took the stand every Sunday afternoon to play for the people in the sun.

Ron Levine and I applied for a permit to use the West Park bandshell some weeks ago and received a flat refusal. Apparently a new ordinance was passed during the winter months outlawing amplified music in the parks so there couldn't be any more concerts, but we knew the people had to have the music. So after giving the matter some serious consideration, including consultations with attorneys and local heads, we decided to just go down to the park and set up and kick out the jams, since the parks belong to the people anyway. Two Sundays ago (July 14, Bastille Day), the MC5 set up in the picnic shelter in the park and played

John Sinclair, photo by Leni Sinclair

MC5 at West Park, Ann Arbor, 1968, photo by Leni Sinclair

Early MC5, pre-John Sinclair, 1965

for about an hour for a great audience of freeks and black people from the neighborhood. The police showed up to douse it out, but the mayor was on the set and held them off until he could talk to us and see what the deal was. I told him that these were important community functions and that we were donating our time and energy to the people so they could have some of the free music they need to survive, and he said he could dig it. He promised to get in touch with us during the week, but two weeks went by with no word from the city, so we decided to make it on down to the park again and rent our own generator so we could play in the bandshell this time. Word of mouth spread the news, and a large grooving audience was there on Sunday ready for it.

The Up played the first set and smoked all the way through, with a short interruption when two uniformed patrolmen mounted the stage in an attempted suppression scene. Lt. Staudemire emerged from out of the audience where he had been digging the proceedings and cooled out the lowly patrolmen. He explained to us that the neighbors around the park were complaining about the noise and could we turn down a little to see if that would work out? Sure. The Up did the rest of their set, and the 5 followed them for an hour with the dangerous jams the people love to hear. When it came time for the magic moment Tyner got the whole crowd to scream "KICK OUT THE JAMS, MOTHERFUCKER!" with him, *three times,* and you could hear it all over town. This brought down the self-righteous wrath of the Birchers in the neighborhood, however, and led to the arrests of Friday.

There was no music in the park this weekend, but one interesting development has taken place: city officials have expressed a further desire to meet with the Trans-Love freeks this next week to see what can be worked out in terms of free outdoor concerts somewhere else around town. Meanwhile petitions are being circulated among Ann Arbor's hip citizenry to demonstrate the need and support for such concerts.

More News as it happens.

FLASH! More news happened. On Sunday, July 28, as this SUN was going to press, the MC5 was traveling to Oakland University to. play on a benefit for ALSAC (Aid to Leukemia-Stricken American Children) when we were met by our equipment crew who had gone on ahead of us. They reported that they'd been at the gig and were greeted by more than 10 Oakland County Sheriff's cars. Apparently the legendary Oakland pigs had warrants for Rob Tyner, Mike Davis and Wayne Kramer dating back to 1966 and were determined to cash them in at Oakland U when we showed for the benefit. We just turned around and beat it back home.

Stay tuned to the paper radio for more news as it happens.

6. FLASH! FREE MUSIC IN GALLUP PARK EVERY SUNDAY! ROCK & ROLL EMERGES TRIUMPHANT!

Following the tremendous success of the first Gallup Park free concert last Sunday local heads and rock & roll maniacs will carry on on the banks of the Huron River every Sunday afternoon until further notice. Last Sunday's concert, which featured the Black & Black Boo Funny Music Band, Billy C. and his Killer Blues Band, and the dangerous MC5, went off with no trouble whatsoever, just groovy vibes all around. No cops appeared all afternoon during the three-hour fest, but Lt. Staudemire could be seen with his lady digging the music quietly from the riverbank on an unofficial off-duty visit. Staudemire, who has emerged as the city's liaison man with the hip community, was instrumental in freeing the Gallup Park location for the free concerts, working in conjunction with Asst. City Administrator Don Borut and Trans-Love heads to find a home for the music the people need.

The Gallup Park location, on the south bank of the Huron River near the corner of Geddes Road and Fuller Road, is so isolated from complaining neighbors that the city called us up Monday morning to see if there had been a concert the day before! When they realized that everything is cool they granted permission to use the park whenever necessary, which is pretty incredible.

This Sunday's concert will start at 3 p.m. and will feature the Wilson Mower Pursuit and the MC5, with other community bands due to fall by for a set. Bands who want to do their thing for the people are urged to bring their equipment out and kick out the jams with us Sunday afternoon. The concerts are presented by the people for the people—free for all!

7. FLASH! MC5 SET TO KICK OFF FESTIVAL OF LIFE! YIPPIE!

The long-awaited Youth International Party Festival of Life will surge into being Sunday, August 25th, in Chicago's Lincoln Park, with a kick-off concert by Ann Arbor's own MC5!

The *SUN* talked with YIP music coordinator Ed Sanders in New York yesterday and got the latest dope on the already-legendary Festival of Life (YIPPIE! CHICAGO! AUGUST 25-30!), which will be held in the Windy City at the same time as the Democratic Party National Death Convention. The YIPPIE Festival will be built around the music of the international youth culture—rock & roll!—and will also focus on two other favorite activities of *SUN* readers—dope, and fucking in the streets. In addition to other YIPPIE! activities, Sanders has scheduled rock & roll concerts for each afternoon and evening of the Festival, which should create enough energy to keep everyone going through the less musical aspects of the program. Other Ann Arbor bands scheduled to play during the Festival of Life are the mighty Up, the Psychedelic Stooges, and probably some others.

In his telephone interview with the *SUN* Sanders (who is otherwise known

Rob Tyner of MC5, photo by Leni Sinclair

as editor-publisher of FUCK YOU/a magazine of the arts, and founder of the fuck-rock group the Fugs) revealed that the Festival will indeed be held and that the city of Chicago is expected to grant the Lincoln Park permit with the added stipulation that the Festival area is to be left alone by Chicago police, who will be busy enough carrying out their assignments at the Democratic Death Convention and trying to keep the candidates from getting murdered on stage in the Amphitheatre.

Sanders and other Festival organizers will be flying to Chicago from New York today to confer with city officials and straighten out this permit business as well as other necessary arrangements. Sanders is confident that the city *will* grant the permit, although they may hold off until the last minute to spread further confusion among the millions of young people who are planning to make it to the YIP gathering. The Festival will go on no matter what the city says, according to Sanders, and the officials are well aware of that fact by now.

With all the other shit going down in Chicago during the week, it should be kept in mind that the Festival of Life is NOT a "protest" of any kind, but is a presentation of an alternative way of life which will provide a sharp contrast to the way of death epitomized by the Democratic Death Convention. Drunken delegates in restrictive ugly suits and ties and wing-tip shoes courting plastic prostitutes will be exposed as the pigs they are by hordes of long-haired freaks in brilliant colors and free bodies dancing to rock & roll, smoking dope, and fucking in the streets and parks of Chicago. For many Americans this will be their first contact with the dynamic Life Culture as legions of maniacs explode into the streets and onto the sacrosanct TV screens of America, bringing some free life to the nightly death news reports. And unlike the Democrat scene, no one will be barred from the YIP Convention, and we damn sure don't need "15,000 police, troops, and FBI personnel" to keep us from murdering each other while we do *our* thing! Kick out the Jams! YIPPIE!

8. FLASH! ELEKTRA BUYS 5!

In a lightning move, Elektra Records signed the MC-5 and the Stooges to long-term recording contracts in New York September 26th.

The move was engineered by Elektra's publicity director, the young Danny Fields, who flew out to hear the bands last weekend at the Grande Ballroom in Detroit during the 5's triumphant return to their old stomping ground for the first time since they were barred after the Blue Cheer hassle June 26th, and at the Union Ballroom in Ann Arbor where the 5 and the Stooges were playing a benefit for the Children's Community School.

The 5's first album will be recorded live at the Grande Ballroom late this month, probably on Wednesday and Thursday the 30th and 31st—Zenta New Year! The two dances will be free for all the people in the community so all the freeks who have supported the band all these years can get on the record too.

A single release is tentatively scheduled for early December, with the album itself due for release around Christmas or early January. A 16-mm color film of the 5 will be produced by Trans-Love Energies for release with the single, which will undoubtedly be "Kick Out the Jams" and probably "Motor City Is Burning."

After the recording is completed the 5 will travel to the east coast, where they will be introduced to the people of New York with a free concert at the Fillmore East right around Christmas. Motor City maniacs who can make it are invited to come out with us and show our brothers and sisters out there what we're doing here. Rock & roll!

POSTSCRIPT

Everybody knows what happened in Chicago that August, but it had a tremendous effect on us because the suppression of the Festival of Life confirmed our suspicions that it was our culture which was really dangerous as a political force in this place. We had been following all the developments in the radical movement throughout the summer, looking for some way to tie what we were doing with rock & roll maniacs in to the political scene, but of all the individuals and groups which were active at the time only the Yippies and the Black Panther Party seemed to understand the revolutionary potential of the people we were working with. We were knocked out by the total assault tactics of the Yippies, and we were even more impressed with the propaganda and the actions of the Black Panther Party, particularly the way Eldridge Cleaver related to our culture and Bobby Seale and Huey P. Newton called for "mother-country radicals" to organize their own people into a conscious political force. Pun got out of jail in September ready for action, and we started talking about how we might be able to hook up with these people so we could give the kids who related to the band a clearer political focus for their wild inarticulate anti-authoritarian thrust. When we got the recording contract with Elektra we knew that we would be able to reach a whole lot more kids all over the country with our total assault propaganda, and the time seemed absolutely perfect for putting our ideas into action. Immediately after we recorded the album at the Grande Ballroom we announced the formation of the White Panther Party, which we conceived as "an arm of the Youth International Party," and from that point on the MC-5 was identified as "the White Panther band." We had thousands of White Panther buttons printed up which we would pass out at all our gigs, and we started rapping about "revolution" before every show in an attempt to put the music and the "cultural revolution" into an explicitly political context. I stopped writing so much about our exploits with the police and started trying to sum up our experience and make some sense out of it so the kids who followed the band could see that they were part of a revolutionary movement and not just "rock & roll fans." The White Panther State/ meant is the first of those documents.

MC5 and The Stooges signed to Elektra, photo by Leni Sinclair

THE WHITE PANTHER
STATE/MEANT

NOVEMBER 1, 1968

First I must say that this statement, like all statements, is bullshit without an active program to back it up. We have a program which is ongoing and total and which must not be confused with anything that is said or written about it. Our program is cultural revolution through a total assault on the culture which makes use of every tool, every energy and every media we can get our collective hands on. We take our program with us wherever we go and use any means necessary to expose people to it.

WPP Red Star sisters, 1970, photo by Leni Sinclair

Our culture, our art, our music, newspapers, books, posters, our clothing, our homes, the way we walk and talk, the way our hair grows, the way we smoke dope and fuck and eat and sleep—it is all one message, and the message is FREEDOM! We are free mother-country maniacs in charge of our own lives and we are taking this freedom to the peoples of America in the streets, in the ballrooms and teen-clubs, in their front rooms watching TV, in their bedrooms playing with themselves or smoking secret dope, in their schools where we come and talk to them or make our music in their weird gymnasiums—they love it!—we represent the only possible contemporary life-style in America for its kids and it should be known that these kids are *ready!* They're ready to move but they don't know how, and all we do is show them that they can *get away with it.* BE FREE, goddamnit, and forget all those old creeps, is what we tell them, and they can see that we *mean* it. The only influence we have, the only thing that touches them, is that we are *for real.* We are FREE, we are a bunch of flipped-out arrogant barbarians and we don't give a damn for any cop or any phony-ass authority control-addict creep who wants to put us down.

I heard Stokely Carmichael in 1966 call for "20 million arrogant black people" as America's salvation, and there are a lot of arrogant black warriors in the streets today—for the first time in America—and for the first time in America there is a generation of visionary maniac white mother country dope fiend rock & roll *freaks* who are ready to *get down* and *kick out the jams*—

ALL THE JAMS—break everything loose and free everybody from their very real and imaginary prisons—even the chomps and ponks and honkies who are always messing with us. We demand total freedom for *everybody!* And we will not be stopped until we get it. We are *bad.* Like Hassan I Sabbah The Old Man of the Mountain we initiate no hostile moves, but when moved against we will mobilize our forces for a total assault. We have been moved against every day of our lives in this weirdo country, and we are moving now to overturn this motherfucker, scrape the shit off it and turn it back over to all the people. All Power to the People! Black Power to black people! And People Power to *Everybody!*

As Brother Eldridge Cleaver says, the shit is going down and there's only two kinds of people on the planet: those who make up the problem, and those who are the solution. WE ARE THE SOLUTION! We have no "problems." Everything must be free for everybody. Money is obsolete. The white honkie culture that has been handed to us on a silver plastic platter is meaningless to us! We don't want it! All we want is our freedom, and we know we can't be free until *everybody* is free!

Our program of rock & roll, dope, and fucking in the streets is a program of total freedom for everyone. And we are totally committed to carrying out our program. We *breathe* revolution. We are LSD-driven total maniacs in the universe. We will do anything we can to drive people out of their heads into their bodies. Rock & roll music is the spearhead of our attack because it's so effective and so much fun. We have developed organic high-energy guerrilla rock & roll bands who are infiltrating the popular culture and destroying millions of minds in the process. With our music and our economic genius we plunder the unsuspecting straight world for money and the means to carry out our program, and revolutionize its children at the same time. And with our entrance into the straight media we have demonstrated to the honkies that anything they do to hassle us will be exposed to their children. You don't need to get rid of all the honkies, you just rob them of their replacements and let the breed atrophy and die out, with its heirs cheering triumphantly all around it.

We don't have guns yet—not all of us anyway—because we have more powerful weapons: direct access to millions of teenagers is one of our most potent, and their belief in us is another. But we will use guns if we have to—we will do anything—if we have to. We have no illusions. Knowing the power of symbols in the abstract world of Americans we have taken the White Panther as our mark to symbolize our strength and arrogance and to demonstrate our commitment to the program of the Black Panther Party as well as to our own—indeed, the two programs are just part of the same whole thing.

The actions of the Black Panthers in America have inspired us and given us strength, as has the music of black America, and we are moving to reflect that strength in our daily activity just as our music contains and extends the power and feeling of the black magic music that originally informed our bodies and told us that we could be free. I might mention brother James Brown in this connection, as well as John Coltrane and Archie Shepp. Sun-Ra. Robert Williams. Malcolm X. Huey P. Newton, Bobby Seale, Eldridge Cleaver, these are magic names to us. These are *men* in America. And we're as crazy as they are, and as pure. We're *bad.* This is our program:

1. Full endorsement and support of the Black Panther Party's 10-point program and platform.
2. Total assault on the culture by any means necessary, including rock & roll, dope, and fucking in the streets.
3. Free exchange of energy and materials—we demand the end of money!
4. Free food, clothes, housing, dope, music, bodies, medical care—everything free for every body!
5. Free access to the information media—free the technology from the greed creeps!
6. Free time & space for all humans—dissolve all unnatural boundaries!
7. Free all schools and all structures from corporate rule— turn the buildings over to the people at once!
8. Free all prisoners everywhere—they are our comrades!
9. Free all soldiers at once—no more conscripted armies!
10. Free the people from their phony "leaders"—everyone must be a leader—freedom means free every one! All Power to the People!

—John Sinclair,
Minister of Information

Stay alive with the MC5! Photo by Leni Sinclair

WHITE PANTHERS ON THE MOVE

DECEMBER 5, 1968

Flash! White Panther Minister of Information John Sinclair announced today that the newly-formed revolutionary organization has named its first Central Committee.

In its first formal meeting the Committee discussed matters of immediate importance to the White Panthers and the world, including the threatened imprisonment of brother Eldridge Cleaver, Minister of Information, Black Panther Party, and the arrest and imprisonment of 13 young brothers and sisters in Detroit for alleged "conspiracy to place explosives with intent to do damage" to police cars, draft boards, the Ann Arbor CIA office, and other "anti-establishment" targets.

The Committee offered a special round of tokes dedicated to Eldridge Cleaver and the strength and daring he has demonstrated in his stunning escape from the mother country police forces. A second round was offered in solidarity with the powerful brother, "wherever he may be." The Committee then dedicated itself to increasing the White Panther attack on all fronts in order to possibly short-circuit any future attempts on our comrades' lives.

"We can't tolerate this bullshit any longer," Sinclair said in a prepared statement. "The shit is really out in the open now and it's starting to stink real bad. If Eldridge Cleaver—or any revolutionary—is fucked with any further we will be forced to step up our total assault on the pig-death culture until the pigs can't stand it.

"We have been shown no mercy and we will grant none until all harassment of all citizens is stopped and the brontosaurus capitalist economy smashed to smithereens. We mean it. We are tired of this shit from the honkies and so are millions of young brothers and sisters all over the planet. We will not rest until it is stopped.

"The problem is getting more serious every minute, and we are responding to the increased pressure of the power structure by building a dangerous power structure of our own.

"Panther Ministers have been meeting with spokespeople of a number of tribes of radicals and freeks and will be moving to establish direct and concrete alliances with as many groups as possible, all over the planet.

"A ten-man guerrilla reconnaissance team will be sent out from our national headquarters in Ann Arbor to meet with people in Boston, Cleveland, and New York City in the next two weeks.

"The spearhead of this attack will be the MC5, who have scheduled appearances at the Boston Tea Party, the Cleveland Grande, and the Fillmore East in New York City in order to get the Panther message to the people in those areas. Minister of Defense Pun Plamondon, Minister of Religion J. C. Crawford, National Captain Steve Harnadek and myself will accompany the brothers in the band, and we will all be looking forward to meeting with militant brothers and sisters wherever we go. All Power to the People!"

The MC5 is a *whole thing*. There is no way to get at the music without taking in the whole context of the music too—*there is no separation*. We say the MC5 is the solution to the problem of separation, because they are *so together*. The MC5 is totally committed to the revolution, as the revolution is totally committed to driving people out of their separate shells and into each other's arms.

I'm talking about *unity*, brothers and sisters, because we have to *get it together*. We *are* the solution to the problem, if we will just *be* that. If we can *feel* it, LeRoi Jones said, "Feeling Predicts Intelligence." The MC5 will make you feel it, or leave the room. The MC5 will drive you crazy out of your head into your body. The MC5 *is* rock & roll. Rock & roll *is* the music of our bodies, of our whole lives—the "resensifier," Rob Tyner calls it. We have to *come together*, people, "build to a gathering," or else. Or else we are dead, and gone.

The MC5 will bring you back to your senses from wherever you have been taken to hide. They are *bad*. Their whole lives are totally given to the music. They are a *whole thing*. They are a working model of the new paleocybernetic revolution in action. There is no separation. They live together to work together, they eat together, fuck together, get high together, walk down the street and through the world together. *There is no separation.* Written as the liner notes to the MC5's Elektra album "Kick Out the Jams," and printed on the first edition of the album. These notes were later deleted by Elektra Records due to pressure from the music industry. Just as their music will bring you together like that, if you will *hear* it. If you will *live* it. And we

will make sure you hear it, because we know you need it as bad as we do. We have to have it!

The music is the source and effect of our spirit flesh. The MC5 is the source and effect of that music, just as you are. Just as I am. Just to hear the music and have it *be* our selves, is what we need. We are a lonely desperate people, pulled apart by the killer forces of capitalism and competition, and we need the music to hold us together. *Separation Is Doom.* We are free people, and we demand a free music, a free high energy source that will drive us wild into the streets of America yelling and screaming and tearing down everything that would make people slaves.

The MC5 *is* that force. The MC5 *is* the revolution, in all its applications. There is no separation. Everything Is Everything. There is no thing to fear. The music will make you strong, as it *is* strong, and there is no way it can be stopped now. All Power to the People! The MC5 is here now for you to hear and see and feel now! Give it up—come together—*get down*, brothers and sisters, it's time to testify, and what you have here in your hands is a living testimonial to the absolute power and strength of this music. Go wild! The world is yours! Take it now, and be one with it! Kick out the *jams*, motherfucker! And stay *alive*, with the MC5!

—John Sinclair,
Minister of Information,
White Panthers
Friday, December 13th 1968,
in the first year of Zenta

ROCK & ROLL IS A WEAPON OF CULTURAL REVOLUTION

DECEMBER 1968

"The duty of the revolutionary is to make the revolution." The duty of the musician is to make the music. But there is an equation that must not be missed: MUSIC IS REVOLUTION. Rock & roll music is one of the most vital revolutionary forces in the West—it blows people all the way back to their senses and makes them feel good, like they're *alive* again in the middle of this monstrous funeral parlor of western civilization. And that's what the revolution is all about—we have to establish a situation on this planet where all people can feel good all the time. And we will not stop until that situation exists.

Rock & roll music is a weapon of cultural revolution. There are not enough musicians around today who are hip to this fact. Too many of your every-day pop stars feel that music is simply a means by which they can make a lot of money or gain a lot of cheap popularity or whatever—dollars and ego power, both of which are just a killer ruse, in fact I would have to say the killer ruse of all time. Money is the biggest trick of all, next to the so-called ego, which comes out of the same scene as money anyway. I mean the ego developed strictly as an economic function, when there got to be too many people on the planet for the planet's natural resources and there wasn't enough for everybody any more. Then people had to start separating themselves out from the tribe and see themselves as individuals, because if there ain't enough for everybody then everybody's got to try to make sure he or she has got enough, and there's always somebody else around who wants to take it away from you.

Before that, when there was plenty for all and the only "other" was the magic force of nature, people were just "there," together, Everyone was brother and sister and they were all in it together, totally. The Paleolithic Age. And for centuries between then and now people have struggled to secure enough for themselves and "their" families. The development of western culture was strictly a function of scarcity economics. No one seems to realize this. It was all strictly necessary. But what is so interesting about being alive right now is that finally the means to plenty for all exist again, even with all the millions and billions of people on the planet, and it is only a small oligarchy which is holding the new age back.

The economy of this country—which controls the economy of the rest of the world—is controlled by maybe 200 families of Euro-Amerikans which

Rob Tyner with tools of Revolution, photo by Leni Sinclair

are inextricably connected through intermarriage and other traditional aristocratic tricks. Check it out—this arrogant clique of super-rich capitalists runs *everything*, and they do it by being so well organized to protect their class interests. They are not going to give up what they've got, and the only way we can deal with them is to organize ourselves and move in an organized manner to seize political power from these greedy pigs and use it in the interests of *all* the people, not just a tiny gang of "owners" and manipulators. If 200 families in America can control the economic and cultural life of 200,000,000 people at home (as well as countless millions around the world) then 200 together "families" or tribes of freeks, radicals and other dope-crazed maniacs could just as easily take it away from them and give it back to the people as a whole, if we would work as hard at revolutionary change as the Rockefellers and Kennedys and Harrimans and DuPonts and their crime partners work at making money and extending their financial empires. But we have to have the full-time commitment to revolution that these people have to capitalism, and we have to set up an interlocking system of alliances and mergers that will give us the collective strength that the rich white folks have. Then we can just turn them out, because we're a lot heavier and a lot more together than they are.

As William Burroughs pointed out in *The Soft Machine* ("The Mayan Caper"), the ruling class doesn't know what it's doing anymore—they just push the buttons and hope that things will keep working out for them. They don't understand how their system works any more than I understand the workings of a Marshall amplifier—they just plug it in and hope for the best. If it doesn't work they have to call in the repairman, like they did with S. I. Hayakawa at San Francisco State a little while ago. The pig power elite called in the expert semanticist to cool out the hard brothers and sisters at SF State, and when they "wouldn't listen to reason" and tried to beat the Tom's ass, he tried to destroy their public address system—what a *perfect* fucking metaphor!

But you see, our scene is tighter than that, and if they destroy our machines we'll just build new ones, organizing as we go by getting people to relate to the honkies' panic. That's why the stomp scene in Chicago was ultimately the most successful ruse the movement has pulled, because freeks were able to organize media people as well as other freeks around the simple gut issue of getting beat over the head by some rampaging pigs. The Violence Commission Report that came out last week bears witness to our success—now we've got the pigs investigating each other. And you can't call that "co-optation" any way you look at it, because *we* co-opted *their* media and used it against them. And that's what we have to keep on doing, at all levels, taking over the machinery and the technology—especially the communications media—of the pigs to use it against them. And we can use it to reach the millions of straight people they've been brainwashing against us—once we control the means of production, including the mass media, we can save the honkoid masses from their pig-induced sickness and fear. If we can get our own messages into those media the masses will start to see things our way and they'll have to dig it, because it's so much better for them that the shit they're stuck with now, under the present system.

Our way is best—that's what we have to start from. We have the most fun. We feel good all the time, even in the most distressing situations, because we *have to.* We haven't got any choice. We've been blasted out of the old way and we can't *take* it any more, no matter what they try to do to us to make us come back. That's why it's so funny to hear people talking about "selling out" and "co-optation" any more, because now anybody who's been opened up to the new universe just can't go back to that other shit. It's impossible.

Actually we co-opt their media, not vice versa. Just like we co-opt their kids. When the son or daughter of an industrialist big-shot starts smoking dope and dropping acid and digging high-energy rock & roll music and taking the money from their father's system and bringing it into our new economy, we can't say they're co-opting the free thing—we have to say that we've copped another of their replacements, you dig?

It's the same way when a creep-o magazine like *Playboy* runs an interview with Eldridge Cleaver or an article on the new age by Alan Watts—we're using their media to get our point across to their people who are our people all the time but just aren't hip to it. We couldn't buy that space, we couldn't steal it, we couldn't make them give

it up, but we did get it by making our thing attractive enough to them on their weird terms that they would use it for their ends too. If we can't do that then we simply don't *get* to the broad masses of the people, because we sure don't have an alternative mass information system of our own—yet. We will have, but until we do we have to use whatever we can get our hands on while we're building our own network.

Westerners have absolutely no respect for content—they're hooked on form image. "Image is junk" is the way Burroughs put it, and once their forms are infiltrated you can get your own content in and they hardly notice the difference until it's too late, as long as they can relate to the form. Americans are the farthest out in this respect. That's how we can disguise ourselves as simple economic forces, like rock & roll bands, newspapers, etc., and continue to carry out our work with the blessing of the power structure, because they are so easily fooled by a graspable form. I think it was Adolfo Gilly in his introduction to *A Dying Colonialism* by Frantz Fanon who said "the new content is creating cracks in the old forms" and bringing about their destruction. We can work within those old forms, infusing them with our new content and using them to carry out our work, which is making people feel good and giving them the information they need to free themselves from the death culture once and for all, and get busy freeing other people.

The answer is for people to start dropping out of the death machine and start getting it together. Find your own personal brothers and sisters and start living and working together. It's not only more fun and more productive, it's also cheaper and easier within the present system to live, work, eat, and do everything else as a communal unit. Plus, you build political and economic power that enables you to get along better and carry out your program with less bullshit from the creeps, or at least a better chance of dealing with it when it does come down. If you have an effective organization you can demand better conditions from the greed creeps, and you will at least have a better shot at getting what you need. Try it.

You know this is true. The system depends on you for its existence. If you don't go along with it, it will fall apart. Believe it. If you—every one of you—would refuse to go into the army there simply wouldn't *be* any army! The same thing for General Motors. They need YOU to keep their thing going. And when you aren't there they miss you. They want to lock you up so if you won't go along with them, at least you won't get to go against them. But they can't keep us all locked up. Shit, they can't even keep *me* locked up!

Think about it. If all the kids in high schools who can't stand that shit would stop going—all of you—then where would the schools be? They have to have you there. If you aren't there they won't be able to eat—they won't have a job any more. Your parents will go crazy too. They'll all have to start giving you what you demand in order to get you to go along with them. And if you don't stop demanding, they'll be on their toes every minute. The second you let up, they'll start to solidify their gains. You can't let up on them, people.

You got to keep on them all the time. You have to live this life every second, or they'll shoot you right out of it before you know what happened.

If you're living at home, start planning for what you'll be doing when you split. Get together with your people who are waiting to split and plan a scene for when you can be together. Start practicing now, on your parents' money and time. Save up your money if you get any so you can buy your supplies and equipment when you split.

Don't waste your time pissing and moaning about how shitty everything is. Start getting it together so you can change it. Everybody knows what a drag it is. You're not telling anybody anything they can use. Exchange information. Get down. And when you *have* split, get your thing together so you'll be able to have a better time than just sitting around smoking bogus dope, dropping bogus speed-filled acid, shooting smack, and listening to brainwash low-energy jams. Tripping out is a dead end and a drag. *You always come down.* If you engage yourself in a total revolutionary program of self-reliance and serving the people any way you can, you will have a guaranteed good time forever (except for when they lock you up from time to time) and will help other people get it together too.

It isn't enough just to drop out though—you have to create new forms which will enable you to sustain yourselves while you're doing your work. The commune is the life-form of the future, it is *the* revolutionary organizational life-form, and the communal relationship must be realized in everything you do. Rock & roll is the best example. That's why I said at the beginning of this rant, that MUSIC IS REVOLUTION, because it is immediate, total, fast-changing and on-going. Rock & roll not only is a weapon of cultural revolution, it is the *model* of the revolutionary future. At its best the music works to free people on all levels, and a rock & roll band is a working model of the post-revolutionary production unit. The members of a rock & roll family or tribe are totally interdependent and totally committed to the same end—they produce their music collectively, sharing both the responsibility and the benefits of their work equally. They work on the frontiers of modern technology to produce a new form which is strictly contemporary in all its implications. *There is no separation.* And that's what it's all about.

The way to total freedom is through the cybernetic revolution carried on in a communal context, which means that the technology will be freed to do the work of the people and the people will be freed to develop their culture—their humanity—as high as they can take it. They will share control over the means of production and share the fruits of the productive process equally Work will be restored to its original meaning—energy freed for use—because the work that people will do in the paleocybernetic future will be totally useful and humanly fulfilling. There will be no waste, because there will be nobody around who can profit from the waste as there is in capitalist society.

Capitalism is obsolete—it is based on the two horrible notions of private property and competition, both of which have to go right now. And the point is, that it's time for them to go, because there's no more room for that old-time shit in the world today. People have got to get it together, not apart. People are now stuck in bullshit jobs, bullshit schools, bullshit houses, bullshit marriages, bullshit social and economic scenes, and there's no need for it anymore. Most of the jobs that presently exist are useless and anti-human, and they'll be done away with immediately once the people are in power and the machines are freed to do all the work.

Likewise most of the products of the present consumer economy—they're bullshit and will no longer exist. Eighty-seven different brands of toothpaste! Millions of junky automobiles! That's all they are—junk—that people have been hooked on by the junk pushers of capitalism. The whole thing is ridiculous! Everything has to be free or else!

It is extremely important for urban groups to organize themselves around some form of popular cultural activity like a rock & roll band, a community newspaper, guerrilla theatre groups, a health clinic, or whatever you can put together. The cultural forms will give you access to the mass media and to mass audiences of pre-revolutionary youth who are just sitting around waiting to get totally turned on. High school groups can organize around newspapers and posters and bands and present a united front in their dealings with administrators and other old creeps I'll try to get more into this next time but right now I've got to split for St. Thomas Aquinas High School. It's time to turn on tune in and *take over!* Up against the ceiling, motherfucker!

TWO VIRGINS

JANUARY 1969

I'm sure everybody's tired of hearing all the psychedelic chatter about the Beatles and all, but there are some strange things going on in Beatledom that nobody seems to be talking about. There's never much need to talk about the music itself, because it's a popular music and anybody who wants to can turn on WABX and hear the music itself even before the records are released. And everybody knows what he or she likes to hear, and hears it. The music is always its own best explanation—especially when people can hear it for themselves, like with the Beatles—but a look at the scene that surrounds the music can be enlightening, especially when we're talking about tunes like their new single "Revolution."

Being the Number One Stars in the whole world, as well as England's richest young men, everything the Beatles do singly or as a group gets to the people immediately. The Beatles can do anything and people will know about it. What this means is that they have full access to the people's consciousness, or at least as full access as is allowed anyone. That is to say, they have access to people's minds in the same term as General Motors or the Army, say, are granted access, and they have the possibility of changing the public consciousness like very few people anywhere do. They have a lot of potential power, is what I'm trying to say, power such as very very few freaks ever get their hands on, and what I'm interested in is what they *do* with that power.

Rennie Davis, Yoko Ono, John Lennon, appear for the media before the John Sinclair Freedom Rally.

When the Beatles' lifestyle changed so drastically in 1966-67, that change was heralded throughout the world by *Sgt. Pepper's Lonely Hearts Club Band*, which got to more young people than any single record in a long time. It was the first time that stone freaks were granted positive access to the mass media, and the effects were overwhelming. That record, and the life-context it came out of and reflected, turned on millions of kids throughout the western world, especially in America, where the kids were really ready for it and could act on it right away. They all got turned on, just like that, and a lot of older people got caught up in it too, and got turned on just as hard.

It seems obvious to me that the Sgt. Pepper phenomenon was, along with Tim Leary and LSD, the major observable influence on the "youth revolution" as it exploded onto the scene as a mass movement. I mean, when the Beatles came out with mustaches and beards and beatnik long hair, smoking dope and coming on like weirdo acid freaks, playing and singing songs about acid and getting high and scenes on the sofa with a sister or two, it was a real bombshell that was dropped into the ruins of western civilization, and its effects were enormous.

For one thing, the Sgt. Pepper ruse effectively legitimized the hippie dope scene for the popular media and consequently played an indispensable role in bringing about the hugest change in a generation's consciousness in human history. I mean if you think things are the same now as before Sgt. Pepper and the all-American LSD year of 1967,

and if you think the Beatles didn't do it, check out where you were at in 1967. Look in the mirror. Ask your parents.

Anyway, it's in the light of their social effect (and their social tactics) of the last couple years and their good but horribly naive intentions that I can listen to "Revolution" by the Beatles without simply throwing up. The only way a program like the one laid out on that record is in any way palatable is if it's ongoing and total, and the Beatles' program in actual practice is sporadic and inconsistent at best. When it goes down it's dynamite, but it's only been going down once or twice a year (when a new Beatles jam is released) instead of daily, and their records since Sgt. Pepper (with the exception of a couple spaced-out singles) haven't been much to talk about at all.

They could own television stations, is what I want to say. They could do anything they wanted to do. They are in a position to propose and to carry out a total cultural assault, the effects of which would be incredible in their quality and quantity, and yet they set up an organization that gives clothes away to rich people and offers as the new musical hope on their own Apple label a female Englebert Humperdinck and the Black Dyke Mills Brass Band. Apple is just bullshit hippy capitalism unless its effects are commensurate with the needs of the people who look to the Beatles for leadership—and they just ain't.

My point is that if any freeks can do anything to change the way things are "peacefully," the Beatles can first of anybody because they've got the money and the power (in terms of positive

"I really thought that love would save us all. But now I'm wearing a Chairman Mao badge, that's where it's at."
—John Lennon, 1971

access to the mass information media) to bring about that change *right now* if they have it in them. There aren't very many of us who have available the kind of capital that's necessary to do anything constructive on a mass scale, and when somebody's got the resources and don't make use of them I don't wanna hear what they're talking about, I wanna see them *do it.* If their program is "changing people's minds" or whatever, there are obvious possibilities here for the rich and famous Beatles which start with personal example and practice and which don't have anything at all to do with "Those were the days my friend, we thought they'd never end," you know?

Some of John Lennon's individual activity is really encouraging in this respect, not that he's doing anything useful with his millions of dollars but at least he's improving the *content* of his message to a certain extent. Lennon has newly defined himself as a real *freek* and of course is getting somewhat shit on by the straight press for what he's doing, but the important thing is that millions of kids are finding out by watching him that *you can get away with it* if you wanna.

First he left his little pop-star wifey of some years and moved into what the *Detroit News* would call a "hippy pad" with the international spaced-out beatnik artist Yoko Ono, who is known and loved by freeks everywhere for her outrageous cultural assaults, e.g., a movie featuring 365 asses one at a time. This was pretty far out for the old Fab Four leader, and people started wondering what was going on. They knew there had to be something to it because after all, this is John Lennon of the famous BEATLES doing all this weird shit, and there must be some good reason for it or else he wouldn't be doing it, right?

Then he and Yoko got popped in their new place (which used to be occupied, according to *Rolling Stone* fanzine, by Ringo Starr, Jimi Hendrix, William Burroughs and other famous dope fiends) for possession of hashish, which was big news again especially since the Beatles had copped out the year before and said they'd quit smoking dope. Well, you knew it was a shuck but what could you say? It *is* interesting to note that their fans didn't start saying that shit but kept right on smoking plenty of dope of their own—which goes to show you that you have to be as fast as the kids all the time or they'll leave you behind, caught up in your twisted image of yourself. You get people smoking that good weed and then try to tell them that's not where it's at, and they just *know* better. "The people are the real heroes," Mao says, and they look up to their idols and leaders only as long as their heroes stay as fast as they are. Once they slow down, forget it. That's what's so beautiful about it.

John Lennon was hip to it after all. Signing an ad in the *London Times* is one mild-mannered way of fighting the marijuana laws, but getting busted on the street just like the hard-core brothers and sisters do and demonstrating to the masses that you get high and it's all right because you're John Lennon of the Beatles is something else altogether. Freeks don't relate too well to symbolic acts and gestures, but they can really get behind everyday reality, and they know what it is to get hassled and busted because it happens to them all the time. They can trust somebody who's like them in his or her daily life, and who shows them how to do the things they want to do and get away with them. That's how the Beatles established themselves as a force in the first place—I mean, you don't think it was the force of the music, right? *I Want To Hold Your Hand?* There's a *whole lot* more to it than the music, and it all has to do with the kind of reflection of themselves the people need at any given time: I guess that's why they're called "stars," because all they really do is *reflect* the level of consciousness of the people, you know what I mean?

Anyway, Lennon's latest caper is really a killer stunt. He and Yoko have recorded a soundtrack to their movie *Two Virgins*, and they put it out with an album cover photo of John and Yoko full-face naked on the front cover, a super-double-beaver shot that boggles the mind. There they are, two nasty old humans with their holy genitals waving in the wind like there ain't nothin' wrong with bein' naked out in the open like that. It's a killer album cover and of course its impact will be huge because *everybody* will see it or hear about it even if they never buy the album or listen to the music. It's a pure social act above and beyond any music industry bullshit, and it was a daring move indeed. The phony "nice-guy," "boy-next-door" image of the hungry early Beatles is smashed to smithereens, and the repressive effect of that kind of brainwashing gets totally reversed with one little photograph. It's a great liberating deed, and I love the brother for it.

Pop artists have been—and continue to be—overly cautious about their public image because they know that if they get too far out they simply won't be allowed to *get the money,* which is of course their overriding desire. It isn't all the fault of the musicians, because their lives are tightly controlled by a bunch of greasy greedheads who have colonized our culture and milk it for every cent they can rip off while the getting's good. But there are some of us now who are waking up to the fact that the greed creeps depend on us to make their money for them, not vice versa, and we're determined to change the structure of the Hollywood entertainment industry—which certainly includes, or which you might say has been replaced by, the pop music scene—and the people whose lives it shapes, as we pass through it on our way to building a whole new structure of our own.

Once you're a star or a mass-media personality people find out what you say and do, and you can have a tremendous liberating effect on millions of people if you insist on injecting blatantly revolutionary content into their cracked old forms. The rock & roll musician has a tremendous responsibility to his or her people, because they look up to their musicians as their own only heroes and idols, and our musicians are going to have to start living up to their responsibilities or they will eventually face the wrath of the people they have been betraying. Because the kids are getting farther out all the time, and they aren't going to put up with wimps and ponks and worthless opportunists much longer. John Lennon looks like he might be trying to get into something worthwhile now, but until he starts putting his money where his mouth (and now his cock) is, out front with the people, using it to fund self-determination programs for our people, I can't feel much better about him than I feel about his "revolution" ruse. He's headed in the right direction, but he's still got a way to go.

COMMUNITY RADIO

*"In a modern telecommunications society, the radio
station is one of the real seats of authority, its
seizure the seal of a successful revolution."*
        —Red Flag/Black Flag: French Revolution 1968

FEBRUARY 1969

I was just now talking with my good friend Richard Stoneman about the
subversiveness of what is so glibly called the "underground radio" or
"progressive rock" scene. We listen to the radio consciously, i.e., we know
what's being aired and we seek it out, and if the people who run the station
aren't getting down then we call them up and tell them what's happening—and they listen to us, because they want to find out, for whatever reason.
The customer's always right, if only on that level. But there are stations that are
different, where subversives are at work, and they're in the business of turning
people on to the cultural revolution in its various manifestations.

With these new radio people, their consideration is the brothers and sisters
who are listening to them on the air, and they're starting to realize that they have
a tremendous responsibility to those people because they haven't any other access to the natural facts—the real thing—unless they get it from their community
radio station. People depend on the radio to hip them to the whole cultural scene:
not only the new records, but all the news of what's going down in the immediate
area as well as around the global village, what's happening on the music scene,
who's in town this week, and like that. The people want to know who got busted,
when, where, and how, they want to know where they can find free medical care,
food, entertainment, materials, energies, whatever—the things that are important
to them in their daily lives.

For those of us who read—a minority I'm sure—the community newspaper
fills in the details and expands the context (visually too!) on a periodic basis,
but the radio is on every minute and has that further possibility of absolute currency—the electric *right now!* that we're trying to get at in our lives—the absolute
quick of things, that will put us right on time and in the middle of the flow.

Barbara Holiday, WABX DJ , photo by Leni Sinclair

The radio—and in our particular instance I'm talking about WABX-FM in Detroit—the radio is beginning to respond very precisely and very accurately to our needs, and we can grow as a community because of it. News gets around, as they say, and with the radio it gets right where it has to go. A sense of community is based upon adequate and accurate communications between the people and the community, whatever its specific geographical specifications. Our culture has needed radio for a long time, and now we have it, or at least we're in the process of getting it. But our own communications with the media have to improve too, just as theirs have to, and are improving. When you know some news and want other people to know it too, call your radio station and tell people there what you want them to know. Sometimes they might not listen to you, having heavy duties on their minds and shoulders, but I would mostly say that you'll find someone listening to you and spreading your word if you're after the good of the community and not just on some weird ego trip. It *might* be the radioworker who's on the ego trip, and in that case you'll just have to demand someone else. It's *your* radio, after all, and you have to act like it when they get too weird on you.

That's our radio, but you know we aren't the only ones listening to it. By virtue of its very definition radio reaches thousands and thousands of people who only have to turn on their receivers, which are standard gear now in most of our people's homes and automobiles. AM is next. Television is next. But with FM radio we have gone so much further than with any of the print media we have invented for ourselves—any of them. And we have the possibility of reaching lots of "neutral" people—people who wouldn't otherwise be exposed to our culture except through crazed articles in the kept press of the greed culture. "Hippies" and all that bullshit, which doesn't do anybody any good.

What we want is for these other people, just as ourselves, to get the information *now!* The real news, of what's happening in our lives. We want them to know, so they can change too. No one can act without the specific information that would make such action possible. Remember that. It doesn't do any good to come down on people for their ignorance—let them know what's happening and they'll at least have a chance to do the right thing. Without the information they can't get anywhere.

The radio provides the information in a super-direct and very entertaining form so it can't be missed. If only the music. The radio subverts people, because they have not been taught to grant the music its rightful and complete legitimacy as a prime term in their lives. Straight people have been taught that they are complete entities, in complete control of their little lives, given a free will that permits them to choose what they want to affect them. They live in their heads and see the world through their mind's eyes instead of their real ones. Their vision is clouded by what's been shoved into their heads, and what they "think" is

Sunny Sinclair in WABX ad, photo by Leni Sinclair

always more important to them than what's actually happening in the world. They'll do anything to preserve their illusions. In fact, to me that's precisely what makes the difference between someone who's straight and someone who's down. Straight people have "made up their minds" as to what will happen to them, and their lives try to be precisely regulated in terms of those decisions, in terms of what they "think" the world's all about. That's why they're so messed up.

Actually, that's only *how* they're messed up—*why* it's that way is something else again. People are the way they are because their economy demands it. In order to maintain a consumer economy like America's, the people in power have to keep a strict brainwash on the other people so they'll keep doing all the stupid things that are necessary to a consumer culture. Information has to be strictly limited—you have power over someone when you control the information they receive. When you can define the terms of a situation then you have a great deal of control over the outcome. But now we're starting to do a little defining of our own, and it will have its certain effect—watch and see.

Radio is really subversive as it acts on straight people because they think they're "just listening to the radio." As if the songs weren't coursing through their cells! As if they couldn't hear and feel our strange voices and our various energy constructs! As if this shit had no effect on them, the saviors of the western world! What a bunch of chomps! But they don't know any better, because they haven't had access to

the information before in any other media. They don't know any better, and the way they'll find out is by being exposed to the information. No matter how long it might take, no matter how long, it's happening to them every second even if they don't think so. The music is fucking them right in their tracks, and they don't even think it has any effect on them. "Oh yes, rock & roll. Hmmm. Where did I put the cat food? Oh dear." And off into the kitchen, with Jimi Hendrix blasting through the radio walls. She never knew what hit her, but that weekend she went to a rock & roll dance and she threw away her brassiere. No shit. I think it was the MC5 that was playing, and she got turned on to some mellow weed for the first time too. Outta sight. The next week she quit her job and went to California. Hmmm. Did this really happen? Who do you know?

Listen to the radio right now—turn on the FM while you're reading this, wherever you are, and check out what those people are doing on the air. If they're bullshitting and shucking and jiving, call them up and tell them to get down. You know what you want to hear. It's *your* radio, don't ever forget that. And I'm not just talking about requests, I'm talking about *community* radio—media for the people. If you don't know quite what you want, just tell them to do something else, you can't get next to what's going down right now and you want to hear something different, so you can educate yourselves. It's always nice to hear what you know, but it's more fun to find out something new.

Radio should be done as a conscious educational tool, a weapon of cultural revolution, to turn people on and charge them with energy and information so they can change their world. Don't settle for a hip 24-hour-a-day jukebox like so many stations try to be. Every program should be an educational experience for all listeners, and if they aren't giving you that then you give *them* some hell until they start meeting their responsibilities to the community.

Radio is our cultural communications system, and we have to have the information. We have to have the music—the strongest and purest music being made everywhere on earth, all the time. We can't do without it, and we don't *have* to anymore. We have to have news of our brothers and sisters too, wherever they are, whatever they're doing, we have to know about it so we can grow with them and *be* them, so they can be us, so we will be united as a people in knowledge, culture and action. When the barricades go up in Paris or Berkeley or Columbia University, we have to know about it so we can spread the word in our communities and act on that information. When people get kidnapped by the police on phony dope busts and held for ransom we have to know so we can get them out on the streets again. We have to know this stuff, all the time, and the radio can do it.

The duty of the revolutionary media is to communicate the news of the revolution—to get the dope to the people who need the information so they can act on it and become revolutionaries themselves, wherever they are. As we start to define this space for ourselves through our people in the media—our media—we help create a situation in which people who get our information start to act in the desired manner, i.e., in a revolutionary way. They start acting for themselves, moving to control their own lives—though not in any sense of *limiting* themselves, but simply *freeing* them selves from the consumer-death ruse.

As we begin to infiltrate and destroy the straight media and straight culture in general we start to set people free who have been trapped inside the pigpen without any information on how to get out. When people see that our newspapers come out every two weeks, or that the music goes on no matter what, that our lives go on freeky as they are—they learn that they can do it too. They can see that they can *get away with it.* And that's precisely the information they need.

The Man at Trans-Love Energies, Ann Arbor, photo by David Fenton

INFORMED SOURCES

*"Power is the ability to define phenomena and
make them act in a desired manner."*
> —Huey P. Newton

MARCH 21, 1969

illard Bain's book was originally printed by the Communications Company in San Francisco the summer of 1967 and given away free in the streets of the Haight-Ashbury. Now it's been picked up by a big publishing house and more people can get to read it.

Informed Sources is the first post-Burroughsian American novel I'd say, post-McLuhan too, and in its intentions and designs strictly contemporary. A series of AP-type news releases unfolds a whole network of plots and weird doings, centering on the takeover of a news service (Informed Sources) by a cabal of crazed anarchists calling themselves Green Dreams. The book is a strange trip and a groove to read, but beneath the plot level Bain (who has the same initials as Burroughs—WSB—strangely enough) has gotten down to the simple major questions of *control* and *power* and what *language* has to do with it.

Huey P. Newton's definition of power is not widely understood. What is meant here is that the people who have the ability or the means to *define* a situation can control those people who are caught up in that situation. People can only act on the information available to them, and if you control the information flow you control their possible action too. Hitler was the master of this technique, but the whole western control system is based on the same assumption. The language conditions us to make certain responses which are limited in advance by the form itself. In the West people ask you "what is 2 and 2?" You would say "four" without thinking, that is, *habitually*, unconsciously, because you have been given the terms of the proposition and have no choice but to accept them. That's as much as they told you, right? But any sane, i.e. conscious, people would say "2 *what*, motherfucker?" because they're hip to the medium and know that its message is *control*.

Can you dig this? Because it's one of the most important things for people to know right now. If we get hip to their language we can start to break their hold on us, because we can then refuse to accept their language as valid and force them to deal with us *on our own terms.* That means our own language, which is a pure and accurate expression of our own culture. The master language, what they call "English," is a control system meant to lock people into capitalism, competition, confusion, separation and death. It has evolved as a function of imperialism and means to preserve that system by limiting the flow of information to the people so they can find out only what the people in control want them to know, which is very damn little, because the more you know the less you want to be kept a slave. The best run-down of this language system I've ever seen is in George Orwell's killer book *1984*, and I wish you would check it out.

Information is the thing that will set people free, or at least start them on their way. Language is the primary non-military control device in western culture. You believe what you see or hear, but if you are given access only to a small fragment of the whole spectrum of information, your possibilities are extremely limited. If you are brought up on television and the daily press and the attendant honkie media (including the church and the American "educational" system) you will be given to believe, until you get the chance to find out for yourself by going out into the world, that everyone lives like a honkie in America except

the crooks, commies, filthy scum dope fiend rock & roll student demonstrators, black power advocates, and other deviates, and these people are all your (and America's) enemies. It's only when you *become* one of these types that you really start to find out how these media have been brainwashing you. You read about yourself in the papers and you can see just how much the honkie media will manipulate information in order to keep people under control.

American television is a precise control device. The American "educational" system is a precise control device. The American kept press is a precise control device. What is news is what the news media promote as the news—nothing else. Everything is happening all the time, but what you get is the story the power structure wants you to get so it can retain control over you. The power structure is in control because it can effectively *define* phenomena (things) and make them *act* in a desired manner. It will control your life until you seize the means of defining yourself and begin to develop a new definition of reality. Everything defines itself, in reality. What is, *is.* We define ourselves through our actions and the context we create for our actions, which gives our actions an organic structure we can constantly relate back to in order to give our work maximum effectiveness.

The purpose of the American information media as they exist now is to keep people chained to capitalism and consumer consciousness. Everything reinforces everything else, and none of it is done by accident. Any system that is functional must create a context in which everything that happens within the system reinforces everything else that happens. It's no accident that the honkie press reports only death, crime, war, weirdo opinions by honkie higher-ups, and the other shit it represents—the power structure that controls the press needs to have you believe that that's all that's going down in the world. If you were to find out that the world doesn't have to be so awful they'd have a hard time keeping you in line doing all the awful shit they tell you you have to do.

When people find out they don't have to get up every fucking morning at 6 o'clock to be at some horrible robot job at 7, eat lunch when they tell you, pee when they let you, go home when they let you, live in your jive-ass little house as long as you pay the rent they tell you you have to pay, eat the shit food they put before you like it's the only way to eat, get drunk, watch television or go bowling or play golf or listen to Frank Sinatra for your entertainment after going through all this shit all day all week all year—whew! Then it'll be hard to keep you toeing that line. How you gonna keep 'em down on the farm, like they used to say.

Can you dig it? That's why they're so down on the revolutionary media, because we're letting people know through our alternative information/communications network that there's a whole new way to do things which they've never been given to see on TV or anywhere else in honkie culture. What they don't know yet, because they can't know yet, is that the revolution we're talking about will solve all *their* problems as well as our own. Elsewise it's just bullshit, and anybody who talks to you about a program that doesn't account for *all* the people when the revolution is accomplished is just as full of shit as the honkies. All Power to *All* the People!

The revolutionary media are developing an alternative communications complex that will enable us to function most effectively within the honkie capitalist culture while working full time at the business of transforming capitalist society into a totally free society by projecting an image of the free future through our own media and the honkie media we infiltrate and destroy, or transform. Actually nothing in the universe can be destroyed because everything is just energy in its various forms, and the *forms* can only be *trans*formed. To talk of destroying the media is not even to the point—the communications media are just an energy form which can be transformed by revolutionary content into revolutionary media. The message is the medium, as well as vice versa, you dig? And the message is freedom. We won't transform this weirdo society only by projecting images of freedom, but by also creating new forms, new life-forms, which are *free* life-forms and which will serve as the basis of the new order that will replace the old. And, we will have to deal with the die-hard reactionaries who will try to block us from freeing ourselves and the whole planet from their grasp, but if we can use our media to expose them we can pull their support among the people out from under them, isolate the virus and douse it completely. This means that it is even more important for us to do everything we can to take over the pig media and use it for our own ends, so we can reach more and more people with our message of liberation for the planet.

Now Bain in his book is hung up on the idea of "unmanning" the media, which he describes (as some radicals do) as "the fascist pig." Green Dreams simply brings the Informed Sources news operation to an end. But the point is to *take it over* and use it for our own purposes. The *pig* is the pig, you dig, and the pig media is the pig media because it carries the message of PIG. When the people control the media, not control it but get *free use* of the media, the message is the people's message and the media becomes the people's media. Dig it. The media is only there, a form, to be *used,* and it will take the shape of the content transmitted through it when it is allowed to function in a free and unified context. When you hit somebody with your hand in a stupid move you don't cut your hand off, you purify the purpose, i.e., that which directs the hand in its uses. When Sun Ra makes a record there's not a goddamn thing wrong with the recording medium—the point is to make all records as useful as that, not to do away with records altogether because a bunch of imperialist robber goons control the means of record production. When you can see a bunch of liberated freeks on television directing their own programs and projecting the possibility of a free life-form so people can absorb the information and act on it to free their ownselves, or so they

will have a further possibility of freeing themselves thereby, then television is being put to human uses, as it should be all day and all night.

But we have to quit bullshitting and get ourselves *together,* people in the media. We have to organize ourselves as effectively and as extensively as the National Liberation Front is organized and effective in its terrain. Their ends are the same as ours: self-determination and freedom for their people, and for all people finally. The face of the imperialist enemy we have to fight is the system that conditions people to submit to conscription and be shipped to Vietnam to fight and kill their Vietnamese brothers and sisters. We don't have to fight those soldiers yet, but you can bet that the pigs who order them around will be sending them in on us just as soon as we are together enough to pose the same kind of threat to their rule as the Viet Cong do. And if we do our job properly we can undercut the threat of those soldiers being sent to stomp us out, because they are our brothers and they only want the same thing we want. They just don't know it yet, and they won't know it until we can get through to them using any media we can get our hands on—any medium that will *reach* them, including the pig media. The people are our real friends, and they are ready to hear what we've got to tell them—our job is to *get the information through to them,* however we can.

One way we can move ahead is to develop our own language, our own media, our own total culture, consciously and precisely, and get the information to the people who are being controlled by the pig culture through its language and other related media. We have to stop accepting the pig's definitions of the world and force them to deal with us on our own terms. It's being done all the time, but not enough people are hip to it yet because our media isn't doing its job properly. Each newspaper, each band, each film, each radio or television program we do, each medium must broadcast the message of liberation, total energy release, total revolution RIGHT NOW! There are millions of straight people out there who are dying to find out about our culture and how it might affect them, and we have to study their media and their life-styles and start relating our message to them in ways they can understand and *relate to*. If they can't relate to it you might as well talk to a wall. We have to distinguish between our own people and peoples of other cultures and relate to each of them in their own terms. It might be a while before we can get through to the honkies, we're still not even reaching all the potential freeks who are ready to break completely loose from the old order, and of course our primary task must be to reach our own people first—but as we do that we have to start thinking and working to win over the straight people too, not by going into their factories and suburbs but by drawing them out of those forms and into our new life-forms and making room for them where we are.

And we can start with the language, taking every opportunity to force our own definitions of reality on the pigs. When they tell you you broke a law, you tell them their laws are not valid and you use their media to beat them in their own courts. When they tell you your language is obscene and disgusting, you tell them their language is criminal in intent and in effect, a control device meant to keep people slaves, while our language means to set people free. When they tell you about drugs and all that shit, you tell them you're ingesting the divine sacrament in a holy religious purification ceremony and *they're* the ones who are hooked on coffee, cigarettes, alcohol, barbiturates, speed, television and control. When they tell you about their schools, you point out that they have no schools but only industrial training centers and youth discipline prisons where they condition their children to honkie culture and force them into its service through strict control of the information available to them. When they tell you this:

SAN ANTONIO, NOW (IN-FORMED SOURCES)—A COM-MUNIST BEATNIK DOPE FIEND KILLED AND MUTILATED A 3-YEAR-OLD BOY TODAY AS THE LAD WAS KNEELING IN PRAYER IN A JUST-DEDICATED METHOD-IST CHURCH.

THE MOTHER OF THE VICTIM WATCHED IN HORROR AS THE DIRTY BEARDED ABOMINATION SEIZED THE YOUNGSTER, BEAT HIS SKULL AGAINST A FONT, AND THEN SLASHED REPEATEDLY AT THE BOY'S GENITALS WITH A SINISTER KIT KNIFE, SHOUTING LEFT WING SLOGANS THROUGH-OUT THE CRIME.

Then you tell them this, you see:

WINDOW ROCK, NOW (IS)—MEMBERS OF RACIAL MINORITIES SHOULD NOT BE BARRED FROM ADVANCEMENT BUT, TO BE FRANK, MOST ARE, IT WAS CONCLUDED TODAY.

"WHITE MEN FOR INSTANCE," SAID ONE LOCAL SHAMAN. "THEY CAN SMELL THE WIND BUT THEY CANNOT FEEL THE TREE. THEY LOOK UPON THE SEA BUT THEY CANNOT HEAR THE RIVER. THEY STAND ON THE SAND BUT THEY DO NOT SIT UNDER THE CLOUDS. THEY SMILE IN THE MORNING BUT . . . WHAT??"

And besides, if you follow their stories along the line you'll find out that they'll tell you *anything* the way they want you to believe it. If you didn't follow the story you'd've missed the ending to the beatnik dope fiend story:

SHE DESCRIBED THE INCIDENT AS THE MOST TERRIFYING OF HER LIFE, BUT SAID IT CONFIRMED EVERYTHING SHE HAD SUSPECTED.

SHE WAS TAKEN TO A LOCAL HOSPITAL FOR OBSERVATION.

THE BOY, WHO SURVIVED THE ORDEAL IN GOOD SPIRITS, WAS SENT TO LIVE WITH RELATIVES.

You might remember the story of the dude in Pennsylvania, a doctor of some sort at a college in that state, who reported that a number of students had been blinded while looking into the sun on an LSD trip. It was headline front-page news and millions of people read the stories and believed them as truth. The next day the follow-up, buried far back in the papers, was that the doctor had been made to reveal that he had made the story up to scare people away from acid, and he was taken away to a mental institution like the kid's mother in the story from *Informed Sources* above. But you'll still hear people talking about LSD causing blindness, because the original story "confirmed everything they had suspected" about LSD, you dig? They are *supposed* to believe shit like that, and they read the lie first. The pigs push those lies because they know that if people were exposed to LSD and grass and other psychedelic agents properly their minds would truly be opened and they would flash right out of the pig's grasp.

Informed Sources is a handbook on media, especially the so-called "news" media. Bain worked for some time as an Associated Press staffer in its San Francisco Bureau, and the whole book is written in news dispatches from Informed Sources reporters. The IS form follows the form of the AP and UPI services, using the same language and writing the same kind of stories which distort everything that happens. Informed Sources doesn't really represent any kind of substantial change from the old system—not because it uses the same (news service) form, but because there is no advance in content. And since Informed Sources is really only perpetuating the decadent form of the established media without changing it, it can be overthrown by purer forces, or Green Dreams in the book. Just as Informed Sources infiltrated AP territory and took over much of it, Green Dreams infiltrates Informed Sources offices and stations and then overthrows it altogether. They "unmanned" the media and shut the whole thing down. But in a mass society without mass communications the people are thrown into darkness—they have to have information, and shutting down the wire services and other media is not the answer. The thing is to take them over and completely *transform* them by infusing them with our new content. We need the media for educational programs and high-energy cultural forms, and we can take them over and turn them into revolutionary media only when we are bent on revolution as a total way of life, only when revolution is our message, only when we dedicate ourselves to freeing the media from the death-grip of the pigs and using them in the interests of all the people.

All Power to the People!

OUR CULTURE IS A REVOLUTIONARY CULTURE

MAY 2,1969

We have to realize that the long-haired dope-smoking rock & roll street-fucking culture is a whole thing, a revolutionary international cultural movement which is absolutely legitimate and absolutely valid. There wouldn't even be a question about this matter if the honkies didn't attempt to deny our validity so vehemently, because our culture is so fully developed by now that anybody can see and know that it exists as a force in the world. The pig power structure and the people it has under its control know it and respond to it in their actions against us, but they refuse to legitimize our existence within their language structure. This task remains ours.

The Up! and friend

What has to be dealt with is the fact that we have developed our own indigenous culture, our own unique worldview, our own language, our own communalist ethics, our own cultural, political and economic values, our own art, music, literature, our own economy, our own total way of life which is based on the highest human principles of love, peace, harmony among peoples, and universal sharing. Many of the new forms we have created are still in an embryonic state, some are maturing more rapidly than others, but the point is that our culture is a whole thing and must be understood as such.

More than that, our culture is a revolutionary culture, a revolutionary force on the planet, the seed of the new order that will come to flower with the disintegration and collapse of the obsolete social and economic forms which presently infest the earth, especially here in the West where the dinosaur of capitalism is writhing in its death throes and lashing out at everything in its path. The emergence and growth of our new culture signals the end of western civilization as we know and hate it, and the more it spreads the closer the old world comes to its inevitable doom. Our culture is not isolated either—it springs up wherever post-industrial productive forms are developed, and it heralds the freedom all people will share in the post-scarcity future when the new post-industrial technology is freed to produce for the needs of the entire planet.

Right now we are caught up in a struggle to preserve our culture and our very existence as people of the future from the greedheads and death merchants of the dying capitalist order who understand what a threat our activity poses to their survival as the bosses of the earth. They understand better than we do that our culture proposes and demonstrates an absolutely workable alternative to their death machine, and they're making a desperate last-ditch attempt to stomp us out before we can move them off the set forever. Our culture calls for the end of imperialism, capitalism, racism, sexism, and honkyism—they are all the same in that they all develop from the same economic base and work together to maintain a single unified control system— and for the beginning of a human renaissance. In fact it *is* a human renaissance in its daily applications.

The pig-death machine is anti-life by definition. It is afraid of life because free life can't be controlled and manipulated to profit a little bunch of avaricious creep "owners" at the expense of the rest of the people on the planet. The whole rotten culture developed by the pigs to perpetuate their rule is directly in contradiction with ours—it's based on capitalism, control, competition, robot subservience, no fun, low-energy fear and trembling in the face of the universe, and it leaves no room for other cultures in its wake. One of the most sickening aspects of western culture is that it is committed to wiping out completely the cultures of the peoples who come under the rule of the Euro-American "ownership" class—the infamous "melting pot" ruse—while what we want is for all peoples to be free to develop their native cultures to their highest possible level.

The pigs of the honky power structure are committed to defending and maintaining the low-energy death culture they represent by any means necessary, just as we are committed to transforming that culture by pumping more and more energy and life into it by taking over its forms with our revolutionary content. There is no way we can possibly be stopped, but the pigs just keep lashing out indiscriminately at our culture and our people. The pig police are the shock troops of cultural repression and as such are extremely interested in snuffing out even the external manifestations of our culture. They pretend that they are "only doing their job," but they follow our cultural developments very closely and get their weird sexual kicks by arresting and beating freeks and other new people. They can't just fuck, they have to try to stop other people from fucking (which will never work) and from even *saying* "fuck." They seem to have no other sex life.

It's only natural that these chomps have picked the great holy year of 1969 for their stepped-up repression of our culture. The holy Zenta double-suck we love is repellent to them. They get their rocks off by arresting us for getting ours off however naturally we can, and by any means necessary. They are sick, insane, perverted PIGS who can't stand to see us having a good time even as we struggle for our freedom. They hate us and everything we do or stand for. They want to cut our hair off because it shows them that we are free from the honkie work ruse and the perverted standards of "manliness" and "femininity" they use to keep people trapped in inhuman sexual roles. They want to stop our high-energy music and art because it keeps people free by pumping intense high-energy force into their bodies and moves them to strike out for more life and more freedom all the time. They hate it. They arrest us for smoking the sacrament and dropping acid because they know these sacraments help keep us free by keeping us in touch with the natural energy flow of the universe. They arrest us for our high-energy language and artifacts and newspapers because these media are expressions of our freedom from the control virus and our determination to put an end to their rule. They hate us because we are free and they are *trapped.*

But what they don't realize, and this can't be emphasized enough, is that our program calls for their freedom as well as the freedom of *all* people. We realize that the pig police forces are merely the ignorant lackeys of the imperialist power structure, and that this power structure is based on an American oligarchy of some 200 interlocking families which control the world's economy through their immense corporations and banks and financial institutions—the deadly money/private property ruse. The third point of our ten-point program calls for the end of money and the free exchange of energies and materials. Implementation of this point will bring an end to their rule—because then all the people on earth will share the collective control of the planet's resources—but it cannot be implemented until all ten points are implemented. These are non-negotiable demands, just as their money will be non-negotiable as soon as it stops being current. The only currency we respect is electric current and the charge of life that runs through our bodies and throughout the entire universe.

The power structure has the rest of the people under its control because it controls the information media. The people can't get the information they need to free themselves unless we pass that information along to them through their own media. They will never get to read our papers or experience our culture properly—on its own terms—because they aren't able to relate to our media. So we have to get it together and relate to their media because it reaches the people and those people have to get their hands on our information. We know what has to be done—now it's a problem of getting that solution to the people so they can act on it and put it into effect.

But the pig power structure does not want the people to get this information and has stepped up its counter-attack of misinformation and repression in order to try to suppress our burgeoning revolutionary culture with fascism and naked control. *Control* is the keyword. The honkie culture is *based* on control (as all scarcity cultures must be), and instead of moving to lessen that control or prophesying the end of state control (as Marx and Lenin did) the honkies want only more and more of it. Corrupt "leaders" tell the people where to go, when to go, what to do, how to do it, when to do it, why to do it, and even worse, what NOT to do, when NOT to do it, ad nauseam. These orders are based not on useful information but on false authority which they have usurped from the people by lying to us and forcing their lies on us through their monied power and armed force. If there must be leaders they must be revolutionary leaders who are moving to liberate their people and lead them to govern themselves—leaders like Mao Tse-tung, Fidel Castro, Ho Chi Minh, Huey P. Newton, Bobby Seale. If our culture has to develop leaders they will have to be leaders who will teach the people how to defend and expand their revolutionary culture and who will dedicate themselves solely to serving the people.

The honkies are in big trouble. Their economy is failing, their schools and other institutions are falling apart, even their armies are crumbling from within, and their control over their young—their scheduled successors—is disappearing because they are engaged in a program of total degradation and total failure to deal with reality. They had better wake up or they won't get a chance to wake up. "You'll wake up one morning, find your poor self dead," like the song goes.

Everywhere the honkie power structure moves against us to stop us, or at least slow us down. They steal our time, our energy, and our pitiful financial resources by arresting us on bullshit charges, holding us in jail in lieu of bonds up to $100,000, stealing our money through their bondsmen who post ransom for us to get out of jail at 10 or 15% of the face value, stealing our time and energy in long court battles with many appearances and postponements (they even get paid

for their time with the money they rip off from the people in taxes and other illegal shit most of our people have no say in), sending us to penitentiaries and stockades when they can get away with it, and generally keeping us from our righteous work and our ultimate freedom by everyday harassment and wholly arbitrary terrorism.

We have to start organizing ourselves, people, getting it together, so we can build and utilize a real power base in our own communities. One thing we can do is organize around the legal battles we are forced to mount and turn that whole mode of engagement back against those creeps. When they take some brothers and sisters to trial for weird political/cultural "crimes," the people of the community should be rallied to their defense. Groups should turn out in the courtrooms every day, fill them up, so the victims on trial can see and feel the strength of the people behind them. It makes a lot of difference when there's a courtroom full of freeks, and it's an effective weapon too. This will draw the pig media and give us a platform from which we can expose and explain the crimes of the pigs and their bosses against the people.

More people should start defending themselves in court whenever possible, demanding jury trials, full pre-trial examinations, court-appointed lawyers, anything to cost the prosecution and the state more money. That's something they can relate to. When you start making them more trouble than you're worth to them, they might lighten up a little. They can't handle it. They're programmed for total control and freak out when they are confronted by free life-forms and free people who are not afraid of them. People who are arrested for marijuana offenses should all plead "not guilty" and enter briefs challenging the constitutionality of the dinosaur marijuana laws. (We have a model brief available for anyone who wants it—write to us and get your own copy.) This takes a long time and fouls up their system no end. It also makes the issues more apparent, i.e., that you're not breaking a law but that the laws are constructed to work as the tools of repression by one culture against another. The marijuana laws and the way they are applied against the people have nothing at all to do with "narcotics"—they're meant to stop people from living and feeling and experiencing the world in a different way from the robotized plastic culture we're threatened with by the honk power structure. Remember, they don't want you to feel free because they can't have you running around free and still maintain their system of greed and control. So they use their so-called "legal" system against us.

There is no LAW in America today—-only the honkie power structure and its victims. We are down to the nitty-gritty now, with our backs to the wall, and the population is quickly polarizing into oppressors and oppressed. The revolutionary youth of this weirdo country are an oppressed people—the victims of a calculated cultural suppression movement planned and carried out by the honkie power structure fronted by Howdy Doody Nixon and Clarabelle Mitchell and backed by the real vampires—Henry Ford, Nelson Rockefeller and his slimy brothers, the DuPonts, Mellons, and other monied interests who are deathly committed to maintaining the decadent status quo. They will kill us if they can get away with it, they will beat and incarcerate their own children if they have to, they would put all of us in jail if they could—all in the name of freedom, democracy, and the unspeakable obscenity they call the "American way."

They maintain their power over us because they control the communications media, the educational (brainwashing) apparatus, and the economic life of the world—the resources and materials all people need to rule themselves and maintain themselves as free peoples. Through an interlocking conspiracy of total control, the rulers define our phenomena and make us act in a desired manner, and when we start to realize that their so-called reality is just a warped image of greed and control and move to redefine reality as it is (not as they would have it), they move quickly to lock us up, to make us flee the country or otherwise go underground where we are separated from our people and limited in our work with them. They move to rob us and beat us and try in every way they know how to stop our program of total freedom for all the people.

They don't move quickly enough, though, and they don't realize that by ALL THE PEOPLE we mean *everybody*—as Eldridge Cleaver put it, there are a whole lot more people than there are pigs. And Huey added, "the spirit of the people is stronger than the Man's technology." He was absolutely right on. We are the spirit of the people, and we cannot be stopped. But, in order to stop the corrosion of our spirit by these pigs, we have to start defining things for ourselves in terms of total reality, and we have to get ourselves in tune with the pure universal energy force that will make us act in the desired—i.e. FREE—manner. Everyone desires to be free—the desire is born into our meat—*we must be free*. We must be free, goddamnit, or we'll leave the planet!

WE WILL NOT SUBMIT TO FASCISM IN ANY FORM, now or any time. We will not allow these creeps to stomp us out, and we will defend ourselves by any means necessary against the fascist terror. This means using every possible weapon at our command, including the pig's own technology. We will rob that motherraper blind, we will steal his machinery, his media, his money, anything he lets us get our collective hands on we will snatch up and take back to our communities where it will be put to use for the people by the people with the people. All Power to the People! The spirit of the people coupled with the strength of the pig's technology in the hands of the people will enable us to turn the pig out to pasture for good!

BACKDROP TO URBAN REVOLUTION: SOME NEW BLACK MUSIC

FEBRUARY 1969

I remember two and three years ago and longer writing columns for this paper and trying to pull people's coats to some new music and never getting anywhere—people just didn't seem to be ready for the high-energy jams for one reason or another. Maybe they weren't eating enough acid like people do now. But I feel very strongly right now that people are ready for a lot more high-energy music than they're getting from the pop stars, and the music is certainly out there waiting for them—waiting for you right now.

All I'm trying to do is turn you on to something I know about, you know? I mean I *know* about it, because I listen to it. And that's all there is to it, just *listening* to it, getting out of your head for a while and down to the natural facts. Because the music I'm talking about will turn your heads *around*, people, and make you hear things you never thought would happen. But then that's what you get for thinking, like I always say.

John Coltrane, photo by Leni Sinclair

Enough of this abstract bullshit. Some of these new records you might like to hear would be: the new Sun Ra jam on the ESP label, which is called NOTHING IS. The album was recorded live a couple years ago while Ra was doing some gigs in New York state colleges with Burton Greene, Patti Waters, Giuseppe Logan and some other maniacs.

Ra is the absolute master of space and time—his music, or the music made by his Myth-Science Arkestra, is like nothing you've ever heard. Believe it, because it's the realest thing there is on this planet. Whew! Sun Ra! The music on the new album is really live and fresh, and if you've ever seen Ra in concert this record'll bring back images of the Arkestra in their cosmic garb, beating drums and shaking bells, marching around the auditorium playing and chanting, singing little melodies in joyous insane harmony. "We Travel the Spaceways." "Next Stop Mars." "Sun Ra and His Band from Outer Space." These are the people to listen to, and "understand." (Which only means to *get down*, "stand under" it and dig it.)

Marion Brown, the beautiful black alto saxophonist, also has a new release on ESP-Disk called WHY NOT. The original title of the album was THE PSYCHEDELIC SOUNDS OF MARION BROWN, and that's just what it is. This music will open you up and spread you with feeling. Featured on piano is former Detroiter Stanley Cowell in his first recording session. Stan played with Charles Moore, John Dana and Ronnie Johnson as the Detroit Contemporary 4 for over a year

just before he recorded this side, and I know a lot of neighborhood people will remember hearing and seeing Stan play with the DC4 at the old Artists' Workshop, at Lower Deroy, Community Arts, on the mall, and everywhere else the old band played. They sure were beautiful!

Also featured on Marion's record is John Coltrane's final drummer, brother Rashied Ali, the most straight ahead percussionist on earth. Rashied is bad. His drumming moves ahead and sideways at the same time, driving with great strength in all directions and covering everything that's going on in the rest of the band. Covering, like "I've got you covered." Taking care of business, is what Rashied does.

Another dangerous ESP-Disk is the first record by a young brother from the lower east side, Marzette Watts, a black painter who traded painting lessons to Pharoah Sanders in return for tenor saxophone lessons, and got it together. Marzette at that time lived a floor below Archie Shepp and two below LeRoi Jones at 27 Cooper Square in New York City. That was a far out place. Marion Brown, Archie, Pharoah, and dozens of other musicians would hang out at Archie's and jam, using various extra-musical stimulants to get them into different musical vistas.

Marion told me once about a day when everyone dropped acid and started playing in Archie's place around noon. Four hours later a huge knock on the door and it was the Tactical Police troopers, riot helmets and all, demanding an end to the music.

Archie Shepp, photo by Leni Sinclair

Out on the street under the 3rd-floor window people were standing gaping on the sidewalk and over the curbs, and traffic was lined up for blocks while stupefied drivers tried to figure out what that *sound* was. It was the sound of crazed men, people, screaming and hollering to be free. Marion said there was dope and shit all over the table but the pigs weren't even interested, they just wanted the fucking *noise* to stop. "It must have sounded like the end of the world," Marion said grinning.

Anyway, Marzette's first ESP-Disk has Byard Lancaster on alto saxophone, Clifford Thornton on trumpet and trombone, Karl Berger vibes, Sonny Sharrock guitar and others. Sonny Sharrock has created one working solution to the problem of plain old line-runs on guitar, licks and shit—Sonny Sharrock plays flashes of amplified sound, weird spaced-out hums and sound drifts, spreading his sound out as far as he can get it until it takes in a whole spectrum of sound. (The other solution is to overpower the simple guitar and make the amplifiers sing the song, e.g. Brother Fred Smith, Brother Wayne Kramer, where the power of the machinery is written into the songs just as the notes and words are written in, or happen. So the sound itself, the totality, becomes the thing, the thing that moves you and makes you scream. Makes me scream, anyway. Just like Archie Shepp does, just like Pharoah.) Just like Marzette Watts' band does on this record, and the song on the first side, "Backdrop to Urban Revolution." If you can relate to that.

Other records you should get—and I mean it, you should get *at least one* of these records, the next time you go to the store, and take it home with you and listen to it when you get a chance. Smoke some good weed first, enough so that you're kind of spaced out and feelin' plenty good, layin' back on a big pillow or on the bed with somebody you dig, got some time to lay around and get down, and then after you play "Sympathy for the Devil" you ease off the needle before the next song and slip on Archie Shepp's record THE MAGIC OF JU-JU, side one first. You might want to turn the volume down a little bit at first so you won't get scared, because Archie starts right off in the middle of a thing and moves straight ahead, right up your spine and into your cells. Let this music inform your cells, and shape them. You'll dig it.

If you don't dig it right then, try the other side. A lovely melody starts it off, "You're What This Day Is All About." The other things are nice too. You've got to listen to it a few times, play it while you're doing something else and let it sneak up on you, but when it does it'll reach right down inside you and *grab* you, and it'll probably never let you go.

John Coltrane's record COSMIC MUSIC is a true testimonial to the gigantic Zenta Saint the late genius John Coltrane. He is joined with his wife Alice on piano, brother Pharoah Sanders on tenor saxophone, and three drummers including the mighty Rashied Ali. The songs include "Lord, Teach Me To Be," "The Sun," and "Manifestation." At one point you can hear John and his brothers chant "Let there be peace, and love, and perfection, throughout all the earth, o God." Yes, yes, yes, let that be, let that be.

One other for now: The one record you *have* to have for further benefaction is the monumental Pharoah Sanders album on the Impulse label, TAUHID, with Sonny Sharrock and other heavy brothers. The album has Pharoah singing, playing flute, piccolo, and alto and tenor saxophones, and the songs are plain beauty and truth. You may have heard, some time ago, the MC5 do one of Pharoah's melodies off this TAUHID album called "Upper Egypt and Lower Egypt," which I wrote some words for Rob to sing: "Got to get out in the music, got to get out in the sun, got to get out of your heads now, got a lot to get done." If you die before you hear Pharoah smoke this masterpiece out you'll deserve it.

Archie Shepp's brand new record, THE WAY AHEAD, is way ahead too. I wish you would buy these records and turn yourselves on to them. I wish the people on the radio would play some more of them too, so you can hear them free and want to buy them for your own home. But they will soon enough. This is the music of the future, and it's waiting for you to catch up with it. Catch up!

KILLER BLUES

"Rulers first fantasize their devils, then create them"
— Tom Hayden, *Trial*

*"We are always searching; I think that now we are
at the point of finding"*
— John Coltrane, in an interview, 1965

JULY 21,1969

I t's killer hard to write about the blues, as it's hard to write about any music, but more so the blues. Blues developed as the formal cultural expression of a dispossessed people, slaves ripped off from their own culture and forced to live and work in a totally alien culture, one that was considerably more than just hostile to their own. Blues was the formal expression of an illiterate people struggling with a language that was totally alien to their mouths and minds, but the only language they had in common with each other (having been snatched from so many disparate tribes in the mother country) and with the oppressor, who was, after all, the subject of their speech, and increasingly, the object as well.

Blues was never meant to be written about. Blues was there to be sung, played and felt. Blues was the articulation of a people's consciousness just as this writing in process here is the articulation of a current people's consciousness. More simply put, blues was the formal speech of that people, and the musicians served as the bearers and carriers of the culture from generation to generation, plantation to plantation, just as in any pre-literate culture. The blues people, for the black Africans enslaved in Amerikkka, served the same purpose as Homer and Hesiod did in pre-literate Greece. The blues musicians were the teachers and codifiers, prime movers of their culture, and the music was not taken lightly—it was simply the formal oral literature of the blacks, born out of their struggle with the white man, the land, the terrible brokenness of their families and tribes, with the alien tongue of the white Europeans in their mouths.

This is very important, because we have been given music as a luxury, and a specious luxury at that. In capitalist society the arts are despised, and at any rate are nothing to commerce and industry, private property and individual gain.

Muddy Waters and Otis Spann

137

"People who come out of prison can build up the country.
"Misfortune is a test of people's fidelity.
"Those who protest at injustice are people of true merit.
"When the prison-doors are opened, the real dragon will fly out."
—Ho Chi Minh, *Prison Diary*

"We can (and must) begin to build socialism, not with abstract human material, not with human material specially prepared by us, but with the human material bequeathed to us by capitalism. True, that is very 'difficult,' but no other approach to this task is serious enough to warrant discussion."
—V.I. Lenin, *"Left-Wing" Communism, an Infantile Disorder*

Amerika's artists are despised and villified, treated as criminals (as indeed we are if we are effective as artists in this hideous space), jailed and shot down in the streets, dragged into courts, tortured in jails, hounded and harassed all our lives by the "responsible" citizens of commerce and industry and trade whose culture is best typified by Ed Sullivan and Kate Smith, or Lawrence Welk and Liberace, whoever, ponks like Glenn Gould held up as the apotheosis of Amerika's formal culture. Entertainment, as something you do on the weekends after slaving in the factory or the office all week, sitting at home at night taking in all the vile pablum spewed out of the television set. Luxury. What You Could Do Without. No sense, these people in this country have no sense of the immediacy of music, the quick feel of it, the way it can shape your life and take your life's shape as you give yourself to it every moment of your life, as a first term in your life.

Blues was like that, and is like that, for the people who live with it as a first term. That's why the blues is so strong, because people *LIVE* with it, breathe it, LIVE it that strong, and in the face of an almost absolute repression that will make you strong if you last or kill you if you don't get strong, just like that. People sleep with the blues at night, fuck the blues, smoke it, eat it, feel it around their chair. The blues is the expression of a living culture, an oppressed culture which feeds on the music for strength as it feeds on meat, and which feeds the music back into the living culture which feeds it back into the music, and each time the cycle repeats itself it gains in intensity and feeling, pushing people higher and higher on the road to liberation. Whew! The killer self-charging and recharging energy cycle that moves people out of stasis and into pure motion.

This may all be too abstract, or whatever, but it's really worth saying even if none of us understand it yet. We will. Because we are going to *have* to know these things, that will make us strong. We are an oppressed people too, now, whether we think about ourselves that way or not, or whether or not we want to admit it. And though the peculiar quantity or quality of our oppression differs from that of the blues people, the oppression is constant and will work to bring our culture closer to theirs—it will unite us in our common struggle against the common oppressor, and the music is what will help us get together as we relate more and more to the music of black culture and feed on it, and feed it back to them through our own music. Dig the Temptations or Muddy Waters' latest sides for that, or Jimi Hendrix and Buddy Miles and for that matter, Buddy Guy. Sly and the Family Stone.

We know the other side of the equation well enough, too—Canned Heat, Paul Butterfield, Fleetwood Mac, the MC5, even the English dandies Clapton, Page, Beck, Alvin Lee, the Rolling Stones, *all* rock & roll in fact is derived from and directly inspired by the blues and its modern forms, rhythm & blues and now soul music. Naming names is beside the point, though, although that act does make for easy reference. The blues music and culture gave rise to our freeky culture, gave root to it, and even if we don't recognize ourselves as the blossom of that root, being the blossom, the root does increasingly recognize this blossom as its own. Blues people, or in the cities rhythm and blues people, are beginning to know us and know that we are with them, strange as it seems, they been catchin hell from our daddies all their lives and here we are almost as crazy as them, or tryin to be anyway, and just look at what we coulda been! Shit, here we are, in all our crazy glory, and we wouldn't trade it for a goddamn thing. That black music has worked its blue magic on our ass, and we love it, even if we can't articulate it worth a shit. We love it, and take it home with us to bed, and fuck it and sleep with it and eat it and feel it inside us, twisting at our guts to bring us out of our parents' heads and into the world.

What I mean to say is that the blues has developed into a bridge between the black people who have inspired our culture, and the freeky white mother country maniac people who have developed out of that inspiration through tons of marijuana and LSD and into our current madness. A lot of us don't even know where we came from, culturally that is, but that is a condition of our oppression just as the first generations of blacks in Amerika (and even now) didn't know where their culture came from either, it was just there with them, in them, *of* them, and they played it out just as we do now. We will teach our generations, though, just as the current black generations are teaching their young about their own sources. I mean there are people who *live* rock & roll and "hate niggers," they know that little about their own roots. But then there are people who hate their mothers. It doesn't do anyone any good to hate where they came from like that—the best thing to do is dig it and see how it worked, dig the process, so you can apply it wherever you can in the future. Dig that.

I would likewise assume that the people who are reading this piece at this blues festival here in Ann Arbor, I would assume that we are at least getting hip to our roots and love them and want to get closer to them now. That's why you're here in the park, right? Because there is no such thing as just relating to the music and not its social context—the music IS the social order, and must be taken in like that, or you are blowing the whole thing. That's one thing that's so beautiful about the blues—the music is so much the life, and the life is so much the music, that it's still a whole thing when and where those conditions obtain. There is no separation. I mean John Lee Hooker is *not* separate from his music at all. Nor is Howlin Wolf, or Son House for that matter. Nor is the Up, or some other people you might not know about yet.

I keep wanting to talk about two different things, or what looks to most of us like two different things, but what I keep wanting to say is that they are NOT separate at all, but the same thing: the music itself, and its singular history; and the music as the expression of a fully developed culture and as the reflection of that culture. And one other thing, that we ourselves are developing a culture that has as its most exciting aspect—outside of the culture itself, and its potentialities—its commonness with the blues culture, black culture, in that our music at its best is a direct expression of the people who make the music, first, and of the whole people out of which the musicians emerge. Which is to say, our culture is a whole thing where and when those conditions obtain.

You can read the list of names for this festival, Jimmy Dawkins, B.B. King, Fred McDowell, J.B. Hutto, St. Louis Jimmy, Junior Wells, Luther Allison, Clifton Chenier, Sleepy John Estes, Roosevelt Sykes, Otis Rush, Muddy Waters, Howlin Wolf, Big Boy Crudup, John Lee Hooker, Big Mama Willie Mae Thornton, Freddie King, James Cotton, Lightnin Hopkins, Son House, Charley Musselwhite, T-Bone Walker, Sam Lay, but remember that for most of them this is not at all a listing of "stars" or anything like that but simply a list of men and women who play the blues, get drunk, fight in bars, gamble, get high, fuck, play the blues some more and live it like that. The music is no big thing, as ART or something alienated from the lifeblood of the culture; it *is* the lifestream of the culture, *the* formal expression of their lives, and unless you can relate to it like that—unless you can relate to it in terms other than those you use for Hollywood productions and museum pieces—you are missing the whole point of the music, and you probably won't be moved much at all. You are missing precisely the quality that makes the blues *The Blues*, and that's really something too high-powered to miss out on.

You can come here and hear the music, or buy records and hear the music at home, so I won't talk about the music itself at all. You can hear it and feel it for yourself, and there's absolutely nothing I can tell you about what that experience should be for you. I wouldn't even want to if I could, and you shouldn't even want me to fix it for you in front. And you can read bios and press releases and little stories on the *Silver Screen* model about the facts of the lives of these men and women, but that ain't it at all. Their lives refuse to be encapsulated except in the music itself. Unlike a lot of white people and white musicians, whose lives as LeRoi Jones once said can be seen on television every hour, there's a lot more to these people's lives than could ever be written down, even if the language were adequate to the terms of their lives. They *invent* their lives, while too

"The leaders had to restrain the exceptional enthusiasm and radicalism that are always characteristic of any youth engaged in building a new world. . . . Only progressively did the political training that was given them lead them away from contemplating the struggle in an explosive form."
—Frantz Fanon, *A Dying Colonialism*

"At a time when many of us only carried the idea of revolution in our heads; we were locked up, isolated in prison cells, but it never occurred to us to think that it was impossible to bring the Revolution about."
—Fidel Castro Speaks

"Without the cold and desolation of winter there could not be the warmth and splendor of spring.
"Calamity has hardened and tempered me and turned my mind into steel."
—Ho Chi Minh, *Prison Diary*

many white people live out lives that were invented for them, if not by any immediately recognizable person or thing (like a press agent or a screen magazine) then by some inanimate thing like television or the movies.

These people—these blues people—live their music full time. And the music isn't at all "made up," or anything like that. It is in no way a luxury—they make their living playing it in murderous bars and dives, and the music flows directly from their lives in these places, in the sinkholes of Amerika's cities where black people are kept penned up and treated like dogs. I mean the blues is natural music, *organic music,* brothers and sisters, and we can relate to it just like that; we can relate to it like that, and we can learn a lot about ourselves and the world if we do. To talk about this music and these musicians in music business terminology is foolishness. It's only a matter of fact that Big Boy Crudup was a "major influence" on the early Elvis Presley, or that St. Louis Jimmy wrote "Goin Down Slow," or that T-Bone Walker was the first popularizer of the electric guitar, or that B.B. King once played and sang with Count Basie's big swing band in the '30s and got sick of being so abstracted from the natural blues and went back home, or that Charley Musselwhite is a white boy from Memphis who hung out with the young white Chicago blues players and now has two of our brothers from Detroit in his band, or that Billy C. used to play with Sam Lay, or that James Cotton was Muddy Waters' harp player for a long time. These things mean nothing to these people, and they don't serve to explain their lives away. The blues is not western "art" in any term, nor is it western history, as some isolated sequence of events torn out of their human context. The blues is a *whole thing.* Dig it like that, and get down in it. It will take you from there, once you give up your head and your body to the music, it will take you as far as you can go. If you can get ready for it, it can take you—as it's taken me since I first heard it as a child—exactly where you were meant to go.

PRISON WRITINGS

TRANSCRIPT OF SENTENCING PROCEEDINGS

JULY 28, 1969

THE CLERK: File No. A-134588, People vs. John A. Sinclair. You were found guilty by a jury July 25th of Possession of Marijuana. You are here today for sentence. Do you have anything to say to the Court?

THE DEFENDANT: I do.

THE CLERK: Speak up.

THE COURT: You want the microphone, Mr. Sinclair?

THE DEFENDANT: Not particularly.

THE COURT: All right.

THE DEFENDANT: I haven't had a chance to say anything so far and I'd like to say a few things for the record. The Court is aware these charges have been fabricated against me by the Detroit Narcotic Squad. He came to me one day and said a month and three days ago, you did this, you gave so and so this, you did that. I had no opportunity, I didn't do that and I had no opportunity to construct a defense. But I know what was going on all along and it was a conspiracy by these people, Warner Stringfellow, Vahan Kapigian and Joseph Brown and the rest of them, to frame me on this case and to bring me right here and to manufacture two marijuana cigarettes and say I gave them to them and then let the rest of you who are in it with them manufacture this cold case and bring me here. The punishment I have received already in the two and a half years since this case started is cruel and unusual, if I *had* committed the crime of possessing two marijuana cigarettes. And everyone who is taking part in this is guilty of violating the United States Constitution and violating my rights and everyone else's that's concerned. And to take me and put me in a pigsty like the Wayne County Jail for the weekend is a cruel and unusual punishment, to sleep on the floor, to have no sheets, no blankets, pig swill to eat. You see, but you can get away with this and you can continue—I don't know what sentence you are going to give me, it's going to be ridiculous, whatever it is. And I am going to continue to fight it. The people are going to continue to fight it because this isn't justice. There is nothing just about this, there is nothing just about these courts, nothing just about these vultures over here.

THE COURT: One more word out of the crowd and I will clear the courtroom.

THE DEFENDANT: Right. And that will continue in the tradition that's been established here. I am not done, but no sense talking any more.

MR. JUSTIN C. RAVITZ (for the Defendant): Your Honor please, Mr. Sinclair is twenty-seven years of age, he is married, he has one child in the audience today, two years of age. A beautiful child, she is there. His wife is pregnant. He's lived in the State of Michigan all his life. He has three prior convictions, two are for marijuana. In each instance, he pled guilty. In the second instance, he never, ever should have pled guilty. It was the subject of illegal entrapment by Vahan Kapigian. He was induced, he was seduced, he was led by Kapigian to be an intermediary. To be an intermediary to a transaction which he never would have been a party to. To be an intermediary to a transaction which the major persons on both sides of the transaction were, of course, not charged with an offense.

John Sinclair stands convicted in Oakland County of assaulting a police officer who wasn't even a police officer. Of assaulting a person who assaulted him. He's been given a sentence of thirty days in that case, which is on appeal. The Court knows something about the history of cases involving alleged assaults upon police officers where the alleged assailants were persons of the nature of John Sinclair.

If there are two crimes in this country which are political prosecutions, they are in one instance, those of claimed assaults against police officers and in another instance, those cases which can be proved easily by fabricated stories and not easily disproved by citizens. Namely, offenses such as the one before this Court.

John Sinclair has another pending case. That pending case is an oddity in the annals of jurisprudence in this country or anywhere else. That case is for violation of the Federal law, which is on its face, palpably unconstitutional. It was stated as many as twelve years ago in the case of *Lamberg versus California,* by the Supreme court. I wonder who it was who came up with the clever notion of saying that John Sinclair is a criminal because he kept a business engagement in another state, in Canada, and went across the line not registering as a person convicted of a narcotic offense? Who else has been charged with that case and when and who is behind that case?* I wonder! But one need not wonder, one need only look. The community's attitude and the establishment's attitude and the narcotics officer's attitude and the unmitigated power which they have to exercise. The only way that power can be checked is by having an independent judiciary. The only way that power can be checked is by having jurors who aren't going to be servants to police state power, who are going to stand as a bulwark against the improper exercise of that power. And we don't have that in America today. We didn't have that in this court this past week and that's regrettable.

*The reference is to Tim Leary, who was charged with the same "crime" by U.S. Customs authorities in Detroit two years earlier.

In America, which has never known anything but the history of racism, and in America which practices those imperialistic and those brutalistic and inhuman wars in Asia and elsewhere around the globe, and in America which sends a man to the moon while millions of its citizens starve, John Sinclair is brought before this Court and he is said to be a criminal. He isn't a criminal. He isn't criminal at all. The criminals with respect to this law are the doctors, the legislators, the attorneys who *know,* who know, because they have knowledge, that these laws are unconstitutional. That these laws defy all knowledge of science. That this sumptuary legislation, like its predecessors and like other forms of sumptuary legislation, is on the books to go after and to impress politically unpopular people and groups and minorities. That's the only reason they are on the books.

This very day, twenty-five percent of the future doctors of America who are studying medicine at Wayne State University Medical School, have possessed marijuana. Twenty-five percent of the future lawyers, indeed future judges who will be sitting on that bench some day, have possessed and have smoked marijuana.

THE COURT: That's your opinion.

MR. RAVITZ: That's my opinion.

THE DEFENDANT: That's a fact.

MR. RAVITZ: My opinion and based on studies.

Persons brought before the bar of the Court aren't the middle class, aren't the popular, they are the oppressed. They are the unpopular. It's a terrible law, it's a criminal law. I know that the Court might not agree with my evaluation of it. I know and ask and hope for only this, your Honor. I think the Court has been involved in enough of these cases to know that the law itself, whether it's unconstitutional per se, is a cruel law and isn't a law that is properly and fairly dispensed. I know that the Court, and I hope that the Court recognizes that the two cigarettes in this case were really—the officers in this case really had utter disregard for John Sinclair. They never treated him as a human being to whom the Constitution extended itself. What I really hope the Court recognizes, and that other judges and other persons of this society charged with responsibilities come to recognize, is that America cannot single out unpopular leaders and go into their arsenal of overkill, be it through stone or rifles or highly punitive sentences and think that the problems in this country can ever be solved in that fashion. Yet all around this country, we see political prosecutions. We see the Tom Haydens, we see the Huey Newtons, the John Sinclairs singled out. And somewhere in the warped minds of those so-called leaders, they think that they are going to cure the generation gap. They think that they are going to stem the tide of revolution by picking out leaders. Well, they are simply not going to do so because leaders are no longer indispensable in this country. Because there are a great many people who are awake to the crimes and the atrocities committed by governments and because it simply cannot work. The only way to deal with it is to deal with it rationally, to deal with it constitutionally and to follow those laws written by those legislators. And I will ask that the Court do just that. And I would ask that the Court insulate itself from public pressures which I recognize to be very weighty. But to be equally irrational. Those are the same public pressures that lead to all those acts that called for the conclusions brought forward in the Kerner Commission Report. And yet those conclusions haven't been acted on in any way by government. I hope that this Court in particular begins to act upon them by exercising some degree of rational thought process and by recognizing the realities of the situation.

Thank you.

THE COURT: Well, in this matter here, Mr. Sinclair was arrested in January of 1967 in connection with an offense that took place on December 22nd, 1966. It's interesting to me that he, and you, assert that he has been violated of his constitutional rights because all of the rights that he's entitled to as any citizen is under the Constitution, have been asserted in his defense. In addition to that, there have been appeals to the Court of Appeals, to the Michigan Supreme Court on his behalf, which have held up the trial of this case for a long and lengthy period of time.

Now, Mr. Sinclair is not on trial and never was on trial in this courtroom because of his beliefs. He represents a person who has deliberately flaunted and scoffed at the law. He may think that there is nothing wrong with the use of narcotics, as many people think that there is nothing wrong with the use of narcotics. Although enlightened and intelligent people think to the contrary and otherwise. And medical studies back them up far more completely than they do the people on his side of the particular question.

The public has recognized that the use of narcotics is dangerous to the people that use it. The public, through its legislature, has set penalties for those who violate and traffic in narcotics.

Now, this man started in 1964, in which he first came to the attention of this Court and upon the offense of Possession of Narcotics, on a plea of guilty, was placed upon probation. We have tried to understand John Sinclair, we have tried to reform and rehabilitate John Sinclair.

In 1966, while still on probation for that offense, he committed another offense for which he pleaded guilty. And this Court again showed supreme leniency to John Sinclair, placing him on probation again while ordering him to serve the first six months thereof in the Detroit House of Correction.

This placed him in violation of his other probation, which resulted in that Judge extending that probation on again, so that for you or for John Sinclair to assert that the law has been out to get him, is sheer nonsense. John Sinclair has been out to show that the law means nothing to him and to his ilk. And that they can violate the law with impunity and the law can't do anything about it.

Well, the time has come. The day has come. And you may laugh, Mr. Sinclair, but you will have a long time to laugh about it. Because it is the judgment of this Court that you, John Sinclair, stand committed to the State Prison at Southern Michigan at Jackson or such other institution as the Michigan Corrections Commission may designate for a minimum term of not less than nine and a half nor more than ten years. The Court makes no recommendation upon the sentence other than the fact that you will be credited for the two days you spent in the County Jail.

Now, as to bond, in view of the fact that Mr. Sinclair shows a propensity and a willingness to further commit the same type of offenses while on bond, and I am citing you to the case of People versus Vito Giacalone just cited by the Michigan Court of Appeals, this is one instance where there is a likelihood of that type of danger and which the Court of Appeals said that refusal to set bond is a good grounds. And based on that, and my belief that he will continue to violate the law and flaunt the law in relation to narcotics, I deny bond pending appeal.

THE DEFENDANT: You just exposed yourself even more. And people know that. You give somebody nine and a half to ten years—(noise in courtroom).

THE PENITENTIARY AIN'T SHIT TO BE AFRAID OF: INTERVIEW WITH PETER STEINBERGER

MAY 22, 1970

Last fall, the Michigan Department of Corrections removed John Sinclair from Southern Michigan State Prison at Jackson (an hour's drive from his wife and children, who live at the White Panther commune in Ann Arbor) to the State House of Correction and Branch Prison at Marquette, in Michigan's Upper Peninsula. This is a 900-mile round trip for his family and attorneys.

He is permitted no other visitors. Reporters are not permitted to speak to him. His mail is of course heavily censored.

The Department of Corrections, in keeping John Sinclair from the press, is hiding a fact which–magazine hereby reveals; something that is not known to the great mass of judge Colombo's constituents, who clearly applaud his deed, nor to the children of these constituents, the great majority of whom probably deplore it:

John Sinclair is a free man.

He greets visitors in a large hall, in the center of the medieval castle that is Marquette Prison.

It is his castle.

He is attended by liveried guards. He is healthy and clear-eyed. And he speaks just as he would if he were at his home in Ann Arbor—no posturings of martyrdom, no hysteria, no venom.

John Sinclair, photo by Leni Sinclair

This reporter was able to see him by showing an attorney's bar-card to the prison authorities, and saying that he came on legal business (which he did, but which cannot be reported here).

Seeing Mr. Sinclair was worth the 900-mile ride, and the slight hassle with prison bureaucrats which preceded the interview.

For outside of prison walls, who can find even by travelling 900 miles a free man?

Peter Steinberger

BIG FAT: *This is your interview. I won't have a chance to read it back to you before we print it, and you're the one who will be most vulnerable to retaliation when the interview is published. So you decide—what do you want to tell the people?*

JOHN: Well, the main thing I want to say is that this is the best thing that's ever happened to me or our organization.

BF: *Why?*

JOHN: Because I have a lot of time to study here, to read and think and figure out what's happening so we can deal with it better. And, it exposes the fascists who put me here.

BF: *Do they let you have access to the materials you need for this?*

JOHN: I get most of the books I need, with some exceptions of course. The thing about the penitentiary is, that when you're on the street it's terrifying to think about going there, because you don't know anything about it. Black people, though, have fathers and brothers (and often sisters and mothers) who've been in prison—for them, it's no kind of frightening thing

like it is for our people. But the penitentiary ain't shit to be afraid of. It's like being a straight person for a while: you get up at seven, eat, work, have a lunch break, go back to work, and then at four o'clock you go off work, and go eat dinner at five. Or if you're lucky you don't have to have a job—you can stay in your cell and read and write all day. But they found out I liked being in my cell, so they made me take a job.

BF: *What work do you do?*

JOHN: Sorting dirty underwear in the laundry.

BF: *How do you relate to the other prisoners?*

JOHN: Generally very well. They all know about my case— they've read about me and heard about my case on the radio. All the prisoners know that it's a meatball (gangster slang for a phony charge). They watch as we keep trying to get bond and so on, and they're aghast. They see that in a lot of cases *they* get bail—or would get it, except for a lack of lawyers, or a lack of money—the same thing, actually. So they're shocked to see the unfairness of my case. They can't believe that I'm being held like this, without bond, but they know about politicians as much as we do anyway, and they know I'm a political prisoner, which is a little strange for them because there aren't very many of us in the state prisons.

It keeps popping up—I had the job in the laundry for about a month when this real good clerk's job came up in the garment factory. I was put in for it by the civilian foreman, but they told him they wouldn't let him have me. And he couldn't understand it. When he asked them why they said we don't want him to have access to a typewriter all day long, because we don't like the stuff he writes. He couldn't believe it, and it blew the inmates' minds!

BF: *As a white person, from the middle class, are you surprised at all by what your fellow prisoners are like?*

JOHN: Well, in the first place, I haven't been a white middle-class person for some time—in fact, like the song says, I've been an outlaw all my life, you know? (Laughs.) And besides, I'd been in prison before—I served six months in the Detroit House of Correction in 1966, so I was familiar with what the scene is like before I got this bit. Prisoners are just proletarians and lumpen-proletarians who got caught in the wrong place at the wrong time, for the most part. They're not a special "criminal class" like the law and order nuts would say. The whites seem to be mostly southerners, and I'd say 95% or more are from a working class or sub-working class background. And the black inmates are just brothers off the block who were trying to survive—"illegitimate capitalists" is what Huey calls them. That's what's so stupid about penitentiaries in the first place. This is just a town where we're all made to work to support the guards and the administration. Maybe 10% of the prisoners should be segregated from the rest of the people because they've been so messed over by the social order that they can't relate to other people except in destructive terms. The rest of us have no business being here at all.

BF: *If you have to stay here for 10 years, will you be able to endure it?*

JOHN: Sure—just as I do now, except for a longer time. I have a lot of study-ing to do, and never enough time to do it in. The point is, that I don't *have* to be here that long, but the only way to get me out is for the people to organize themselves politically to do so, which is what we're trying to do now.

If you are a political prisoner the only way you can be released is through political action. You can try legal action—appeals and all that stuff—but the contradiction there is that by law I've got no business being here in the first place. That's one mistake we've made so far: we've defined the problem for ourselves as a legal problem, and it's not that at all. As far as the legal aspect is concerned, you can have your shit really together, but unless you mount a political offensive to force the reactionary judges and politicians to move, they'll just keep on doing their thing on you. In my case, as soon as someone reads all my briefs and rules according to the law, they'll have to cut me loose. So they keep me off the street by denying me an appeal bond, which is unheard of in a case of this (legal) nature. That's why we insist that I'm a political prisoner, because there's no real legal basis to keep me here whatsoever.

BF: *Tell me about the youth culture, the White Panthers, and so on.*

JOHN: Essentially, we have a well-defined culture, which is a reflection of economic conditions—well, it would take us all day to deal with that. So I'll just say that since we have this shared culture, which defines us as *a people*, what we must do is gain political power for our people. Frantz Fanon says that all culture is first and foremost national—it can't be separated from the political conditions of a given people.

So we start with our culture, which everyone can relate to because it's so visible, so evident, you know, and we bring it into a political context, starting with where the people's consciousness is at and working from there. The point is to work dialectically, starting with the people's actual consciousness, and creating a real people's movement by serving the daily needs of the people and educating them so they will see that the only way they can get what they need is by creating a whole new social order for themselves. *That's* what's political. Most of the things that people are doing now on campuses is not really political—or else, it's reactionary, to a great extent.

BF: *Explain that.*

JOHN: The stuff going on now, trashing buildings, demonstrations and protests, is reactionary in one very functional sense of the term. The students are just reacting against the pig power structure and the way it sets things up. To gain political power we must first define the situation in our own terms. When we start defining the situation in our own terms, then we start to get real power. Until then, the struggle takes place on their ground. That's why we are pushing our analysis of youth as a colony, the need for a national liberation movement for young people, and the whole *national* thrust—that gives our struggle a new definition and opens the way for us to make use of the experience of other revolutionary movements, besides being correct in itself. Fanon also said something like, it's dangerous for a people to develop social consciousness before the stage of nationalism, because then the people

get hung up in frantic demands for social justice outside of a usable context, and the movement breaks down into anarchism—he said "primitive tribalism," which translates into small separated groups of people working against each other in effect, pressing for things which cannot be accomplished at this stage of the struggle.

Another thing is that the student movement is still all being done in spontaneous risings, things like that. If we talk about revolution—well, you don't *have* a spontaneous revolution. Spontaneous risings are beautiful in that they show the energy and the anger that people have built up from being oppressed. But that energy and anger have to be transformed and channeled into *political* terms, so we can move to create political power for our people. The black colony learned this lesson a few years back, and the stuff that's going on now on campuses and in the streets of the youth colony is essentially what went down in the black colony three or four or five years ago—Watts, Newark, Detroit—only on a different scale of course. We have to learn the same lesson that black people learned, that is, the point is to seize control over the institutions in your own community and make them operate in the best interests of the people of that community, using them to build a revolutionary base from which to move for liberation.

BF: *So, you want activities analogous to the Black Panther Free Breakfast program?*

JOHN: Yes, and we've had this to a certain extent already, but in an embryonic form of course. The Diggers, free stores, and so on. The beginnings of all this were there, but it was not put into an explicitly political context. That's the key to it, you see, not only doing this stuff but at the same time placing it within the context of national self-determination for the youth colony.

Take the campuses, where a lot of our people live: they are centers of technology. The students there are members of the youth colony, and they have to start regarding themselves as such instead of as a special class apart from the rest of young people. Students have to start relating to their objective situation as part of a youth colony which includes street freeks, high-school students, young factory workers, soldiers, young playboy types, secretaries, young housewives . . . all of these people are part of our colony, of our nation, whether they are aware of it or not. I can't say that *all* young people are part of the youth colony, because like a lot of young industrial and service workers, and a lot of young housewives, for example, have been abducted entirely into the mother-country culture. But there *is* an objective basis for this distinction which has to do with people being born into the post-industrial or electronic world, as distinct from people born into the industrial culture before the second world war, you know what I mean? I wish we had a tape recorder because I'd really like to go into all this!

BF: *What is the content of what you call the youth culture?*

JOHN: This is the thing that unites young people and can be used consciously to unite them even more. Almost all the people of the youth colony relate to rock & roll, to begin with, and the whole culture that has grown up around the music in the past five years or so. This in part is what makes rock & roll so exciting to me, aside from the musical experience itself, of course.

Rock & roll music is about rebellion—that's *its* content. Years ago it was listening to Little Richard and Jimmy Reed, you dig, when we were supposed to be listening to Pat Boone. It's about getting *high* instead of getting drunk like you're supposed to—like we did back then, for example, before kids could get their hands on some weed. They want you to drink alcohol because it is an integral part of the honkie culture complex—it makes you go along with all that low-energy bullshit for the straight life-style and job structure. Young people who work in the factory are doing that essentially because they don't see anything else to do, they-haven't been able to see a viable alternative which could make more life possible for them, and it all goes along with working in the factory anyway—getting drunk, bowling, hunting, buying furniture, establishing a nuclear family, buying a new car, sharp clothes, going to beauty parlors, all that shit. Or else you go into the army for three years and then into the factory. Or some other job. That's the way it was when rock & roll first jumped off, in the '50s, when I was coming up. But it's really beginning to change now.

Ten years ago, you just accepted that shit. And if you went to college you rejected rock & roll as a teenage thing, because college was like a way-station where you gradually assimilated yourself into the real "adult" middle-class culture, you know? So you listened to Dave Brubeck or Peter Paul & Mary (PPM have come a long way, but their music is still a low-energy thing—likewise Joan Baez, and all that "folk music," until Bob Dylan came along and made it a real folk music, that is, the music of *our* folk).

You can see now the same process at work as in the late '50s—the more high-energy our music got, the more the established order tried to kill it: they sent out Frankie Avalon, and Fabian, Bobby Vee, exemplars of honkie culture. Lawrence Welk as a teenager, shit like that. Now it's James Taylor and that whole low-energy scene, which is being pushed so hard because it serves the same purpose. Listen to Little Richard, and then listen to "Venus" by Frankie Avalon, to see the difference between high-energy and low-energy music, and the effect they have on you. The music industry, which is an integral part of the wholes military-industrial complex, was trying to sell the low-energy thing to white youth who had been turned on to high-energy rock & roll and all the possibilities it proposed.

The contradiction I'm trying to point out is between low-energy life forms and high-energy life forms, you know? Low-energy culture prepares people to fit into the passive consumer system—the death culture—consume, kill and shit out, that's what it's all about, you know?

A high-energy culture prepares you for revolution, for change, constant high-energy change. It's the difference between eating something and turning it into shit vs. turning it into energy to build things with. Does that make sense to you?

BF: *Very good sense. What chances do you have to listen to music here?*

JS: I've got a record player in my cell and a pretty nice little record collection, under the circumstances. But I can't get any more, because they say I'm not supposed to have the record player, you know? I bought it off another inmate when I first got here. But Leni used to send me records all the time, and then I've been reviewing records for *Jazz & Pop*, so they sent me some too.*

I listen to Big Brother & the Holding Co.—*Cheap Thrills*—and Jimi Hendrix's *Are You Experienced*, and *Kick Out the Jams* of course, by the 5, which is the highest energy rock & roll record ever made—too high-energy for anyone except stoned freeks and 16-year-old maniacs. Those are the three paramount rock & roll records of all time to me. And *Freak Out*, the Mothers' first album, which is a masterpiece in itself. And of course I listen to the Stones, and Bob Dylan's classic works, and whatever else I can get up here. But my biggest love is that other music, the original high-energy charge—John Coltrane, Pharoah Sanders, Archie Shepp, Sun Ra, Cecil Taylor, Albert Ayler—I have a lot of their records with me, as always. I listen to blues a lot too—Elmore James, John Lee Hooker, Muddy Waters, Paul Butterfield, Johnny Winter—and old rock & roll jams from the '50s, cultural history you know. Plus all

*Four of those reviews have been collected into a book published by *Jazz & Pop* called *Music & Politics*, by John Sinclair & Robert Levin.

the Detroit/Ann Arbor bands like the Rationals, SRC, Bob Seger, the Up, all that stuff. The music really keeps me alive, you know?

People used to look on their music listening as separate from their other life, but that just isn't true. I want to say, and to insist, that the music you listen to shapes your life. You listen to high-energy music, and then when people come to you with low-energy forms, you just can't stand it.

That's why kids hate school so much—school is the ultimate low-energy trip (next to the penitentiary, of course, which is just another form of the same thing). Total separation. You separate the kids into rooms and the knowledge into "subjects." It's done to change and shape you, so you'll be ready to work on the assembly line or in the office. School doesn't start at 8 and end at 3:30 by accident. It's done to start you on an industrial work-shift. So this is why we push the high-energy thing—when you become inundated with high-energy culture, you simply become incapable of operating in a low-energy context without rebelling against it. You just can't accept it. And once you get so you can't accept it you go on to invent new high-energy forms for yourself.

The straight life-style and the straight culture is all about separation. That all has to do with industrialization. None of it happens by accident. People have their own little houses, instead of living in tribal or clan groups, communally. They're isolated into tiny nuclear families, as industrial production units, so they can be more easily manipulated by the big "owners." And television is the ultimate low-energy trip. You don't *do* anything. (I'm. not denying McLuhan's idea of observer involvement, but that's in a different sense—to get involved in it you have to chain yourself to it first.) I mean you just sit there. You don't have to do anything except just sit there in the chair—which is right where they want you.

Now say that because of economic conditions you're stuck in a factory—you have to stay in a low-energy frame of being to stand it. That's why barbiturates and heroin are so big among black factory workers and kids in school. If you were righteously stoned on weed or hash you couldn't stand that life. That's not to say that a lot of kids and workers *don't* go to the job righteously stoned, but it just heightens the contradictions when they do, you know?

So our plan has always been to push high-energy music, high-energy lifestyle, bright clothes, weed, acid, and communal living, which is, because of its volatility, a high-energy thing. Rock & roll, dope, and fucking in the streets—that's our program! Get people into these forms and they relate to them. Because that's what people are supposed to be—*free.* The whole push of the industrial world is to enslave people. The corporations are just modern versions of the old feudal system—in fact they call the factories "plants," which is short for "plantation," you dig? A very few people control all the rest of the people. Everyone works for the handful that owns all. So the way you start breaking this slave system down is by building people who can't and won't relate to that. You get enough such people and it can't go on. Right?

BF: *(nod)*

JOHN: It can only go on as long as people go along with it. Take LSD a few times and you become physically incapable of having anything to do with it, especially if an alternative into which you can channel your energy exists. Without that alternative people just get messed up—they feel trapped inside forms they can't stand any more, and often they just flip out. That's why we stress the absolute necessity of creating alternative life forms. Because people get to the point where they can't relate to the death culture any more, and they move out of it to try to create a new life culture or a new form for their life.

That's the story of my own life. I rebelled all through high school, but I went to college when they sent me there and I tried hard to accept it. It was awful, but I got turned on to a lot of high-energy things when I was there—John Coltrane, Allen Ginsberg, you know? I could see that there were other things you could do besides go along with the program. I didn't know what they might be, but I had to do *something* because I couldn't stand that other thing any more. And that's a beautiful position to be in, because then you have to create something for yourself. And since you've already become involved in a high-energy cultural scene, what you create has to be based on and comes to reflect this same high-energy principle.

So you create communes, and you create other institutions on the same basis. All your institutions are on that same high-energy, participatory basis. Because, in a commune, surrounded by high-energy comrades all doing the same work, you are living in a high-energy environment, and so your creations become a high-energy thing too.

Like Mao says, high-energy or revolutionary culture prepares you for living in a revolutionary society. What he found out, years after writing that, was that you can't have a revolutionary society *unless* you have a revolutionary culture. So he promoted the cultural revolution. And this is also why in Cuba they talk about the New Man and the New Woman, without whom they know they can't have a new social order. In China, after 16 years of revolutionary government, they had to stop everything and say, "Wait a minute." They were concentrating on industrialization and found that they wouldn't be able to develop a real socialist society unless they got people to relate to new terms, to strip away all the cultural garbage which had been carried over from the old society and which was beginning to be institutionalized within the new industrial order. They had to push out of positions of power the individualistic, bureaucratic, western-culture-oriented people and involve everyone in a thorough-going cultural revolution.

I keep getting back to culture, because that's your daily life. And you can't separate people from their daily lives. Just as you must not separate theory from practice. So if you're talking about creating a revolutionary social order, well, it can't be created unless everyone in it acts, in their daily lives, in a revolutionary manner.

BF: *How did you get into all this? You said you rebelled all through high school, and you got turned on to "high-energy" experience in college, but what happened after that? What does marijuana have to do with it, for example?*

JOHN: Well, in my case anyway, and I have to say for the culture as a whole, marijuana really has *everything* to do with it, you know? Both in terms of what it does to you, the way it puts you into a whole different state of being if you get into it, and in the effect it has as a radicalizing agent, simply because it's illegal to get high in this society. That part of it is primary I think, I mean the fact that it is western post-industrial society which is the setting in which we get high, that's what makes smoking weed a radicalizing thing above and beyond the intrinsic effects of the sacrament. I don't know if I can make myself clear on this, but what I'm trying to say is that weed is and has been the perfect catalyst, or the perfect tool, precisely in this time and place, because its effect on people's consciousness is to make us really aware of the artificial barriers which have been erected inside our heads to keep us apart so the power structure can keep us in line, right?

See, the thing is that weed helps put people back in touch with their *senses,* it helps people *feel* more, and in a social order which has successfully dehumanized and desensified people in order to make them into cogs in the great industrial machine that's really a subversive function. Industrial society demands a very serious attitude from the people who are caught up in it, it demands subservience to the "owners" and to the machine itself—it demands allegiance to the concept of efficiency and control, and it severely limits the possibilities for life and consciousness among its people. But marijuana makes people aware of alternatives to the machine life of industrial society—it demonstrates in a very specific term that there are more exciting possibilities for life in this place than whiskey and football games and ulcers and a lifetime on the assembly line or in the office, and it makes people wonder why this old-time shit is still going on. Instead of deadening people's consciousness, marijuana helps bring people back to life and expands their awareness of the world and the possibilities for more life in that world.

Marijuana helps prepare people for the future, for the kind of life we'll all be able to live when the post-industrial revolution is completed—it promotes communalism, sharing, ego-loss, increased sensitivity to the needs of other people, creativeness, a heightened awareness of one's natural possibilities, and other traits which will prepare people to live in the age of post-scarcity abundance. And, by doing this, it heightens the contradictions between the old order and the new, and it brings people into conflict with the control addicts who run the capitalist system, which helps make them see the absolute necessity of rejecting and abolishing that system and its culture and replacing it with a whole new social order. People start getting high and really digging it, and then the pigs come down on them just for doing that, and they can't understand it at first—but the more it happens the more they begin to realize that it's all part of a pattern, that the control addicts don't want them getting high because that

The Sinclair-influenced revolutionary band Up!

shoots them out of the pig's grasp, and they begin to understand that the only way they can live the way they want to live is by doing away with the old order altogether. It doesn't happen all at once, and it certainly doesn't happen to everybody who gets high, but I know that's the way it worked in my case and with a lot of people I know, and that's why I have to consider weed to be a revolutionary force in this time and place.

But you can't take it out of its context, because it's precisely the fact that marijuana has emerged as a force within the context of western industrial-capitalist society that gives it its social utility and its important role in the world revolution. Marijuana isn't much of a force of any kind in the under-developed world, because people in those areas have a lot more basic things on their minds—they still have to be primarily concerned with feeding and clothing themselves, housing and educating themselves, with defending themselves against the imperialist armies and the colonizing exploiters who are determined to rip them off, and they don't have much time available for getting high and enjoying the fruits of abundance as we have here in the West. But the point is that marijuana is indigenous to *post-industrial* culture, and that during a transitional period like the one we're now in, where you have a bunch of industrial dinosaurs trying to hold back the post-scarcity society, getting high goes against the whole grain of scarcity culture and draws severe repressive measures from the capitalist state.

So the act of smoking marijuana and getting high in this context is a po-litical act, not only because it carries heavy political consequences but also because it has definite economic and cultural effects within the context of western society. It's like George Orwell said in *1984*, where he was talking about how fucking was a political act within the context of the Ingsoc system: "You could not have pure love or pure lust nowadays. No emotion was pure, because everything was mixed up with fear and hatred. Their embrace had been a battle, the climax a victory. It was a blow struck against the Party. *It was a political act.*" You dig? Not in itself so much, but because it took place, as everything takes place, in a political context, and because the state had set itself up as against the spontaneity and freedom inherent in the act of love. If the state makes fucking illegal, or getting high illegal, then fucking and getting high are political acts, and people who get high and fuck are engaged in a form of struggle against the state even if they don't consciously want to be involved in "politics" at all. And like I said before, as the shit gets heavier they begin to understand that the only way they can carry on the way they want to is by first doing away with the repressive state machinery, and the economic system which it serves.

There's like a double effect—marijuana puts people in a position of conflict with the dominant *culture* by heightening their sensitivity and making them incapable of living and working willingly within the confines of the death culture, and at the same time it puts them into a position of conflict with the *political* machinery of the capitalist state, which is determined to stomp out all subversive elements, that is, everybody who rejects and rebels against the basic assumptions of scarcity capitalist society. Once weed-heads are treated like criminals and subversives they begin to develop what we call "outlaw consciousness," and they realize that somehow, without really meaning to, they have become enemies of the state, right? So they start to think about the nature of this state that considers such a beautiful benevolent act a crime, and they begin to see just what it is they're fighting against and what has to be done about it—they see that the whole repressive political and economic and cultural machinery of the capitalist state must be dismantled and thrown onto the junkheap of history. And then they smoke some more weed, and start to get down.

I know that's the way it worked on me, anyway, and marijuana has been central to my experience ever since I first got turned on to it ten years ago. When I started smoking marijuana, in 1961, I was still in college, trying to come to some sort of accommodation with the system. I was more or less aware that things weren't what they were supposed to be in Amerika, but I felt essentially that it was just the fault of a few elected officials or Ed Sullivan or something, I didn't know and didn't much care as long as I could go along my own way and do what I wanted to do, which was listen to music and get high and read and write poetry and just have a good time the best way I could. Marijuana fit right into the kind of life I wanted to live, and it made things even hipper.

But the more weed I smoked the less I was able to stomach the stupidity and irrelevance of the so-called educational system I was caught up in—going to class wiped out on weed really makes you realize how ridiculous the whole western system of "education" is, how little it has to do with learning anything useful and how destructive it is of real intelligence, curiosity and creativity. The contradiction between the way I felt when I was high and doing my thing, and the oppressive feeling I had sitting in school trying to deal with that shit got so great that I couldn't take it any more, and I dropped out of school so I could spend all my time with the kind of people I really related to—black brothers off the block, jazz musicians, beatniks, people who smoked weed and dug music and didn't have anything to do with the dominant culture at all. I got myself together to a certain extent during that time, mostly through smoking a lot of weed and doing a lot of heavy rapping behind it, and when I went back to school I had a whole different orientation, like I was into picking up as much information as I could which might help me get myself more together, you know? My parents were paying my tuition and my rent, so I decided to stay in school as long as I could do that rather than getting a job or something like that, and after I got my degree I moved to Detroit where I could be around more people like myself. I was going to graduate school at Wayne State University on a government loan, but the only thing I was really interested in was hanging out with beatniks and heads and getting some kind of alternative scene together.

Just about everybody I met around Wayne in the first few months I was in Detroit I met through the marijuana underground—that was the one thing we had in common, no matter what else we were doing, and I got into a lot of different sets because I was dealing quite a bit of weed at the time. I had connections with some brothers on the west side, dudes I knew through the black jazz scene, and I had like the only steady reefer supply in the campus area, so my apartment got to be like the meeting place for all different kinds of heads, musicians, poets, and other incipient freeks, right? This is in 1964, when there was nothing going on at all, and what happened was that a bunch of people who were hanging out at my place started talking about *doing* something about the fantasies we were steadily smoking up together. The Artists' Workshop came out of that summer's joint conferences, and the thing about it was that the Workshop was actually based in the dope scene more than anything else. People who didn't have anything else in common other than their common interest in getting high were able to come together at the Workshop, and the more we got into it the more possibilities we were able to see and actualize.

Just before the Workshop opened I got busted for the first time, in October 1964, but I got a slick lawyer through a friend of mine and got out of it for $400 and 2 years' probation. I was really the first person in our community to take a bust for weed, but it was like a fluke—a black dude I knew from Jackson, Michigan, came down to Detroit to bust me because he had a sales beef of his own he had to get out from under—so we didn't think very much of it at all. I remember though, when the pigs came busting into our crib to arrest me, it was like a movie or a television show—I mean we didn't have any sense of being criminals or outlaws or anything like that, it was a total surprise and we even thought at first that it was a trick some friends of ours were playing on us, you know? And I got out of it so easy that I didn't think very much of it after that—I just wanted to carry out our plans for the Workshop, and my probation officer was pretty cool, so after a couple months of being paranoid and shit I just forgot about it altogether.

Well, during the first year of the Workshop we managed to expand our operation almost week by week—we started out with a house we rented in the neighborhood by getting 16 of us to put up $5.00 each for the first month's rent, and we put on free jazz concerts, poetry readings, exhibitions of paintings and photography, electronic music concerts, avant-garde film screenings, whatever anybody in the neighborhood was doing the Workshop provided a place for it to happen. Then we started like a free school on weeknights, self-education classes where people who could play music or write or paint or make films or whatever would share their information with other people in the community who wanted to do it themselves. We started renting houses on the block around the corner so everybody who was working or hanging out together at the Workshop could live together too, and within a year we had like six houses and two storefronts all on the same block, with a printshop, a new performing and meeting center, three communes and a number of cooperative living scenes where we would rent rooms out to individual artists and other heads. We never made any distinction between people who did different kinds of art work and people who just hung out, got high and dug what was going on, because we knew that we were all the same, that it was about being part of a culture or a community which had as its common term not so much our art work but the fact that everybody *got high together,* you dig?

Now, during all this time we didn't pay very much attention to the outside world at all—I mean we were very much aware of it, sure, but we didn't want to have anything to do with it if we could help it, and our thing was that we were engaged in building up an alternative to the death scene which we would control ourselves and by means of which we would eventually be able to take care of all of our most immediate needs. We thought the creeps who ran the death system would be only too happy to get rid of us, and we really did everything we could to keep the news of what we were doing to ourselves and our own people—we never publicized the Workshop's programs outside the immediate community (except to establish ties with other alternative communities around the county through our poetry magazines, newsletters, books and a couple of trips to the east and west coast with our band, the Detroit Contemporary 5, or the Workshop Poets), and when straight people or newspaper reporters would

come around we would run them out before they could spoil everything with their weirdness. We knew that what we were doing was completely opposed to the death system and even to the whole thrust of western civilization as a whole, but we didn't think *they* were hip to it, right? We also had contacts with brothers and sisters in the "civil rights" movement and the incipient anti-war movement, who were always telling us that we were just copping out on the struggle, but we kept trying to tell *them* that what we were doing was *really* political because it wasn't predicated on the actions or practices of the established order like theirs was. I mean we weren't at all unconscious of the wider social realities—we just thought that we could get around them while creating an alternative to them which would survive what we considered to be the inevitable collapse of western civilization under the weight of its own internal contradictions.

But the problem was that our analysis soon proved to be wrong—we operated on the assumption that we could do what we wanted to do if we stayed out of the power structure's way and just did our own thing, right? But they couldn't stand to let us alone—the police and the people who gave them their orders evidently figured that we had to be stopped before we attracted any more converts from their university campuses and their suburban living rooms. We weren't doing anything illegal except getting high every day, and we really didn't make a big thing out of that—it was just something we *did,* you know?—but that one thing served as the excuse for the pigs to move in on us and try to shut us up by terrifying us before we could do any more harm to its sense of order. We were too naive to see it like that at the time—we thought it was just a personal vendetta being carried out by the narcotics squad goons—but, objectively, that's what was happening, although it took us a long time to understand it.

I got popped again in August of 1965, two weeks after we got back from the Berkeley Poetry Conference in California where we met a lot of our culture heroes for the first time—Ed Sanders, Allen Ginsberg, Charles Olson, Robert Creeley, and a whole lot of people who were trying to do the same kind of thing in their communities as we were doing in Detroit. The narcotics police sent an undercover agent in with instructions to get some weed from me, and he followed me around for three weeks until I decided to burn the dude to get rid of him, right? I hadn't ever burned anybody before, but this creep was so obnoxious and so persistent that I didn't know any other way to get rid of him than to put him in a trick. A friend of mine who I copped from all the time had scored some lemonade reefer and got stuck with two pounds of it, so I decided to do him a favor and get rid of this chomp at the same time by taking some of it off his hands and selling it to the creep at some exorbitant price. The dude drove me across town to the dealer's place and then back home, but as soon as I went inside the house the goon squad knocked the doors down again and rounded all of us up.

This bust was really a super set-up—the narcotics bureau sent out press releases saying that they had broken up a big "campus dope ring," and it made the headlines in the next day's papers. I was billed as the "ring-leader" in the papers, and the narcs laid all kinds of threats on me as soon as they got me downtown in their sty. I got out on bond the next day and went back to work, still thinking this whole thing was just a personal vendetta, and me & Leni decided that the best thing we could do was to quit smoking weed until the heat got off us so we wouldn't have this kind of trouble any more. See, we still thought it was like a legalistic ruse, you know? And our work was the most important thing in our lives, so we were willing to do anything, even giving up weed if we had to, in order not to jeopardize our work. We got even deeper into the Workshop and the housing project, which we were managing along with Robin Eichele, and at the same time we decided to start fighting the Michigan marijuana laws so we wouldn't be bothered with *that* shit any more. I got a job in a parking lot next to the Dodge Main plant out in Hamtramck so I could pay the lawyer we hired to challenge the marijuana laws for us, and we left the whole legal thing up to him while we concentrated on getting the Workshop together enough so we wouldn't be so vulnerable to assaults like that in the future.

Well, two weeks before the scheduled trial date the lawyer called me up and told me that we wouldn't be able to fight the case—the judge had ruled that entrapment was no defense, cutting off our most likely chance, and there was no possibility of winning on the constitutional issues I wanted to bring out, so the lawyer refused to fight it and insisted that I had to take a cop to possession because he wouldn't take the responsibility of me getting the 20-year minimum that sales carries in the state of Michigan. He promised me that he'd fixed things up with the prosecutor and all I'd get was some more probation and another fine, but when I went for it the judge came with six months in the Detroit House of Correction, right? I flipped right out—not so much at the judge and his well-paid assistant as at my own stupidity in trusting a creep like this fine liberal lawyer I had retained. I *knew* how crooked the whole "legal" ruse was from the last time I got caught up in it, but I let myself go for this double-cross and I was really pissed off behind it. I did the six months and hated every minute of it, thinking about how much work I had to do and how the motherfucking state was able to use these ridiculous marijuana laws to hang people up with, and when I got out in August of 1966 I wanted to start fighting the laws any way we could so we could get rid of them once and for all.

I still didn't draw the larger conclusion, though—I mean it still seemed to me that the solution was to get even farther out of the mainstream of the death culture (which I remember Leni calling "a perpetual sewer" in something she wrote around that time), and to get our alternative scene so together that the pigs wouldn't be able to rip us off like that any more. I hadn't smoked any weed for a whole year and I was talking about people shouldn't smoke any weed any more until we could get the laws changed, because what we were doing was too important to let it get slowed down by silly shit like that, you know? Our music and our poetry and the institutions we were creating for ourselves had to be free to develop even if it meant giving up the sacrament, and I couldn't see how we could afford to spend all that time fighting dope cases and doing prison time just because the police could use that as an excuse to keep us from our work.

So I came out of DeHoCo issuing statements that all heads should stop smoking grass and start working for a change in the marijuana laws—as if those two things were incompatible, right?—because we were just going to get arrested all the time if we kept on breaking the law like that and giving the police an excuse to round us up and get us off the streets and into their jails. But this beautiful thing had happened during the six months I was locked up that time—like there was this huge "hippie explosion" going on everywhere, even in filthy old Detroit, and it really turned me around. See, when I went to prison in February there really weren't that many people like us in the whole country, and there *certainly* wasn't any kind of *mass* possibility for what we were doing, but all of a sudden there were hundreds and thousands of teenage maniacs running around smoking weed, dropping acid, growing their hair long, playing and singing and dancing to rock & roll music which we hadn't even paid any attention to before. We had been into John Coltrane and Archie Shepp and Sun Ra and *that* whole thing, and we had like an elitist attitude towards the Beatles and the Stones and all that stuff, but there were so many people like us who were into that now that we really had to check it out, and it was a *motherfucker!* Actually I really got into it when Cecil Taylor turned me on to the *Revolver* album, right? I mean I had been deep into rock & roll all through my school days, but after I got out of high school and got turned on to jazz I didn't pay any mind to it any more at all, and it was like discovering it all over again. Whew! It blew my mind completely—*Revolver, Sunshine Superman, Jefferson Airplane Takes Off, Freak Out!* by the Mothers, the first Love album— those were the records that were out by that time, and what killed me so much was that all these crazy motherfuckers *obviously* got high and shit, right? That was far out to me because I had thought that people who got high like naturally got into *jazz* (except for dudes like Bob Dylan, who was *always* into it even when he was strumming on an acoustic and playing like a "folk singer") because that's where the high-energy possibilities were, but now these *freeks* were digging the energy scene through electric guitars and amplifiers and all that stuff, and they added another dimension to it by *singing* too. And their songs came right out and talked about dope and the whole psychedelic consciousness thing that all of us were into, which was just *amazing.*'

Anyway, that happened like all at once, and then I met the MC5, and Grimshaw, and a bunch of other people who hadn't been around before, and the Grande Ballroom opened in Detroit, people were doing light shows, there was all this tremendous new energy around and I was ready to do anything I had to do to plug into it, you know? Leni hadn't been able to dig this thing really because she'd been so caught up in trying to keep the Workshop together while I was gone, I mean she had to do it *all,* and besides, I guess it all happened gradually so that people who were on the street all the time didn't realize how much everything was changing. But I had been locked away for six months, and it hit me right between the eyes as soon as I got back home. I could see that it was stupid to talk about giving up weed when all these maniacs were running around smoking all the reefer they could get their hands on, so I threw that idea out of my mind and started smoking dope and dropping acid every chance I could get in the hope that I could maybe catch up with everything I'd missed.

Dope was like the link between the neo-beatnik culture we had been involved in prior to 1966 and the new hippie culture which was just beginning to spring up then, but more than that, it was also the link between all the different strains of hip people within the new open scene just as it had been earlier, when our scene was much more a *closed* thing and weed was like the automatic credential, right? The spirit was the same too, although most of the manifestations of that spirit were different as between the neo-beatnik and hippie scenes—but in each case it was weed that was central to what was happening, just as it was weed which did provide the dialectical link between the older scene and the new one. Acid was a big part of it too, but acid was indigenous to the new culture whereas it wasn't really integral to the older one—acid is what really opened people up a lot, and it was easy to make the transition once you had taken acid a few times, but weed was the everyday connection that couldn't be broken.

Anyway, me & Leni went through a lot of changes during that period, we hooked up with a lot of new people and got into a whole lot of new things, trying to bring some of the older sensibility and seriousness really, to the hippie scene and the rock & roll scene—we could sit down and smoke a few joints with people and turn them on to some of the things we had been into with the Workshop, and at the same time they could turn us on to what *they* were into, so we could all arrive at some kind of new high-energy synthesis which would make the most of both sources. What we found right away was that these kids were just as alienated and disgusted with the old-time shit as we were, although they couldn't articulate it as well as we could maybe, but it was all about the same thing in the end, and we were constantly pushing our line of building alternative institutions and keeping control of them in the hands of the people who were creating them. There were all kinds of new institutions shooting up anyway—head shops, underground papers, the Ballroom, rock & roll bands everywhere you looked, light shows, posters, more and more communes and dope dealers and hip craftspeople and artisans, and we were trying to expand the context of the old Workshop so it could take in all of these phenomena and help define them as components of a single thing, which

we were calling the cultural revolution, you dig?

We had moved down to this place called Plum Street, which was like an early attempt at hip capitalism, so we could keep a close check on what was happening there and so we could be closer to the *Fifth Estate,* which had moved its offices down there during the summer. We took over the Fifth Estate Bookstore and were using it to slip poetry books and magazines and avant-jazz records in with the regular psychedelic stock which was paying the rent, always trying to use the thing people already related to in order to get them into something a little bit deeper and a little higher energy. Grimshaw was living in the layout room of the *Fifth Estate* office, right across the hall from us, and he was doing all the posters for the Grande as well as the light show there, so we got to be very close with that brother from the beginning. He had gone to high school with most of the dudes in the MC5, who were all living in one little apartment over on Canfield with Frank Bach (Frank was emceeing at the Grande and writing a rock & roll column for the *Fifth Estate*) and some other people, and we all started hanging out more and more, especially me & Rob Tyner and Grimshaw and Emil Bacilla, another brother from Lincoln Park who was doing the High Society light show with Grimshaw. A lot of us would take acid together at least once a week, and we were *always* smoking plenty reefer and talking about all the shit we might could do with all the possibilities that were opening up at the time.

Well, not very long after Leni & me

moved down to Plum Street this narcotics detective who had busted me both times before was down there one night cruising the scene and checking it out—there were tons of kids hanging out down there every night, pouring in from the suburbs looking for something to do, and weed was everywhere, so naturally the pigs came snooping around. This chomp, Warner Stringfellow his name is, and his partner were walking through our building (we lived in a tiny 2-room apartment right over the store) and came to our apartment door which was standing open at the time. I was fixing a light socket—I remember this *so* well!—and turned around to see these two pigs out there in the other room, right? And Stringfellow says, like, "Remember *me*, John?" "Sure." "How did you make out at the House of Correction," all that shit, talking real nice and coming on like I was one of his normal criminal victims who put up with that shit, right? I got pissed off and told him to get the fuck out of my crib, and then *he* got nasty and started threatening me—"you won't get away so easy the *next* time, you worthless prick!" You dig? They pulled up right after that and I went back to what I was doing, but when Leni came home (she was working in the post office for a while to get some money to buy a new camera with) we talked about it and then I wrote the poem for Warner Stringfellow after she went to sleep that night.

Stringfellow had been watching us very closely since I got out of DeHoCo, and he had already sent an undercover snake into the community to try and bust us, but after that night he put this pig named Kapagian on us full time. I remember I gave a poetry reading at Wayne a couple weeks after that, where I read the Stringfellow poem for the first time, and in the police reports that turned up at my trial it comes out that Kapagian was assigned to that reading as his first assignment on my case. We didn't think too much about the police at all—we were too busy trying to get all this shit together and we were dropping acid one or two times a week on top of that, going to the Grande every weekend to dig the 5 (they were the house band there) and be with the people, running the bookstore, trying to get the Workshop back together, and everything else—we heard about the rock & roll benefits they were putting on in San Francisco, so we decided to do the same thing in Detroit, and that was one of our major projects right then too. Plus we had started a Detroit chapter of LEMAR (Legalize Marijuana) and were setting up speaking gigs for attorneys and hip doctors at WSU to give out legal and medical information pertaining to reefer.

So all of this was going on, and everything was getting farther out all the time, and the police were getting very freaked out behind it—they thought they were going to put a stop to us when they sent me to DeHoCo a year earlier, but now the whole fucking scene was getting out of hand and we were right in the middle of it, right? So they laid out this whole strategy for breaking up the expanding hip community before it could consolidate itself, and they carried it out right down the line. The snake Kapagian was sliming around on

Plum Street and in the Warren-Forest neighborhood around Wayne, copping joints and matchboxes and half-lids and whatever he could get his hands on, and they picked the week before our first big benefit to pull their big raid off. *Guerrilla Lovefare* was supposed to go down at the Grande on January 29th, with poets, rock & roll bands, jazz groups, light shows, plenty of weed and acid, the most explosive gathering of freeks in Detroit's history—the posters were already out and everybody was talking about it when BAM! January 24th the shit hit the fan, 56 people were arrested all in one night, the papers came out with more campus dope raid headlines, and me & Leni were both cracked this time—me for "dispensing" two joints (giving them to Kapagian's policewoman partner who was disguised as a sister) and Leni for possession of our stash at home.

They got the whole neighborhood, hitting like five or six communes and a bunch of people who owned or worked in stores on Plum Street—they got the Magic Veil Light Show (Jerry Younkins and Ron "Anarchy" Frankenberg), people from the staffs of the *Fifth Estate* and *Guerrilla* (which Allen Van Newkirk, Grimshaw and myself were putting out), people who were at the Workshop for poetry classes and a LEMAR meeting, and my whole band. Oh, I forgot to tell you about that—Jim Semark & me put this band together, called the Downhome Tyrannosaurus of Despair, which was like a rock & roll space band—two saxophones, two guitars, two basses, two drummers, and Semark on electric piano and composition with me singing and holler-

ing. We were playing music like "A Love Supreme" by Trane, "Sexy Ways" by Hank Ballard & the Midnighters, B.B. King tunes, Bo Diddley jams, all kinds of spaced-out improvisation and chanting and original compositions by Semark, who was one of the original Artists' Workshop people—"Death Dwarves in the Street," "Trackin Down That Old Downhome Tyrannosaurus of Despair," "Sea of Tranquillity," weirdness personified, right? We were practicing in the Workshop for the Guerrilla Lovefare benefit the night the bust came down—I think we had changed the name of the band to Detroit Edison White Light Company by that time—and "A Love Supreme" was blasting away when the pigs came to arrest us. I'll never forget *that* either! We told them we would go with them as soon as the tune was over, that's the kind of consciousness we were into at the time, right? The music is stronger than your guns, all that idealistic shit.

Anyway, everybody got out in the morning on bond—43 of the 56 people weren't even charged, they were just dragged in so the headlines would be more sensational in the morning papers—everybody got out except me, and I had to stay in the Wayne County Jail for a week on a probation holder until our attorneys could get me back out. I had that whole week to think about what was going down, and it woke me up like nothing else had been able to do, up to that point. The benefit had to be called off, the whole scene was in a panic, people were like cutting their hair off and putting their brassieres back on, right? Splitting for California, shit like that. When I got out on bond finally I went out in the streets and people were still *terrified*, man, sitting around talking about how they had quit getting high and they were gonna get jobs or go back to school—I mean they were *terrified* behind it, you dig?

The pigs had set out to demoralize and disintegrate the whole community, and it worked for a minute, but after a couple weeks of rapping to people and spreading plenty reefer around we were able to get the spirit that had been growing for six months back up to the level it had reached before the bust, we scheduled the benefit again and got Allen Ginsberg and sister Diane DiPrima to come in for it, and Jo Jarman and Roscoe Mitchell and their space band from Chicago, and the Detroit bands, the 5, Billy C. and the Sunshine, the Spikdrivers I think, all the poets read and people really got together and overcame the weirdness that the police tried to lay on us. (It was funny in a way, but my band never got back together because the bass player's mother and the guitar player's mother wouldn't let their sons hang out with us any more, right? So we just hooked up closer with the 5 and Billy C., because they were making the music anyway, and that was the point.)

The thing was that it was so *obvious*, man, that this was a *political* act on the part of the police, and everybody could dig it like that because it was so plain, and it really had a tremendous effect on everything that happened in Detroit after that, for the next two years and a half anyway, until they finally locked me up behind that two joints ruse. Trans-Love Energies grew

directly out of January 24th, and the legalize-marijuana movement in Michigan, and the rock & roll scene we had there, and everything else really was tremendously influenced by the experience we all gained that night. There was never any question in Michigan that marijuana was a political question, and if you can dig all that you can see why they've made such a big thing out of my case, right? Because we went on from there and just continually flaunted the pigs' mistake in their faces—the whole ruse had backfired, and instead of breaking up the community they just brought everybody closer together. It was pretty far out.

From that point on we used the marijuana issue increasingly to educate kids to the political aspect of the cultural revolution, and we hooked it up I would have to say inextricably with rock & roll and everything else that was going on. Like we used to make it a point to smoke joints on stage at the Grande everytime we played there in those days, to show kids that the pigs weren't shit, and we constantly pushed the outlaw thing so they could understand that our culture, this thing we were all engaged in, was a political phenomenon above all. That's how so many "non-political" kids, like thousands and thousands of them, were able to get into the White Panther thing in 1968, because we based all our propaganda on rock & roll, dope, and fucking in the streets, and we said, dig, *this* is the revolution, people, this is what they're attacking us for, getting high and having a good time, they don't want us to get like this because they want us all under control,

174

but that ain't nothin, we can smoke dope and get high any time we wanna, we might have to fight for it but if that's what we gotta do then that's what we'll *do*, goddamnit! You dig?

BF: *Yeah!*

JOHN: OK, that's what that was about, and it was really central to our whole experience—weed, that is. The higher we got the more the pigs were determined to stomp us out, and the more they tried to put the douse on us the farther out we got in terms of "politics," right? Because we could see that what we were doing was actually undermining their whole thing, and they just couldn't have that at all. We could analyze what was going down because it was so *obvious,* man, and it was obvious to all the people who we reached through the band and like my writings in the *Fifth Estate* and the *Sun,* right? And everything else we were doing. We were dangerous because we understood what was happening and we were running it to the people so they could understand it too, so the pigs had to go to extremes to slow us down at least, if they couldn't stop us. That's why they laid this sentence on me, and no appeal bond, and the bombing conspiracy ruse, and all that shit, but just like everything else they've tried it's just backfired on them. I would have to say that my case and the sentence I got from that pig Colombo have done more than any other single thing in the state of Michigan to expose the repressive nature of the state not only to young people but also to a lot of straight people who just can't understand what the fuck is going on. Two joints of weed! Whew!

BF: *Well, how does this tie in with the Movement, or what people usually think of as "political"? I know you've kind of put down demonstrations and a lot of the more traditional forms of political activity in the past—do you still feel that way?*

JOHN: Yeah, pretty much; I mean *living* in a revolutionary way is what is finally a threat to the established order, and that's what's finally going to make the difference. Whereas a demonstration finally is not a threat, and you can see this objectively in the kind of time they hand out—you see that you get 9½-10 years for smoking weed and promoting revolutionary culture, but for taking part in a demonstration or something, if you get busted you get like 90 days, or a fine, you dig? And even if they lower the penalties for marijuana possession it won't be because it's not a threat any more, but because people are forcing them to do that—not *forcing* them with demonstrations or woofing or shit like that, but because there's so many of us now, man, there's so *many* of us that they *have* to respond to us, and the more they resist something like legalizing marijuana the more they expose their repressive nature, even more than with "violence" and shit like that, because the average person just doesn't see any *reason* for locking people up for getting high. They don't understand it, but the more they think about it, and the more information they get, the more they start to put things together, and the more they begin to see what it's all about.

Now the good aspect of demonstrations is that they get a lot of people together and, hopefully, unite them around one issue, at least momentarily. But that's as far as they go. After the demonstration, everyone goes back to their individual rooms with their one roommate, and goes to classes and watches television, consuming, sitting around waiting for the next demonstration to happen. It doesn't provide an alternative *life context* for people who want something different, you dig?

As far as getting large numbers of people together is concerned, if you can get them together for a rock & roll dance or a festival, it becomes more than, and better than, a demonstration. Because you are doing it for yourselves, you're *creating* something, you're not just reacting against some insane action on the part of the government, and it's a positive thing which raises the energy level of the people and hopefully, which gives them a direction, or an idea of a direction, in which to move. Not always, not even very often yet, but we're always thinking about the future, and we relate very strongly to that possibility, you know?

There are other problems with demonstrations too, most of which stem from the problem of the pig's defining the situation in his own terms. When petty violence is used, or when verbal diarrhea by demonstrators causes the pigs to attack the crowd, the primary issues raised by the demonstration are covered over by the phony issue of "violence," and the pig power structure only uses that issue to organize the straight people against the students.

Of course there are two sides to this too—the repression of protesters by the pigs has helped considerably to raise the consciousness of young people, and it helps heighten the contradictions in the death culture by polarizing people into the life camp and the death camp, but at this point in our struggle we have to start reaching across the cultural barrier and try to unite with the broad masses of straight people. We have to show them that their real enemy is not *us* but the pig power structure itself, which uses both of us against each other. And the phony "violence" ruse really contributes to this problem. The straight people see it as a direct threat to them, and it pisses them off. Besides, the point of polarizing people is to see what you've got to work with, to draw the line and set up your opposing camps—it isn't the end but only the beginning. That's when the work of organizing the people in your camp starts, you know?

Look at the difference between the Chicago Convention scene and Woodstock, two of the major turning points in our culture's history so far. In Chicago, the Festival of Life was supposed to be like Woodstock finally was, only more beautiful because we ourselves would control it (and not some rich dudes and pop stars). But the violence at Chicago blew all that. I'm not saying it didn't have its very positive aspects— it certainly intensified the level of the struggle, and made millions of people see how serious this whole thing is.

But my point is that everyone finally was perceived as just "demonstrators" in Chicago, people who went there to provoke the police and disrupt everything. There was no finally positive image projected out into Amerika, you

Abbie Hoffman

know? I certainly didn't go there to demonstrate—except to demonstrate the existence and beauty of our alternative culture, the Life Culture. I thought that's what we were supposed to be doing there, showing people that we *did* have an alternative and that we *were* practicing it—that it *could* be done. I wouldn't walk across the street to demonstrate against the Democrats!

The reason why the whole thrust of the Festival of Life was obliterated so completely was that *it was such a dangerous image.* The pigs wish they could have obliterated Woodstock, too. Because our big gatherings obliterate all the myths and lies they spread about the youth culture—about our people.

In other words, here at Woodstock you had 500,000 or a million long-haired kooks, right? Who are always portrayed in the papers as misfits, people who can't relate to anyone, who can't take care of themselves. Yet, against overwhelmingly lousy physical conditions these people lived together in a big field in the rain and helped one another out, and did fine, survived, and had fun.

So what was successful to me about Woodstock was that it wasn't set up as a protest. They couldn't even say anything bad about it. The pigs didn't beat anyone up, so they couldn't say it was "violent." So a new myth was created—our culture is a positive thing. This was something new in terms of our relations with straight people. We could have done this at Chicago in 1968, but of course we didn't have the money to buy off the pigs, and pay the bands, and rent the land, and insure the success of the Festival of Life like that. But before

long we'll be able to produce our own Woodstocks, which will be controlled completely by our own people, and which will be real demonstrations of what we're all about.

But you see, that's why we keep emphasizing the Woodstock thing, because even the reactionary press has had to accept it as a Positive happening. In Chicago, where we tried and failed to pull it off, the media defined the situation in their own terms: a negative demonstration against the established order, and the masses of the people were rallied to the defense of the government.

Always, it was portrayed as a negative, destructive thing. *They couldn't let the Festival of Life go on.* It would have exposed all their myths about the hippies. We could have shown that we had that we were, a real people, a whole new possibility for people. And they couldn't let that happen.

That's the important thing about Chicago to me, given everything else people already know and feel about it. And they've kept it all hid ever since. The Festival of Life is completely forgotten—it was only a violent demonstration, right? That's why they wouldn't let me go down to Chicago and testify at the Conspiracy Trial, because that was going to be my testimony. I was supposed to be the first witness for the defense, but they refused to honor Abbie's subpoena. And the government (which included the judge, of course) doused all references to, or demonstrations of our culture in the courtroom, because that would've meant that we had the power of definition of the terms of the trial, and they couldn't have that at all. No singing allowed in the courtroom. And the prosecutors portrayed the defendants as being destructive, tear-it-down nihilists, which the papers projected too. It's all about controlling the terms and images that are projected, you see? At least at this point.

But Chicago was beautiful finally, like I said before, because it convinced us of the seriousness of the threat we posed to the ruling elite, that they took us a lot more seriously than we did ourselves. That was a mind-blower, and a lot of us still don't realize it. They *know* how dangerous we are to their rule, and they will do anything to stop us. We certainly saw that earlier this month, huh? At Kent State? It won't work, though, because our time has come and theirs has passed. We are the positive force which will triumph over their negative force. That's why we must project positive images, because we *are* positive and not negative at all. Only the government has an interest in portraying us as a negative thing.

Only by projecting positive, high-energy things will we build the youth colony up into a powerful political force, and even win over the straight people. The Revolution is for all the people, and it can't be won without the people's support and participation. So all I can say to end this is what I always say—All Power to the People! Life to the Life Culture and Death to the Death Culture! And thanks for coming up to see me, brother, I really dug it.

Rainbow Party icon

WE ARE A PEOPLE!

MAY-JUNE 1970

Brothers and Sisters—

I t is time for us to realize a number of very important things. We are a people, we recognize each other as brothers and sisters united in a common struggle for our freedom, for our survival, and we recognize each other because we share a common culture. We do the same things, we live the same way, we listen to the same music, smoke the same sacraments, we are united by our age, our common values, our common vision of the future. We want the same things—freedom, self-determination, peace, justice, harmony and equality for all people. There are millions of us, we are a people, but until now we haven't started to realize our strength because most of us have been primarily concerned with our *individual* freedom, our freedom as separate individuals, and we haven't really been aware of the need for our freedom *as a people.*

We've been giving too much attention to our individual selves, or to our separate little families and tribes, and what we have to realize now is that none of us can really be free until *all* of us are free. That's what we have to start with. We have to go beyond our spaced-out individualism, which has brought us up to this point in our history, and we have to start thinking about our freedom as a people, as a vast nation of free brothers and sisters who must unite with each other in a struggle for our *collective* self-determination and freedom. We have to get ourselves together, we have to unite on the basis of our commonality, we have to come together and emerge together as a powerful new political and social force which is capable of bringing about the changes we all know have to be made if we're going to survive and grow into our full human potential as a new people on this earth.

181

Rainbow Party icon

We all want to be free, and we all want all the people on earth to be free—that's what we've always wanted, right? There's never been any doubt about that. But we've been going about it all wrong. We've been asking and begging the established order for our freedom, like they're going to give it to us as a favor, and we've got to realize that we're not going to get what we want without a struggle. We have to struggle for it. We have to understand that the creeps who now control our lives, the "ownership" class here in Babylon, are not going to give up any of their power or any of their control unless we *make* them give it up, and the only way we can do that is to start from where we are right now and move together in an organized fashion to get what we need. That's the only way we can do it. And the first step in that direction is to start re-defining reality in its own terms, in our own terms, in terms which will make it possible for us to realize our collective strength and to use it in our own interests.

We have to force our own definitions on these creeps, and the very first thing we have to do is seize control over our own images. We have to make it clear that we are *not* simply a "protest movement" but a *liberation* movement, a movement for total change and total revolution which will not be satisfied with anything less than the total freedom of all the people on the planet. And once we do that, once we define and advance our own image of ourselves and our people, then we can start moving in the right direction. We can get out from under the definitions the pigs have put on us, and we can force them to start dealing with us on our own terms.

How do we do this? We start out by saying that *WE ARE A PEOPLE.* We are a people. We are not a bunch of isolated protesters, or one side of a "generation gap," or a collection of weirdos and misfits, or anything like that. *We are a people,* and we have been a colonized people, an oppressed people, we have been a people with no control over our own national destiny, we have never enjoyed the ownership or control of the means of production of the goods and services necessary to our survival, we have been subjected to the classical type of colonialism in which the mother-country "owners" have come down into our communities and ripped us off not only for our labor but for our national resources as well, and they take our resources back into their economy and refine them and adulterate them and then sell them back to us at exorbitant rates, with all the profits from our energies and materials going not to us but to the mother-country exploiters. Check it out. You can start by thinking about the example of Woodstock, which is something we're all familiar with. Woodstock was something *we* produced out of our own national genius and energy, it was a beautiful experience for hundreds of thousands of our people which we produced ourselves, but the mother-country record companies and movie companies and vampires of all kinds swooped down on it and grabbed it and took it into their factories and cooked the reality of Woodstock down into records and movies and shit which they now sell back to us at $3.50 and $12.00 a shot. We control no part of it, yet it's entirely produced by us. And if we do get any share of the wealth our energy and labor and genius has generated, then we are trained and pushed by the mother country "owners" to squander that wealth on their products, their plastic junk, their degrading entertainments and products which they use to keep us under their control. They pump us for all we're worth, and they make sure that we don't get any control over our own economy.

That defines us as a colonized people, that objective situation defines us as a colonized people above and beyond our national culture which is only the visible manifestation of our peoplehood. We are exploited as a people, we are oppressed as a people, and we are denied our freedom as a people. But there's more to it than that—our whole relationship with the mother-country system is a colonial relationship. We are impressed into the mother-country armed forces and sent to fight its wars under threat of imprisonment or death. Right? We are not permitted to vote or otherwise take part in the mother-country political process, those of us who aren't "old enough," and those of us who do "get to vote" don't have any say in the selection of our candidates for public office since the mother-country political process is controlled by small cliques of professionals who are responsive only to the big business interests who bankroll them. We don't have an effective voice in the mother-country government so we can't say anything legally about what wars are fought or where our

taxes go—we do pay taxes, and those of us under 18 are literally subjected to what our ancestors called "taxation without representation."

We are conscripted into the training and brainwash centers of the mother country—the schools—and all of us are forced under pain of imprisonment to stay enrolled in those centers until we're at least 16 years old—until they can be sure we've been pumped full of their poison. We are forced to accept the ugly death culture of the mother country under pain of imprisonment. If we try to say anything about it, about how rotten it is, we are beaten or arrested and jailed by the mother country's troops. Or else we get away with it, but we still have to worry about getting beat up or arrested and locked up, because we know that's what's happening to our brothers and sisters and we're bound to be next We're bound to be next. Or we might get shot down for trying to demonstrate against the death machine, we've seen that already, we've seen our sisters and brothers gunned down by the mother country troops just for walking across the campus at the wrong time, or for carrying a sign saying End the War in Cambodia, or for calling the troops names fitting their functions. Die it. And if we try to build an alternative to the death culture, if we try to create an alternative order which suits our needs, it's even worse.

But the point is that we are a colonized people, subjected to the classical methods of colonialism by the Amerikan ruling class just like colonized peoples all over the world. That's where we have to start. And we may

184

have the highest so-called "standard of living" of any oppressed people in history, but this "standard of living" is ours only so long as we toe the line, only so long as we accept the terms of the death merchants and reject our peoplehood with our brothers and sisters in the colony. We can't do that, and we can't accept the bribes of the mother country either, because we know that its "high standard of living" is only possible through the colonization and exploitation of millions of other people around the globe who get ripped off so the Euro-Amerikan people can have all those color TVs and electric toothbrushes and new cars and shit, so we have to reject it on that basis also. Besides, having had access to the so-called fruits of this exploitation, we know how *worthless* they really are. This is one advantage we have over other oppressed peoples, many of whom are still struggling to attain the privileges and material well-being which were given to us at birth and which we have now rejected as worthless.

We've had it, we've had the whole thing, and now we've rejected it and we will keep on rejecting it until all the people in the world can have the same advantages that we've had, and until the death culture is finally junked on the scrapheap of history. We don't want any of it until *everybody* can have it, and we won't be satisfied with anything less than total freedom for everybody on earth. We can't be bought off, no matter how hard they try, because nothing they can give us or sell us is worth as much as the freedom of the people.

We are a colonized people, but there is one quality of our situation which is not shared by any other colonized peoples, and it is the condition which gives our struggle for liberation a very special role in the international revolutionary drama. Our colonial status is supposed to be merely a temporary stage of our development, since we are expected to "graduate" from colonialism into the mainstream of the mother country social order. We are the expected heirs and successors of the mother country's ruling class, and we are the heirs and successors of the mother country's working and management classes as well. If the mother country's socio-economic order is to survive we must be persuaded or forced to step into the shoes of our mothers and fathers. There are no replacements for us. If we refuse to toe the line, if we refuse to step into the roles we are expected to play in the mother country system, then that system must collapse.

Check it out. It will collapse without us. That's why our secession is so important, above and beyond the fact that we must have our freedom, because we are indispensable to the economy of the mother country. We are indispensable to its survival. They have to have us as workers and as consumers, and if we won't go for it then their system falls apart. No other colony has ever enjoyed this distinction, although with the contemporary form of economic imperialism which is necessary for the survival of international capitalism, all colonial peoples are necessary as *markets* for the consumer economy. Imperialism has to have markets for its degrading products, and it can't afford to let people reject its imperialist culture or else its own domestic economy will fall apart. They have to keep expanding their markets, they have to keep smearing their ugly death culture over the face of the earth, and when any people stands up to them and says they don't want it, that creates a tremendous crisis for imperialism—especially when that people is determined to fight back for the right to control its own destiny.

So we have to see how important our struggle is within the context of world revolution—we are not only an oppressed people, but our liberation is the key to the liberation of *all* oppressed peoples. If we can free ourselves from the grasp of the imperialist octopus which keeps us oppressed—which we can only do by cutting the head off the octopus and dragging its corpse off the stage of history once and for all—then we remove at one blow the force that is keeping all other peoples on the planet in a state of exploitation and oppression. It's as simple as that. We have been expected to step into the shoes of the oppressor and run the death machine, but if we refuse to do that, if we instead strike out for our freedom as a people, the death machine itself will fall apart, because it can't run on by itself—there have to be people to operate it. If we break free from the deathgrip of the octopus, if we refuse to go along with its program of exploitation and greed, if we do the one thing that can liberate us from this beast— that is, if we cut off its head—we not only free ourselves but we create the conditions of freedom for *everybody.*

That's why our struggle is so important.

But in order to do that we have to get ourselves together and we have to move as a united people to win our freedom. We can't get any freedom as individuals—all we can win for ourselves as individuals is a place in the driver's seat of imperialism. And that isn't anything at all. That's what we're trying to get away from, because that just keeps the system going when what we want is to put an end to it forever. *There are no individual solutions—none of us can be free until all the people are free.* And we can't free ourselves without a struggle, because the people who have the power now are not going to give it up just because we want them to—they never have, and they never will. More than that, they are not even going to let us survive without a struggle, because they can see even better than we can that our existence poses the most serious threat of all to their continued rule. They are going to keep trying to stomp us out, and if we want to survive—let alone realize the fulfillment of our vision—we're gonna have to fight.

Now this goes against the grain of our whole thing, because what we want is peace—we don't want war, we *hate* war, we want to eliminate all wars, but what we have to realize is that we are not going to have peace until everybody on earth has their freedom, and there can be no freedom without a struggle. We have to fight for it. That may be hard for a lot of us to accept, but unless we understand that we are going to have a very hard time of it indeed, and we will not be able to survive. *We have to fight.* That doesn't mean that we have to run out into the streets right now with rifles and shit and start shooting down all the pigs we see, but it means that we have to start thinking about the future of our culture, the survival of our people, the development of our struggle for the liberation of the rainbow colony over a protracted period of time. We have to start thinking about how to move, when to move, where to move, who we can move with, who we are moving against, what they will do to stop us, and how we can overcome all the obstacles they will be sure to place in our way, to stop us from gaining our freedom.

We have to start thinking very seriously about *revolution*, brothers and sisters, because that's what this is all about. And we have to understand very clearly that the revolution is more than just an apocalyptic armed struggle which comes in a big flash, which happens all at once, is fought out and decided on the spot. That's just the way it is in the movies—in real life, *the revolution is the entire scope of the people's efforts to achieve self-determination,* and armed struggle is merely one tool of the revolutionary people which can be used in our cause. It is a tool, and it should be picked up and used when it fits the specific task to be undertaken, and then it should be put down and replaced in the people's hands by other tools of liberation: revolutionary education, revolutionary economics, revolutionary technology, revolutionary culture. The revolution is a process which develops according to the given conditions in a given time and place, and it encompasses all of the efforts the people make in their struggle to achieve self-determination.

Right now our revolutionary culture is our most powerful tool, because it brings us together and inspires us to keep pushing for what we know has to come to pass. It unites us around a high-energy core and gives us the strength to go on even when it looks like things are getting worse and worse for us all the time. Our culture helps us see that we really *are* a people, that we are a *new* people, that we really *do* have a vision which can light up the earth and take everybody into the future. What we have to do is to start developing our culture to higher and higher levels, consciously and precisely, purging it (and ourselves) of the poison and filth that the death culture has implanted in it (and in ourselves) so it can lead us more directly and more perfectly into the New World. We have to put our vision out in front where everybody can see it for what it is, and we have to temper everything we do in the heat of that vision, letting it lead us and inspire us to new heights of creativity and struggle until we finally emerge victorious over the forces of death and destruction which want so desperately to wipe us out. We have to build our culture into a powerful force for a revolutionary change, and we have to defend it (and ourselves) against the constantly increasing attacks on our way of life.

We have to realize, as brother Che said, that it is time to moderate our disputes and to place everything at the service of the struggle. We have to do that. We have to see that all of us are engaged in a single struggle against a single enemy, which is the imperialist octopus with its tentacles spread all across the globe, strangling and choking whole peoples in its terrible greed. We have to come together *as a people*—freeks and students, musicians and scholars, radicals and radio technicians, factory workers and filmmakers, lawyers and laborers, dope fiends and deviates of all kinds—and we have to move together to free our whole people from the death machine. We have to start looking beyond our own immediate interests and see that none of us will survive intact unless all of us survive, that none of us can grow and develop unless all of us do, that none of us can have our freedom unless we can have our freedom *as a people.* That's where we have to start.

We have to be concerned above all with our survival (self-defense), because if we don't survive we don't do anything else either. And we have to be concerned with our political and economic development (self-determination), so we can grow and maintain ourselves during our struggle for the liberation of our people. We have to survive, and either we move to insure our survival as a people or else we face genocide as a people, because the death culture is *not* going to let us carry on like this. It can't afford to. We *all* represent a serious threat to its continued rule, whether we realize it or not, and the point is to start moving *consciously* to get ourselves so together that we can turn that threat into an actual act of liberation, a prolonged blow against the very roots of imperialist control which will free all of us from its grasp.

Now a lot of our people have already been rising against the oppressor—or at least against the symbols of oppression and the storm troops of the oppressor, on the campuses and in the youth ghettos—people have been rising spontaneously and striking out in their own individual ways, striking out against individual policemen and buildings and shit, but we have to realize, we really have to realize that spontaneous risings are not enough, that they are far less than enough, that in fact they usually play right into the hands of the oppressor, because their actual physical effect is minimal at best and the pigs use them to organize the broad masses of the people against us.

Spontaneous unarmed risings against an armed, disciplined, highly organized, brutal and technologically far superior force are not in the best interests of the people. They are beautiful in that they express the people's righteous anger, and the people's energy, and the people's intense need for change, but they are no more than that. In fact, when you break it down you will see that spontaneous risings are really just a form of ego-tripping in a lot of cases, where a brother or a sister makes himself or herself feel better by smashing a few windows, or throwing a rock at a pig, or shouting slogans which have no basis in reality at the time. They are expressions of the people's frustration and our feelings of powerlessness, and as such they are wrong—because in reality we are really very powerful, we can do a lot more than that, we can really make some changes, but we can't do it un-

Up! drummer, Scott Bailey, photo by David Fenton

less we get ourselves together, organize ourselves, and make the fullest possible use of our tremendous energy and our collective genius.

I don't mean to put down the brothers and sisters who have been moving spontaneously like that, because they've been a great inspiration to a whole lot of us and they've certainly made us see that we can't just sit around waiting for something to happen—they've taken the initiative and they've moved to do *something* about their condition, which is certainly right on. But what I *am* trying to say is that now we all have to start carrying on our struggle *consciously*—we have to start thinking about the effects of our actions, we have to start thinking about doing specific things to achieve specific results, and we have to start bringing all of our activity within the framework of a conscious revolutionary program which will bring about the liberation of our people. We have to relate to the fact that these risings have to be part of an overall strategy, a strategy which calls for and which can promise the collapse of the death machine. Too many of us don't see the difference between *strategy* and *tactics,* and we tend to make our tactics our strategy too much of the time without relating to the need for an overall strategy which incorporates all kinds of different tactics. If demonstrations and risings will advance the people's cause and bring us closer to victory, then right on, but we have to start figuring this shit out in front and picking our shots, choosing our tactics in accordance with the objective conditions in any given place and time, making sure that any given

tactic is in line with the overall strategy for victory, and then moving with all our collective energy and rage to make each tactical battle a success.

We have to start organizing for our struggle in earnest. Smashing windows and throwing rocks at armed troops, without thought for the consequences, is not in the interests of the people. Even shutting down the universities is not in the interests of the people finally, although organized strikes against the universities are certainly more effective than a few rocks and bottles thrown spontaneously through some windows or at some pigs in the streets. Shutting down the schools might show people that we are determined to do *something* about our situation, but that isn't enough any more. What we have to do is start *taking over* the schools so we can use their facilities in the best interests of our people—use them to teach the people what they need to know to survive and grow. We have to take control of the schools, and use them to further the growth of our culture, to further the growth of our people and to provide for our collective needs. We can use the facilities and the incredible technology which is at hand on the campuses, we can use the radio stations and printing facilities, the television equipment, the scientific equipment and laboratories, the dormitories and cafeterias and auditoriums and stadiums, all those buildings and all that technology, housing and dining and meeting facilities, we can use all of this for *our* people, and when we control our schools we can also throw them open to *all* the people in the communities in which these tremendous physical plants are located. The people need that stuff a lot more than General Motors does, or North American Rockwell, or Standard Oil, or Dow Chemical, or any of the other greedhead institutions which now control the schools and use them to keep the people enslaved. And we can get it. *We can get it!*

We can get it through organizing our people, and educating our people, and banding all of our people together so we can operate at our full strength. That's the only way we can get it, and all there is to it is to start *doing* it. The people are ready for it, and all they need is a program for action which makes sense to them and which has room for them to take part in it. Millions of us are tired of this shit and want to change it, millions of us are ready to start moving to determine our own destinies, millions of us are ready and waiting to take the steps which will spell death for the death culture and life for the life culture, but we've been more or less paralyzed so far because we haven't had a clear picture of what it is we want to happen. And it isn't just young people who are fed up, although we're the ones who are most ready to move—there are millions and millions of straight people, Euro-Amerikan people, who are sick to death of the kind of life that's been forced on them but don't know what to do about it. We have to reach across the line between our two cultures to draw all those people into our movement too, we have to make our vision available to them, we have to give them a clear idea of what it is we're fighting for and what we plan to do when we do win our victory.

We have to realize that the masses of the people in the mother country are never our enemy, that the masses are our friends, our real friends, that objectively speaking the masses of Euro-Amerikan people are as beaten down and oppressed and colonized as we are—as Huey says, *all* Amerikans are colonized by the "owners," or the ruling class—but subjectively, in their heads, they have been made to believe that we are their enemies and that we are trying to destroy them, to destroy their way of life just as they have been trying to destroy ours. The oppressor has been able to brainwash them so successfully that they identify with their own oppressor against the people who are fighting to try to free them from their own oppression. It's weird, but that's the way it is, and we have to recognize it and come up with ways of dealing with it so we can bring them together with us to make the revolution against our common enemy.

Another problem we have, which is just the other side of that one, is that so many of our own people, people in the rainbow colony, still have the feeling, the subjective, incorrect, totally wrong feeling that the Euro-Amerikan people are *our* enemy, that we are carrying on our struggle correctly if we attack the masses of Euro-Amerikan workers, policemen, army troops, bureaucrats, storeowners and other elements of the masses. That is not true. The masses of the people are our real friends, even if they don't know it, and although we may be forced to struggle against them to protect ourselves at certain stages of the revolution, we have to keep firmly

LONG AGO THE ANCIENT ONES TOLD US
THAT THIS WOULD BE.
THE WHITE MAN WOULD KILL THE SPIRIT OF THE PEOPLE,
AND TAKE IT TO A FAR PLACE,
BUT AFTER A WHILE IT WOULD COME BACK AGAIN,
IT WOULD BE BORN AGAIN.
IN TIME A NEW SPIRIT WOULD COME INTO THE WORLD
AND WE SHOULD LOOK FOR IT.
LIKE THE RAINDROPS GATHERING IN THE CLOUDS OF SPRINGTIME
SO WOULD THE SPIRIT COME TO A THIRSTY LAND AND A
DYING PEOPLE.
LET IT GROW! LET IT GROW!
THIS LIGHT YOU MUST FIND.
WHEN YOU SEEK FOR YOUR VISION ON THE MOUNTAINTOP
YOU WILL BE TOLD HOW TO FIND IT.
FOR IT WILL BE SOMETHING SO BIG AND SO WONDERFUL
THAT IN IT ALL PEOPLES OF THE WORLD CAN FIND SHELTER
AND IN THAT DAY ALL THE LITTLE CIRCLES
WILL COME UNDER THE BIG CIRCLE OF UNDERSTANDING
AND UNITY
THE RAINBOW IS A SIGN OF THAT WHICH IS IN ALL THINGS.
IT IS A SIGN OF THE UNION OF ALL THE PEOPLES
LIKE ONE BIG FAMILY.
SEEK THE VISION. BECOME A WARRIOR OF THE RAINBOW!
LET IT GROW! LET IT GROW!

in mind the fact that the people are our real friends, and that only the "owners," the big capitalists who control all the means of production and information in this country, are our real enemies. Our job is to educate and teach the masses of the people that we are their real friends, and that the "owners" are their real enemies. We have to do that. It's not going to be easy, but then none of this is going to be easy anyway—it's *never* easy to win your freedom, and we're fighting against the biggest monster humanity has ever known. But just because it *is* so difficult that only means that it's even more necessary for us to get ourselves together and move in a conscious fashion to do what has to be done. We *can* win over the masses, and if we are going to *have* a revolution in this country we *have* to win them over and unite with them and with all oppressed peoples to defeat our common enemy—the Euro-Amerikan ruling class. Otherwise we're not even *talking* about revolution.

Now, these things I've been talking about are what we might call our strategic objectives—these are the things we have to accomplish in order to realize our goal of liberating the rainbow colony and winning freedom for our people. We have to develop a strong sense of peoplehood; we have to develop our collective consciousness and direct it toward liberation for our people; we have to educate and organize ourselves for self-defense and self-determination; we have to purify our culture and hold it up in front of us to light our way to the future age; we have to win over the people of the mother country and unite with them to make the struggle against our common oppressor; we have to *come together* on all levels and *move together* to develop power for our people. Which means that we have to create political machinery for ourselves which will enable us to become powerful, we have to organize our economic development *as a people*, and we have to create new social and organizational forms through which we can move to survive during the struggle and to build up the new order which will sustain the people after victory is won.

We have to build *a whole new nation* on this continent, a whole new social order which will be capable of dealing with the needs of all the people, not just the ones the pig power structure sees fit to take care of. We have to build a *new nation* which will be the *last* nation in this place, which will be the bridge from the old society to the new, from the old order of the capitalist dinosaurs to the New World of our spaced-out visions. We have to destroy the old order, there can be no doubt about that, because there's no way we can have our freedom with the dinosaurs still around—they want everything for themselves, and that's just not happening any more. But as we destroy the old order we have to build our new nation in its place, so we can survive during the struggle and so all the people can see what it is we're trying to make available to them. *That's* the way we can win their support, by demonstrating that we *do* have an alternative to the death culture, an alternative which is every bit as open to them as it is to our own people, the people of the post-western rainbow colony.

We've got to do two things at once—we've got to build the new order starting right now, building it up within the shell of the old, but we've also got to *crack* that shell and smash it completely open so our new world can come into life on its own, free from the strictures that bound it to the past. This isn't going to happen overnight, but it has to happen or else we'll just be suffocated within the shell before we can truly be born as an independent thing.

The gestation period—the time we're insulated and contained within the egg of the old society—will be fairly long, longer than we used to think, and as we grow we will find our situation more and more confining, more and more oppressive, until we no longer have any choice but to break the egg, crack the shell, step out of it altogether and leave it behind us to crumble into dust, empty and useless without us. It will keep us contained as long as it can, but our liberation is inevitable, and it will come when the time is right, when we have reached our earliest maturity, when *all* the conditions are right for our freedom, and it won't come before that.

This means that we have to look upon our struggle for liberation as a *protracted* struggle, a long and arduous fight, and have to do the things at each stage of this protracted struggle which are right for the particular time and conditions. Our development must proceed carefully, from one stage to the next, and, we can't leave out any stages or try to skip them because we'll fail if we do. It's like breaking an egg open be-fore the life inside has matured past the first stage of its development—all you'll get instead of a baby animal strong enough to climb out and walk around on its own is egg yolk sprayed all over the table, and the pigs will just fry it up and eat it. You dig? So we'll have to be very careful in that respect—we can't go on the offensive until we're strong enough to handle it, to complete our victory, or else we'll just get crushed like an egg in the hands of a giant.

A protracted liberation struggle historically goes through three main stages: the strategic defensive, when the revolutionary forces are relatively small and scattered and survival is a problem; the strategic stalemate, when the revolutionary forces and the reactionary forces are fairly evenly balanced (although the new revolutionary forces are in the ascendancy, and the old reactionary forces are going downhill); and the strategic counter-offensive, which leads to the final victory of the revolutionary forces over the reactionaries. Right now we are in the first stage, the strategic defensive, and our tactics—the things we do to advance our struggle—must fit that condition. We can't go on the offensive until we're strong enough to survive, until we have consolidated all the scattered energies and resources available to us, united all our people, and won the tentative support of the masses of the people in the mother country.

That's why our primary goal right now must be to unite our people, spread revolutionary consciousness, and start moving together to defend ourselves against attack and to ensure our survival on the economic front. If we can't do these things we simply won't survive, because we're up against the most powerful, the most well-organized machine in the history of humankind, and it wants to crush us before we can get ourselves together. That doesn't mean it's invincible—in fact, the case is just the opposite, because the machine is falling apart at its center and it's got a whole lot of internal problems of its own above and beyond the trouble we're causing it—but it's still plenty strong, it can still do a lot of damage, it still carries itself along on its own momentum, and in order to stop it from crushing us we have to be just as well organized, just as tightly put together, as the death machine is. We can't stop it any other way.

And in order to unite our people we have to have programs that the people can relate to—programs which deal with the people's needs while at the same time holding up the vision of the new order we're working to bring into being. We have to have programs, and we have to develop the machinery through which these programs can be carried out. And again that means that we have to *organize* ourselves, on all levels, so we can deal with our common problems. We can't keep trying to attack these problems as individuals, because no individuals are powerful enough to overcome the problems by themselves. It's only through *unity* that individuals can gain political power, and economic power, and whatever other kinds of power are necessary for the people to be free. Without unity we can only get farther behind all the

time, and eventually we'll be crushed for good. That's real, and that's exactly where we have to start.

We have to build unity within the colony, among all the segments of our people, and we have to give that unity a political meaning, because our struggle is first and foremost a political struggle—we're fighting for the power to determine our own destiny as a people, and that fight is a political fight. We have to start from that understanding, to make ourselves *consciously* political—we're all political beings anyway, whether we *want* to be or not, and the only question is whether we'll be consciously political or remain *unconscious* and thus ineffective. We need to unify our people, and at the same time we have to formalize our unity so everyone will be able to see what we're about. Since our struggle is a national liberation struggle, we need a symbol which embodies and consolidates into a clear image the particular nature of our movement for the liberation of the rainbow colony. The symbol I want to suggest is this one:

In this drawing the two cross-sticks represent a rifle (on the left) and a guitar (on the right), with a peace pipe full of the righteous sacrament crossing them and bringing those two elements together. We can't have the guitar without the gun or we won't survive, we can't have the gun without the guitar or else we'd just be more of the same old shit we are trying to do away with; and without the sacrament that gives us our vision neither the guitar nor the gun would amount to anything worthwhile.

Further, the conjunction of the three sticks draws a tepee, symbolic of the shelter our new nation provides for its people. The whole thing is contained within a circle, which is the circle of understanding and unity. And the circle has flames bursting out of it, flames which symbolize the sun, the most powerful source of energy and light known to humanity—the sun which is our source, which shines through the storm to lead us through it to the Rainbow on the other side. And underneath it all is the word NATION, to remind us and everyone else what we're fighting for—a new nation of free people which will serve as a bridge into the New Age, where nations and classes and wars will no longer exist, where all the people of the world will live under the sign of the rainbow as brothers and sisters of the New World.

We can use this Nation symbol as a formal image for our struggle, as a sign of our life and of our determination to make that new life available to everybody on the planet. At first the New Nation will be primarily the people of the youth colony, our closest brothers and sisters, the People of the Future who are the natives of the New World even now—but it can't be limited to that, because we want *everyone* to join us in our struggle to create a whole new world, and as our struggle develops more and more people will join with us to fight against the monstrous octopus of imperialism which is our common enemy. We want a nation to end all nations, a nation of free people which is dedicated to doing away with all unnatural boundaries and realizing the global unity which is necessary to

the survival of all humanity. That's the nation I'm talking about.

This Nation symbol can be embraced by all of us to show that we all relate to the same thing—it should be a sign of our unity, a formal image of our common aspiration for freedom and self-determination. My hope is that all the people of the rainbow colony can relate to this symbol and use it to give definition to our dreams of unity and solidarity. The Nation symbol should be everywhere—on all the products created by our people, on record albums, newspapers, books, in people's windows at home or in their cars, on their guitars and drums, on flags (yellow on red) waving in the air over homes and demonstrations and festivals, on their shirts and jackets and t-shirts, around their necks, painted on the sides of buildings, in the middle of the streets—everywhere our people are the image of our new nation should be seen. And when people see it and ask about it, the sisters and brothers can explain to them what we're about, so they can understand what we're doing and join us in our struggle and make themselves one with us. Because that's what it's all about.

But it's also about being together in reality too, not just on paper or in drawings and symbols—the symbol has to stand for the reality which we want that image to reflect. We have to organize ourselves on all levels so we can gain our freedom and bring our new nation into being—it isn't enough to have the image in our minds, we have to construct the machinery which will make it possible for that vision to become reality. It's like if you hear a song in your head, that isn't really music—you have to get a guitar and an amplifier maybe, in order to flesh it out, and then you have to get together with some other musicians and organize yourselves into a *band* to give the music its fullest definition. The music we all love doesn't just spring into life spontaneously—it is highly organized and it comes into being the way we hear it only as a result of hard work and killer dedication by the people's musicians. I think you all can relate to that.

My point is that we have to organize our whole people as tightly and as effectively as our bands are organized, so our whole lives can become the kind of brilliant music we all need for our daily inspiration. We have to organize ourselves to deal with our daily problems, to protect ourselves from the pigs, and to ensure our survival during this stage of our struggle. We have to start in the towns and cities and communities where we live and organize ourselves at the most basic level—we have to organize ourselves into communes, into collectives, into councils and coalitions which will give us the power to deal with our most immediate problems, and we will grow from there. We start with our bands and move to regain control over our music, which has been ripped off by the octopus of greed and competition and profit—we develop our own ballrooms and concert places, our own recording studios and record companies, our own distribution networks and radio stations, our own presses and television stations, our own *means of production* which will enable us to support ourselves and to spread the word of the revolution we are making. We start on the most basic level to seize control of *our* lives and make them ours for once. That's the first step toward self-determination.

We start in the towns and cities and communities where we live and organize ourselves into *Tribal Councils,* community councils which are set up to deal with the needs of the people on the most basic level. The Tribal Councils should be the basic political unit of our new nation at this point—they will be the models for our new state machinery, and we can see for ourselves how the new order will work by putting it into practice in our communities right now. The Tribal Council is based on the government forms of the native red people who once flourished on this land, who lived then like we want to live now and in the future—we are the electric aborigines of the New World, and it is only natural that we should organize ourselves into the same forms as our aborigine brothers and sisters did before our European ancestors came over here to wipe them out.

The Tribal Councils are the political organizations of the rainbow community—everyone in the many youth communities should take part in the Tribal Council programs, because everyone in the communities shares the same problems, and those problems can only be solved collectively, by all the people working together to solve them. Within the Tribal Councils many various committees can be set up, people's committees made up of the most dedicated individuals in the community, who will commit themselves to serving the people by helping them solve their problems in an organized fashion. We need *People's Food Committees* to grow food and to organize food cooperatives which supply food to the community at the lowest possible prices; *People's Defense Committees* to set up bail funds for people who get busted, to obtain lawyers and bondsmen, to train the people in self-defense techniques, to provide security at our gatherings, and to organize teams of Psychedelic Rangers who will serve as the people's peace force; *People's Health Committees* to set up and coordinate the work of Free Health Clinics, anti-smack campaigns, and drug treatment centers in the community; *People's Music Committees,* to create and operate People's Ballrooms and community centers, to organize and produce free concerts in the parks, to set up booking and recording cooperatives for the bands in the community, to build equipment and recording studios, and to get as much music as possible out to the people who need it; *People's Information Committees* to produce local newspapers and get the news out to the sisters and brothers in the community; *People's Education Committees* to set up liberation schools, communal child-care/education centers, and to teach the people what they need to know to survive and grow; *People's Communications Committees* to organize communications, set up switchboards, bulletin boards on the streets, and full-scale information networks in the community, to hook everybody up with everybody else so we can have real communities where

we can all grow and develop together, not separately, not alone but totally *together* at last like all people are supposed to be. We need People's Housing Cooperatives, People's Radio and Television Stations, every kind of institution which is necessary for our survival must be created and controlled by the people themselves—that's how we start to build self-determination for our nation!

This is what we can do to start with, and it's something we *have* to do or we won't survive much longer. That's for real. Our struggle has really only just started, and if you think the pigs have been bogue so far you've got a lot of weird surprises coming—because, believe me, they haven't *begun* to be repressive like they will be before it's over. The snakes and rats and vampires of the octopus power structure use the pigs—the police in uniform—as their shock troops, and as our new way of life becomes a greater and greater threat to the established order in this country, as our nation grows and begins to consolidate itself into a powerful political force, these vampires and other animals will step up their repression more and more in their insane attempts to stomp us completely off the set.

But if we *organize* ourselves and get ourselves together on all levels, if we move for self-determination and self-defense on an organized basis, if we all unite under the banner of the Rainbow Nation we're fighting to bring into being here on this planet, and if we keep our vision of the future out in front where everybody can see it and pick up on it for themselves, we can survive anything the pigs throw at us, and we can come out of this period much stronger than we are now. We are a people, we are just beginning to define and develop ourselves as a people, but if we get straight on what we're doing and what we want to do from the very beginning our struggle will be a lot less difficult and a lot less confusing for all of us. We've been stumbling around in the dark, feeling our way around, trying to figure out what's happening to us, and we've made a lot of mistakes that we couldn't help but make. This is all new to us—we're a whole new people anyway—but now we're starting to put it all together, and armed with a revolutionary analysis and our powerful revolutionary culture we can move to give flesh to our holy visions of the Rainbow World of the future. All Power to the People! Rainbow Power to the People of the Future! Revolution Is the Way to Life!!!

—John Sinclair,
Chairman, Rainbow People's Party

BRINGIN' IT ALL BACK HOME

I ain't gonna work on Maggie's farm no more
I ain't gonna work on Maggie's farm no more
Well I wake up in the morning
Hold my hands and pray for rain
I got a head full of ideas
They're drivin me insane
It's a shame the way she makes me scrub
  the floor
No I ain't gonna work on Maggie's farm
  no more

—Bob Dylan, "Maggie's Farm"

JUNE-JULY 1970

I don't think it's news to people now that the rock & roll scene is incredibly messed up, and that things in our culture generally aren't anything like the way we all know they should be. I mean we know that the music we get to hear, and the conditions we get to hear it in, aren't anything like what they started out to be, and that those conditions especially have changed so much that they have less and less to do with the music and more and more to do with the sickness and greed of the death culture the music originally rose up against, to liberate us from the death machine and turn us on to our free human possibilities and make us *whole* again. We know that the whole scene isn't at all what it was supposed to be, but it's so weird that generally we just don't know what to do about it, the whole process seems to be so far beyond our control that we just go along with it

Photo by Leni Sinclair

as much as we hate it. This isn't what we got all excited about and thought would change the world, but we don't see what we can do about it as individuals and so we just accept this shit as a necessary condition and go along with it and keep hoping that some day people will wake up and things will be better for us in our world, so we don't have to put up with so much shit just to get the little things we need for ourselves—our music, our sacraments, our culture, our lives themselves.

We know we can't always get what we want, but what I want to say is that if we try real hard, we might find, that we'll get just what we need. And I want to suggest that there *are* ways we can try real hard, there *are* ways we can start changing things, ways we can move to bring it all back home where it belongs, and that the best place for us to start is right here with our music and the conditions which prevail in the music business and in our culture as a whole, because that's where we're strongest in a lot of ways even though it seems sometimes like that's where we're weakest. There are things we can do to break the strangle-hold the greedheads have on our culture and our people, to break the music and ourselves and all our people free from the death culture altogether. I won't go into a long rant about how bad things really are, because everybody who reads this paper knows what's happening better than I do anyway—I've been off the streets for a year now and it's easier for me in the penitentiary, if you can relate to that, it's easier for me than it is for you out there, because the repression here is constant and predictable for the

most part, and out there you can never tell what's going to go down next.

You know what it's like out there better than I can say—getting rode down on by the police when you go to concerts or festivals, paying ridiculous prices to get in to hear and see and be with, to be a part of your own culture, having to hear music in stupid places and be treated like dogs when you do go to those places to be in the music, trembling every time you see a squad car turn down your street, the way you have to live with the fear of getting hassled and arrested and locked up for getting high, or for going out to be with your brothers and sisters somewhere in public, or just for going out on the street to cop something to eat, or some weed, or some records, or some groceries from the store. You never know when the shit might come down or when you might get caught up in it, even though you don't have anything to do with it or don't wanna have anything to do with it.

The repression part is bad enough, but what's probably worse is the way the music and our culture as a whole has passed out of our hands and into the grasp of the pig—it *was* in our hands when we started developing it, but now we have been relegated to the role of simple consumers and our music and its byproducts are controlled by an amazing oligarchy of outsiders, of people who don't have anything to do with our culture at all, and they use our culture against us to keep us in our place. Freedom starts with self-determination, and is manifested most precisely in self-determination, and when a people's culture is controlled by forces outside the culture itself the people are reduced to the status of colonials or neo-colonial subjects of the people who control them. What we wanted was to be free, and our music and our culture developed as an expression of our freedom, we controlled it and the way it developed at first, and now we no longer have control over where it goes or how it gets there. That's the worst part of the present situation, and if we want to be free we have to recapture our culture from the people who have ripped it off from us and put it back in the service of our own people, so it can inspire us and lead us on to freedom on all levels.

Before I go any farther here I had better make one thing clear: I'm not some kind of "radical" or "political" manipulator who's trying to "infiltrate" or "co-opt" the rock & roll scene in order to "radicalize" or "politicize" it, or some shit like that. I grew up on rock & roll music, I've been involved and caught up in the music all my life, well at least since I was 11 years old, and everything I've learned about America I've learned through being involved with and inspired by the music. Rock & roll has been the major motivating force in my life ever since it first leaped out of a radio into my consciousness, "Rock Around the Clock" by Bill Haley & the Comets, "Gee" by the Crows, Little Richard wailing "Tutti Frutti" into the hidden corners of America. And one thing I've learned from being moved by this music, from the ways and the directions in which it's moved me, is that the rock & roll scene is *already* "politicized"

and has *been* politicized ever since it first erupted into the cancerous consciousness of plastic Amerika. Rock & roll is "political," whether we want to dig it that way or not, just by virtue of its existence as a high-energy charge-force in the middle of the most deathly, most anti-human low-energy scene in history, and it not only has "political" origins but it is thoroughly "political" in its effects, on every level.

Because the main thing I've learned over the years since I first heard Chuck Berry and the Flamingos is that *any act which has a political consequence is a political act*—and that includes smoking weed, which can get you 9½–10 years on the Penitentiary in the state of Michigan, for example, and growing your hair long, which you can get beat up by the police for, or even going to concerts and pop festivals and other cultural events, because you can get arrested and beat up at those things like a lot of brothers and sisters in Cincinnati, for example, just did, and you also have to realize that the money that you pay for those things, and for records and other cultural artifacts you buy in the stores, is used by monopoly capitalists and domestic imperialists to keep the consumer economy rolling on, so the war can keep on, and the pigs can stay in power, and CBS and RCA and people like that can keep on making obscene profits for themselves at our expense.

I know it isn't pleasant to have to think about these things, but it's a lot more pleasant than the things themselves are, and it's much hipper for us to examine these things and figure them out and move to change them than it is to just go on accepting this shit and letting these people perpetuate their hideous death-style while they wreck our culture and rape the lives of people all over the world. Because if we study the way the pig has infiltrated and taken over and manipulated our culture, we can not only discover how to put an end to this exploitation but we can also see how monopoly capitalism and imperialism works in the larger society as well. What we have to realize finally is that everything that happens in the macrocosm of the American consumer culture can be seen in detail at work in the microcosm of the rock & roll world, and if we can combat the consumer mentality in our culture then we can combat it in the mother country culture too, and save ourselves and eventually all the people of earth from destruction at the hands of the greedcreeps and "owners" who are causing all of us all this grief.

One other thing before I go on—I want to make it clear when I use the despised word "politics" here I mean it like Huey P. Newton has defined it, where he says "Politics are merely the desire of individuals and groups to satisfy first, their basic needs—food, shelter and clothing, and security for themselves and their loved ones"—and I have to add, the desire to create and nurture and support and defend their own culture too, because a people's culture is at the base of their entire being. Politics means analyzing a given situation, and checking it out in all its complexity, and devising a strategy for dealing with the situation so that the people's needs will be satisfied, and then moving from that analysis and that strategy to change the situation so it will be in line with the people's needs and desires. That's something all of us do every day, one way or another, and all of our actions are political because finally we live in the world, we interact with other people every day, and everything we do or which is done to us changes the shape of our lives one way or another. Whether we want to accept it or not, everything we do is political finally, and what I want to say is that we have to start acting consciously and resolutely in such a way that we can make the changes in our lives and in the life of our people as a whole which will make things the way they're supposed to be. And, that we *can* make the necessary changes, if we act and move correctly.

Our culture started to develop about five years ago as a real alternative to the death culture of the straight world. We started out from where we were then, which was almost nowhere, and we built up our new culture from the ground, basing it on our new dope-opened consciousness which told us that we had to get together and love everybody right now. We dropped so much acid that we started to see that we had to move beyond our ownselves though—we saw that we had to turn on everybody in the world, if possible, to what we had found out about ourselves and our possibilities for living beautiful human lives. Prior to 1965 we had slowly evolved a hip subculture which was pretty much a closed thing, an elitist trip meant only for the enlightened few, and when acid exploded onto that

Leni Sinclair protesting, photo by David Fenton

hip scene it transformed us so we knew we couldn't possibly keep hoarding all that enlightenment and beauty for ourselves, because that was just being like the creeps we were trying to get away from.

This is important to remember, because this is what got us into the mass culture scene in the first place, and this is what made the new rock & roll culture different from the hip beatnik-folkie subculture of the late '50s and early '60s. We had been thinking about ourselves primarily, about getting away from the established scene and into something that would make us feel good, and we had a predominantly elitist sense of things that said, forget the rest of the world, it's too messed up to bother with, politics is a drag, most people are a drag, we're where it's at and all we want to do is get high, dig some jams and stay out of the pig's way.

Then we started gobbling all that good LSD and got turned on to the rest of the world, and at the same time we started hearing and feeling an incredible new music in the air—Bob Dylan's rock & roll masterpieces, the Beatles, the Stones singing "(I Can't Get No) Satisfaction"—and this potent combination moved us out of our shells and pointed us toward the mainstream we had dropped out of. Our ranks began to swell, we started seeing more and more weird people like ourselves everywhere, and in America a whole new rock & roll music erupted out of the advanced neo-beatnik culture of San Francisco and Los Angeles and started spreading back across the country, turning on more and more

people by the day. Where our music and our life-style had been intensely private, now it was growing more and more into a strangely public expression which effectively involved more and more people. Folk guitarists started investigating the new electronic possibilities introduced by Dylan, the Beatles and the Stones, they started plugging into amplifiers and adding drummers and microphones, and the music began to move out of cellars and living rooms and coffee houses into more public places which allowed for a much wider participation than ever before.

Some people started getting bands together, jamming and working out arrangements; other freeks discovered overhead projectors and slide projectors and oils and weird combinations of images and colors, and started mixing their "light shows" with the music; still others started thinking about places where these beautiful elements could be put together with the people so everybody could get off like the musicians and light people and their friends were doing; and more and more non-performers began to relate to what their brothers and sisters were doing and gathered around them whenever and wherever they got the chance. Ken Kesey and his Merry Pranksters (among whom were people like the Grateful Dead and Stewart Brand) organized and brought off the astounding Trips Festival in San Francisco in which all of these elements were brought together and catalyzed with some powerful acid, and a whole new scene was exploded onto the world.

What was beautiful about this new scene was that it was a wholly organic expression of a people's lifestyle—it grew out of the consciousness of the people and was brought into being by the people themselves, and it had absolutely nothing to do with the established entertainment industry, which was known to one and all as an incredible drag on every level. The new expression was a *communal* experience, a direct extension of the people's highest consciousness, and it was motivated by great feelings of love and brother- (and sister-) hood rather than by any commercial or cynical interest. Everyone who was involved, from the bands and inventors to the dancers and listeners and general participants, was aware of the huge significance of what was happening—we were sure that what we were doing was going to change the world, and we felt very strongly that it was just going to be a matter of time now until the ugliness and filth of plastic Amerika would be transformed through the force of our music and love into some beautiful and holy thing.

It's hard to describe the feeling we had, especially since it doesn't exist like that anymore, but it was really powerful and everybody believed in it to one degree or another, everybody that is who was taking all that acid and dancing and screaming in the music and uniting on every level with everybody else around them. All of our experiences were unbelievably visionary, we had a whole new vision of the world and what its possibilities might be, and we *knew* that everything would be all right once the masses of the people got the message we were sending out through our music, our frenzied dancing, our colors and illuminations, our posters, our outrageous clothes and manners and speech, our mind-blowing, consciousness-expanding, earth-shaking dope. Everything we did was part of the *whole* we were making of our lives, and everything fit in with everything else— it was an organic explosion of beauty and life unlike anything that had ever appeared on the planet, and the deeper we got into it the purer it got.

The important things about our culture when it first started to develop were (1) that it was an organic expression of the lifestyle of a people, (2) that this life-style was based on love and freedom and thus these forces inspired and motivated the formal cultural manifestations of our people, starting with our music and continuing through the whole spectrum of our personal and public activity, (3) that we not only invented and created this new culture but we also controlled the means through which it was disseminated among ourselves, into our community and out into the larger world, at least in the early stages of its development, (4) that our culture, by virtue of its very nature and the ways in which that nature was expressed, was a powerful force for change, and (5) that the change embodied in and demanded by our culture—again, starting with the music, the core, and moving outward—was a revolutionary change with a decidedly political effect, since it addressed the dominant culture at its very roots and insisted that the basis of western civilization be shifted from competition, greed, cold lust and death to cooperation, communalism, love, life and freedom for everyone.

These things have to be understood before we go any further. Our new culture was more powerful in its possibilities than most of us could understand. We knew it could change the world, but what was more important even than that was that the people who control the world as it is knew it too, and moved to stop us from doing just that. They attacked us at our weakest point—our naiveté and our great feeling of love and trust—and they mounted an essentially two-pronged counter-offensive, co-opting and assimilating the least dangerous elements into their own consumer-culture, and attacking and repressing the most liberating features of our culture. The musicians were bought off, the music was adulterated and repackaged and sold to us like hamburgers, the dope was monopolized and cut and almost wholly defused as a weapon of cultural revolution* (and people who remember what acid was like before the Summer of Love know what I mean—there wasn't any speed in it then, in fact there was very little speed around at all, and smack was just something you read about), and the new forms of mass celebration we had created—dances, be-ins, love-ins, multi-media energy explosions —were taken over by hip capitalists, perverted, hyped up, dehumanized, monopolized, and shoved back at us as the latest revision of the standard plastic Hollywood version of mindless entertainment. And the people who wouldn't go along with this shit were painted out of the picture, stomped off the set, hassled, driven crazy or locked up in penitentiaries to teach everybody else a lesson.

Where the bands used to play for the people because they loved the music and the people equally, now they are motivated by the money they can get and the fame (ego-charge) they can buy with it, and the bigger they get (in terms of the capitalist market-economy) the less they have to go out in front of the people to perform. Where the music was powerful and exciting, pushing at the limits of the form and charging the people with huge blasts of love-energy, now it is mostly weak and tame and easily digested by even the blandest consumers out there in television-land, and those bands that refuse to be sucked into the death-trap are put down by the self-righteous pop star-makers as "tasteless" and "unimaginative," as if that isn't what rock & roll is all about and has always *been* all about, destroying and spitting on the standards of the plastic death culture with every scream and every simple amplified blast of sound.

Where the LSD was righteous and pure, and every trip a ticket to the farthest reaches of the known and unknown human universe of love and compassion, now the dope is hopelessly adulterated, powerless, full of speed and death, sending people off into nightmares of paranoia and egoness and bumming them out completely, or else it's the Plague, the stupid smack-o scene which kills all love and creativity and will for change and puts

*See "Operation Jones"

208

Leni Sinclair, 1971

the brothers and sisters right where the pigs want them, under the thumb, on their asses, sitting in the corner drooling and moaning and out of the running altogether. Speed and smack, the pig drugs of all time, pushed into the veins of our people by Nixon and Mitchell while their creepo agents run around trying to stamp out weed and keep acid from ever emerging again, using the insane marijuana laws to terrify all of our people on a daily, on a minute-to-minute basis, hounding us, tapping our phones, making films of our lives, following us around in their beards and bandannas and bare feet, busting down our doors and pulling us off to their lousy stinking jails and courts and penitentiaries, building up their dossiers so when the shit comes down for real they can round us up and pack us in boxcars like they did the American aborigines and pen us up in concentration camps.

And the worst thing of all, the worst thing of all, is what's been done to our beautiful celebrations, the dances and festivals and free outdoor gatherings that were the crowning glory of our culture, where all of us came together in the music and the light and the people, where we charged ourselves up and moved out from that incredible ecstasy to build our communes and our whole communal, high-energy, sound- color-light-orgasm lifestyle with each other, moving together every day and in every way just as we moved together in the music. Whew! These PIGS! They've made our music and our celebrations into cheap consumer products, they've destroyed the use-value of our culture and converted it all into dollars and cents, anti-feeling and anti-sense, all in the name of profit and greed, and most of our people don't even know what they're missing because the pigs did this so fast that it's the only thing most of us have ever known—concerts where you sit down in a goddamn seat all night and watch the S*T*A*R*S parade across the screen, I mean the stage, sitting on your ass just like it's the Ed Sullivan show, and you're out there in television-land, part of the studio audience, and three or four or ten or twenty all-star pop corporations are propped way up there in front of you doing 30 or 40 or maybe 50 minutes if they're BIG enough, of their all-star golden box-office hits, going through their little acts and collecting 5,000 or 10,000 or 20,000 or 50,000 dollars a night for it, the Stones ripped off over a million and a half dollars from their BIG AMERIKAN TOUR, and they leave us the way they found us only a little more frustrated and a little more messed up, and all the money goes out of our community and into the pig's banks one way or the other, to be used again to keep us deeper in our seats.

We started out controlling our culture and the ways in which it reached the people, and now we don't have control over it at all. We started out making a new life-form in which all of us could Participate equally, and now we have the same thing we were trying to get away from, only it's worse because our original creative impetus has been blunted and perverted and channeled into the same old dead-end Hollywood shuck which insists that the only relationship we can have to our vital art-expression is as consumers, as buyers and consumers who just keep paying and Paying more and more for less and less of what we need.

This is what our new push for life and freedom has come to, and the dream we had five and four and three years ago has been wiped out, or if it still remains in our heads and cells it's been strangely twisted, or it's barely holding on for dear life, or it comes to us in the night in penitentiary cells and shacks stuck out in the middle of nowhere where our people have been taken or have run away to, to get away from the monster that's been made of our culture. This is what it's come to, and it's *awful,* and all of us know it, even the musicians who are making tons of money and flying around the world getting drunk like Jackie Kennedy and creeps like that, even the musicians know it and the people *really* know it because they have to take all the bad shit and they don't even get rich, they just get frustrated and disgusted, they just keep taking this shit because they have to have the music and they'll put up with whatever they have to put up with in order to get near the music and be *in* it.

The dream has been wiped out or twisted around, and the people who have been twisted the worst are the musicians and performers themselves, because they've gone the farthest into the bizarro world of the music industry and they've been subjected to even greater pressures than the rest of us have. Their music and their selves have been made into cheap commodities, bought and sold as the terms of the mother-country consum-

er market dictate, and the powerful use-value they once had for our people has been overtaken by their market-value which is determined not by the people but by the pigs. What started out as the antithesis of the consumer culture has been transformed into the very thing it meant to eliminate, and the people are suffering from it—not just economically, because it's always been this way economically for us, but also culturally and spiritually, which is what hurts us the most.

Local culture has been replaced by universal (rootless) culture in the market economy, the music and the musicians are cut off from their roots in the people and stuck into the capitalist melting pot where they get mixed around by the "owners" and dished out to the people in various insipid combinations of the same old beef stew. Bands aren't shit any more until they are accepted by the industry "owners" and their spokesmen, packaged according to the standard formula and pushed for all they're worth until the people get tired of them, at which point they're replaced by the latest superstar products and dumped back on the people they left to join the Hit Parade. At any one time maybe twenty BIG Amerikan bands are making it in the industry, and their fortune are determined and controlled at all levels by people who have as much to do with us and our culture in its positive sense as Richard Nixon and Spiro P. Agnew. Maybe twenty or thirty more bands and single performers are allowed to play for the people and make a living at it, but their entrance into the market has nothing to do with the music at all—it has only to do with the laws of monopoly-capitalist economics.

If this sounds absurd do as I just did and check out the bills for the BIG money festivals this summer—the same acts are rotated from cow pasture to baseball stadium as the "owners" see fit, and nobody else gets in to play at all. Fewer and fewer people control the performing conditions under which the bands are able to work, and they pack more and more of us into their extravaganzas with no regard for our health, education or welfare, just the big buck and the power it brings them. The big money drives the independents and local promoters, who aren't really much better but who do offer different opportunities at least, out of business or into the arms of the greedheads in ridiculously profitable merger scenes, and what was an expansive and exciting possibility gets more constricted and less vital every day. The anti-ethic of the pig has usurped the life-force of our culture, and all of us are affected by it whether we realize it or not.

The point is to do something about it, something which will put an end to this economic and cultural exploitation and return our culture to the people who gave birth to it and nurtured it to the point where the pigs could come in and rip it off from us. Our life culture can't survive much longer in this form, and even if elements of it do most of their force is gone, most of their utility as agents of revolutionary change is gone, they will only thrive as they come increasingly to serve the perverse interests of monopoly capitalism and the death merchants who "own" all the capital. And they are having their

problems too—Their monopolization and concentration of the energies and materials of the rock & roll culture is even killing off their own profit-making power, and they're starting to get worried as they look into their ill-gotten pot of gold and see the nasty old bottom of the barrel winking back at them through the glitter. They're getting worried too, but their fears and failures are generated by the irreconcilable contradictions inherent in their system. They can't keep plundering the rock & roll culture as they have been and still get the booty they want without at least making an effort at real economic development, and that can't happen without a change in the basic structure of imperialism as it is practiced by these pigs.

"The reactionary forces and we both have difficulties. But the difficulties of the reactionary forces are insurmountable because they are forces on the verge of death and have no future. Our difficulties can be overcome because we are new and rising forces and have a bright future."
—Mao Tse-Tung, "Self-Reliance and Arduous Struggle"

The point is that the present situation is bound to change, and the question then arises, what direction will this change take and who will bring it about? If the people of the rock & roll culture continue to consume and support everything the pigs hand them, the capitalists and rock & roll imperialists will determine the future of our culture just as they have determined its recent past. If, on the other hand, the people of the rock & roll culture start to get themselves together and work out solutions to their problems and unite with their bands and workers and diggers and start implementing these new solutions, the people will be able to recapture the control of their own culture and move for righteous revolutionary change. It's time to make the decision, people, the time is right and what we have to do is SEIZE THE TIME, come together and "retake their universe of fear, death and monopoly," as Burroughs puts it. We have to act now, before it gets any worse, and we have to act in such a way that the people's interests will be protected, and in such a way that those who act against our interests, against the people's interests, will be powerless to rip us off any more, whether they be capitalist record companies, rock & roll imperialists (promoters and booking agents), or pig-oriented bands and performers who are on individualist ego-trips and greed- and power-trips instead of people-trips.

Revolution is the only solution to rock & roll imperialism, just as revolution is the only solution to imperialism and neo-colonialism out in the rest of the underdeveloped world. We are certainly an underdeveloped people, and we are at a point now where we have to determine whether our economic and cultural development will be free and healthy, in the best interests of all our people, or whether it will be as fouled up and unhealthy as it has been for the past three years. Now we have the potential for this kind of action, and we have the necessary elements already developed in our collective community, and what we need is to bring all these things together and put them in a new framework, a new perspective which is focused on the needs of the people and which can see that the needs of the people can be met through collective action. We have the energy we need, we have the materials and resources we need, we have the spirit necessary to the achievement of this dream, and all we need now is the unity and the consciousness which will bring all of these things together and place them directly in the service of the people.

The consciousness is the primary thing, because all the other elements are already present within our culture and they're just waiting to be brought within a new context so they can be used in the people's interest. We have a lot of capital on hand, which is necessary to finance and initiate certain programs and get them off the ground, but this capital is presently held by a relative handful of people—bands, promoters, young record industry geniuses—and is being used to further individual profit schemes and consumption sprees. We have the energies and skills we need to bring off a comprehensive self-determination program—again, starting with the bands and music industry workers and going on to artists, technicians, hip accountants and economic geniuses, promotion maniacs, radio and other mass media operators, craftspeople, builders and planners of all breeds and disciplines who share in common an expanded and expansive view of the world and its people—but so far they've all been working separately or in small combines on individual projects.

We have a communications network, starting with the people's newspapers and radio broadcasters and extending down into our neighborhoods and communities, where word of mouth gets the news around before it can be written up most of the time—we have this extensive communications network which has to be consolidated to the extent that it will be able to keep the people informed and knowledgeable in terms of what plans are being developed and how they are manifesting themselves in specific actions and programs and happenings. We have this possibility, but so far it's been used the same way our other resources have been used, in a splintered, scattered fashion, with various people and groups often working at cross-purposes, and now it has to be unified and organized, at least minimally, so we can use it to educate the people as to the need and the possibilities for self-determination and how they can support all self-determination programs.

We have access, in our community, to all the energies and resources we will need to build self-determination, all the elements are present, and what we need now is organization and Planning on a large scale—coordination—so that all these people and things can be mobilized in the interests of the community, the Nation, as a whole. And as this is being done, there are two things that we have primarily to address ourselves to: (1) building collective economic power, so we can bring all of the products of our imagination and labor as a people and as individual members of a Nation of people under our own control; and (2) transforming our culture, which is simply the whole range of the formal expression of our National lifestyle, into a truly liberating culture, into a true revolutionary culture, bringing it back to where it started from and clearing the pig-shit off and out of it and building it back up from this purified base so it can be a wholly (holy) rejuvenated extension of what it was when it first started to emerge.

In other words, we have to build a consciousness among all our people, from the performers and professional workers through all the people who are reached and affected and inspired and moved by their creations, which is a revolutionary consciousness, a collective consciousness, a unified national consciousness, and which is finally the cosmic consciousness we used to talk about before it started to sound corny—and we have to realize that it only started to sound corny because there were so many cynical creeps around us who were laughing at our naiveté and ripping us off for what we had created out of it at the same time. We have to build and extend this consciousness on every level throughout the rainbow colony, and the chief builders will have to be the bands and media workers—simply because they already have access to the people and are in a position to turn the people on to cosmic consciousness once and for all, and to show them how it can be used in the service of liberation and self-determination.

The bands and the artists and the media workers of our culture have already demonstrated in great detail how much they can do to influence and inspire a people—now it's time for all of us to start directing our influence and breath toward liberating all of our people, not just ourselves, and toward creating the New World we've been dreaming about. The pigs have tried to buy this dream off, and they've been disastrously successful to a frightening degree, but their death-grip on our music and our culture—our people—can still be broken if we start working together to break it. They won't just go away because we want them to, or because that would be best for the people, or because they're messed up and are messing us up too, but they *can* be driven off the stage and chased out the door if we do the things that are necessary to bring that consequence about.

It starts with unity, it starts with consciousness, it starts with collective organization for self-determination and goes from there. We have to get ourselves together, and get together with 244 ourselves, all of us, and start thinking about our people and what we can do to help liberate them. This is essential. We have to start bringing our bands and cultural workers together, and our economic workers together, and our listeners and participants and diggers together, and we have to start figuring out ways that can move for self-determination and freedom on all levels. We have to develop a unified collective consciousness, and then have to put that consciousness into action on every front. Otherwise things will just get worse, and I don't think any of us can relate to that, even the people who are making millions of dollars playing in bands and doing those other things that the pigs pay money for.

I'm not going to lay out an extensive program for self-determination now because we have to develop our national consciousness first, and we have to do one thing at a time so we will have a solid base upon which to build our national life. But I will make some tentative suggestions about ways we might move once we get ourselves together, things we might start thinking about and working toward right now while we're still in the first stages of coming together as a people. Because there are a lot of things that can be started now, programs which will develop in scope and intensity as we start to organize ourselves and work for the realization of our national goals, and these things should be known to everyone concerned so the more advanced workers and diggers can move on them now.

For one thing, bands which are already established as top earners and top drawing powers can play more benefits and more free gigs for the people. They can join with local people's action groups and help raise funds to start implementing local self-determination programs which already exist and are just waiting for enough money to be put into action. In Ann Arbor, for example, the community's Tribal Council is working toward the creation and establishment of a People's Ballroom, a place for the People's music and culture which will be operated by the community in its own behalf on a cooperative, non-profit basis to provide a steady place of work for the people's bands and a place where the people can come together with their bands to dance and get down together. The Tribal Council also serves the needs .of the Ann Arbor rainbow colony by maintaining a community information center, a free health clinic, a People's Food Co-op, and other services, and this organization is always in need of funds to continue serving the people for free like they do.

There are organizations like this in a lot of cities, and the bands have helped keep them alive in the past, and what I'm suggesting here is that more bands start thinking about contributing to the support of people's organizations like this wherever they exist. They can do this by playing more benefits when they are in a certain area or by contributing lump sums of cash in other instances. They can also serve the people better by working wherever and whenever possible with community production groups rather than with pig promoters, although I know that there aren't too many of these groups operating yet. But as our national consciousness grows there will be more and more of such operations emerging, and the established bands and performers can help their people grow by working with these people's organizations whenever the opportunity presents itself.

Another thing we can do is start working toward the creation and implementation of a People's Recording Cooperative, which would record and produce and package and market records by our bands instead of letting the pig companies do all that. This is an ambitious plan but it will certainly emerge with time, and all I'm saying is that bands have to start thinking in terms of operations like this. A People's Recording Cooperative could start by recording new, unattached bands and releasing their products through established capitalist companies to build up some operating capital, while at the same time, as the Cooperative develops, established bands could relate to it and start working with it, producing their records through the Cooperative wherever possible and releasing them as before, through the established labels, until their present contracts run out. Then they could throw all their weight behind the People's Recording Cooperative if they found it worked well for them.

This Cooperative would have to be operated on a thoroughly businesslike basis, even better than the capitalist companies, with the distinction being that the profits from record sales and royalties would go back into the Nation instead of into the pig's banks and corporations. As the Cooperative starts to accumulate working capital it could purchase recording studios, film studios, printing plants, radio stations, even television stations, and make these facilities available to our people. It could branch out and start funding other self-determination projects, buy buildings for cultural centers and community service facilities of all kinds, and it could even buy pieces of land so we could set up incredible Earth People's Park projects in the wilderness. All of these things are possible with enough seed capital, and all of them will help us build up our Nation as the Pig Nation slowly (or quickly) crumbles into history.

Another important project we could start working on right away is a People's Booking Agency, which would contract jobs and other performance opportunities for the bands involved in the Recording Cooperative. This agency could operate on both a national and a local scale, booking bands into established situations and also producing and promoting concerts under its own auspices, the profits from which events would go back into the Nation to help fund the other programs that would be initiated within the people's cooperative movement. Again, this agency would have to be operated on a thoroughly professional level by people who know the business inside and out, and it could be built up on bands which are not already committed to the big pig agencies. The established bands that relate to the cooperative movement could also take bookings through the cooperative agency whenever possible, and if it is successful they could switch over to the People's Booking Agency when their contracts with the established agencies run out. The difference, once more, is that the profits realized from the operation of this program would go back into the Nation, and everyone would benefit from it in the end.

I won't go any farther right now because this should be enough to get people thinking about some of the possibilities open to us, and as I said before it's important to concentrate on one or two major programs at any one time so we won't try to do everything at once and spread ourselves out too thin at the beginning. The beautiful thing about these proposed programs is that no one would have to give up anything out of their own pockets to get them off the ground—initial funding could be raised through a series of two or three major benefit/festivals for which a number of established bands could donate their services for one day in the interests of serving the people and promoting national self-determination. When this funding was acquired a number of experienced business heads could commit themselves to work full-time setting up and operating the People's Recording Cooperative and the People's Booking Agency. They could draw a living wage from the cooperatives and do something that would be more satisfying and more exciting than I could possibly describe here.

The initial operating capital would be used to secure space for the cooperatives to work out of, install telephones and secure business equipment, produce the first series of albums (including the music, packaging for the records, and the advertising/promotion campaigns necessary to get them off the ground), and to start Producing community-oriented dances and concerts.

The people's press, starting with this paper and drawing on liberated newspaper outlets all across the Nation, could report on the progress of the programs and keep the people informed as to what was happening and how they could support it in their communities.

People on campuses all across the Nation could tie in with the cooperative movement and work with the People's Booking Agency to bring bands and other performers into their enclaves instead of working with the big pig talent outlets. Radio people could carry on educational and informational campaigns on these programs and push the cooperative programs whenever possible. Once all of us get into a unity trip we will find out precisely how great our existing resources and energies are, and as we all get turned on to the possibilities of self-determination music we will increase our power and effectiveness by leaps and bounds.

The important thing to understand is that we aren't going to get what we want right off—it will take some time to get this movement underway, and it will take even longer after it gets started to achieve the maximum results. But it has to get started in order to grow, and we *can* get it started right now. We have to realize that we're talking about a period of *years*, not just a few months or a few seasons, and we have to keep the overall plan in mind during every stage of the development of our program. At first it may look to the apocalyptic rebels among us like we're just doing the same thing that the pigs are already doing, but the first difference will be that we are starting to control the means of production for ourselves and our people, and the second difference is that the profits being realized from our work will be going back into our own Nation for the benefit of the people as a whole and not just a few rock & roll imperialists with huge egos and grasping hands.

Like I tried to say before, the Revolution is not an apocalyptic upheaval characterized by a few days of street fighting and a period of chaos afterwards—the struggle for self-determination and liberation is a protracted struggle which is fought on all fronts, particularly on the cultural front, and it has to be waged by the people as a whole because it will affect every person in the Nation when it is accomplished. The Revolution grows as the people's consciousness grows, and once the people as a whole understand what is happening they will support all the manifestations of the revolutionary spirit, especially as these things relate directly and immediately to their lives.

I don't know how many people can relate to these ideas now, but I have to put them forth just so people can have some sense of what possibilities do exist for them, and how they can make use of these possibilities so as to move for self-determination and liberation on all levels. We have a lot of talking and a lot of studying and a lot of planning yet to do in order to bring things like this off, but there are already a lot of people who are committed to working for their people in the cultural arena, and I know there are a lot of other people out there who are just waiting for something beautiful to happen so they can get behind it. The musicians and artists of our culture have to lead the way, we have to unite with each other and present a unified consciousness and a coherent plan for action to all of our people, so they can understand what's at stake and support the programs which are designed only to serve their needs.

The thing now is to get together with each other and start working out our differences so we can come to a common understanding of our situation and how it can be transformed into the beautiful thing we know we must have. Those who can't relate to any of this now may be able to dig it later, after these things start to develop on a visible, measurable plane, but we certainly don't need everybody who's already active to make this thing work—we just need one or two bands at the established level, and a few people's bands from the intermediate level of the Biz, and a few unestablished bands in different local areas to get our self-determination programs started, and we can go from there. We also need a few people in different parts of our Nation who know the Biz and have experience in it, and who are ready to commit themselves to the people's cause and make our programs work. It's the only way we are going to get the control of our culture back out of the grip of the greedheads of pig nation and into the arms of our own people. We got into this mess because we didn't know any better, for the most part, but now we know that it doesn't have to be like it is, and all we need now is for enough of our musicians and workers to get together under the banner of liberation and self-determination and start serving the people instead of just themselves.

Our music and our culture were born in freedom and now they have to return to liberation. We *can* move, we've *got* to move, we *will* be moving, and we need all of us to move *together* in the music and build on the music so all of us can be free. Build National Consciousness! Move for Self-Determination! Liberation for our Music and our People!

THE LESSON OF GOOSE LAKE

"The enemy of our enemy is our friend....We must support what the enemy opposes and oppose what the enemy supports."
—Mao Tse-tung

"To guard its domination, imperialism tries to destroy the national, cultural, and spiritual values of each country...."
—Resolution on "Colonialism and Neo-Colonialism" at first Tri-Continental (OSPAAAL), January 3-12, 1966

OCTOBER 25, 1970

Two weeks ago, Richard Songer, owner and promoter of Goose Lake Park, was indicted by a Jackson County (Michigan) Grand Jury for "aiding and abetting in the sale of narcotic drugs (marijuana and heroin)" during the Goose Lake Pop Festival held the weekend of August 7-8-9. This development of course follows on the heels of a court order closing down Goose Lake Park on the grounds that it is a "public nuisance" which "contributes to the delinquency of young people."

I wasn't at Goose Lake, all I know is what I've read about it and what I've been told by the people in the White Panther Party who worked on getting the Festival together and who were there working among the people, but I know that the overwhelming fact of Goose Lake is that thousands and thousands of our people gathered there to get down together for three days, and that this freaked the pigs out no end, because the last thing they want is for us to get together in huge masses and demonstrate our strength and togetherness in a creative, non-destructive fashion.

You can see from the reaction of the established order, from Gov. William G. "Traverse City" Milliken on down to the lowliest snake in Jackson County (who would have to be Prosecutor Bruce Barton for my money), how serious a threat they feel Goose Lake posed to their security, and what we have to understand is that no matter how many shortcomings or bogus aspects it had, Goose Lake was killer important if only because it struck so much fear into the flinty hearts of the control addicts. If they're so shook up behind it, there *must*'ve been something good about it, and that's what we have to deal with.

Written as a White Panther Party study paper and circulated internally

John Sinclair

Maybe I'd better deal with these shortcomings and bogus aspects first, so everyone will know where I'm coming from. The main thing that people seem to be saying about Goose Lake and similar ventures—including Woodstock and all the mass gatherings of freeks—is that they are "cultural rip-offs" perpetrated by straight people who are just interested in exploiting our music and taking our people's money as fast as they can grab it out of our hands. This is certainly true, there can't be any doubt about it but it *isn't* the primary aspect of the mass festivals, and we have to start with the primary things first.

The primary thing about Goose Lake is that there were 100,000, or 200,000, or however many people there—a huge mass of people anyway, the largest group of freeks ever gathered together in the state of Michigan before. And the other primary thing about Goose Lake is that it scared the shit out of the pig power structure, which knows better than we do that it doesn't really matter, in the primary term, whether it's a "rip-off" or not. The thing that matters to the pigs is that all these freeks were able to come together with each other, get high, take their clothes off, get down in the music and have a good time, and that *there was nothing the police could do to stop them.*

Now you would think that if this gathering was primarily a bad thing for us, for our people, the reactionaries would be *happy* to have it happening, because it would weaken us and make us more messed up than we are already. If it were bad for us they would get behind it and promote it, like they promote schools and prisons and dope laws and methadone addiction and football games and shopping centers and television and shit like that. But they not only *don't* promote it, they're doing everything in their power to make sure that nothing like this ever happens again, that we can't possibly get together in groups of more than what did Milliken say? 5,000 people? That we can't possibly have another gathering even remotely resembling the magnitude of Goose Lake, because when we come together like that we're *out of control* and we can't be effectively "handled" by the state's armed forces.

And now that the state has moved against Richard Songer like has moved against so many of us, using its ridiculous dope laws as a cover-up for political repression (and I should note here, in case you missed it, that the freeks the police and newspapers made such a big deal of busting as they left Goose Lake almost all got off with $50 fines, which demonstrates precisely the political and not the legal motivation behind their arrests), we have to think about Goose Lake and what it means all over again. Songer was supposed to be the big enemy of the rainbow colony, according t the local "radicals," and yet here he is being indicted by the state as an outlaw just like the rest of us. That should lead people to reconsider some basic things, and to draw some different conclusions.

Now I don't have any illusions about Dick Songer one way or the other—he says he's always had a dream of building a park where young people could get together and have a good time, and now that he's made a million dollars or so in his own construction business he's using his money to make that dream come true. But whatever his motivations, and however much money he may hope to make off this project, the important thing to me is that he's trying to establish and maintain a place where thousands of freeks can get together out in the open, and since we don't have any places like that of our own yet, our best shot is to try to work with those people who do have them and who are open to us. *In the absence of an alternative,* that is, we either work with people like Songer, or we don't get together in the thousands and hundreds of thousands at all. And as the STP (Serve the People) Coalition said during the planning stages of the Goose Lake Festival in an official statement, "Dick Songer seems to be a man we can work with."

Too many people just put promoters like Songer down as capitalist rip-off agents without going into the full realities of the situation. I will insist that there's more to it than that, and that to maintain that position is doing a serious disservice to the people. People like Dick Songer can be very useful to the development of our culture, and like I said, *as long as we are not yet prepared to offer an alternative*—because this is something the people obviously want and need—as long as we are not yet prepared to put on our own festivals, our own mass gatherings, we had better try to combine and work with people who will give us a chance to work with them, even if they aren't everything we'd like them to be. We can't operate on the basis of "fantasy or else"—we have to start with conditions

as they are and work from there to make our ideals real. Otherwise we're just worthless dreamers with nothing to offer our people at all.

Here in Ann Arbor we should know how this works, because we've had experience with it, we know that you can start with what you've got and work from there to get what you need, and we also know that things aren't over with just because the pigs say it's time to quit. Our experience with the free concerts in the parks has taught us that the people can get what they need if they unite on important issues, organize themselves politically and take effective political action to bring about the desired results. We have been able to take care of our most immediate cultural needs, in the summertime at least, with the free concerts in the parks, but we can't forget about our brothers and sisters around the state who don't have a situation like we have here—who haven't organized themselves yet as we have started to do, and who are therefore powerless to provide for their collective needs.

For these thousands of young people, festivals like Goose Lake are their only chance to come together with their sisters and brothers in the music and in the flesh, and until every city and town in the state—in the midwest—in the whole Nation—can organize itself and provide for the needs of its people, gatherings like the Goose Lake Pop Festival are going to continue to be very important to the development of our culture, of our sense of peoplehood, and of our struggle as a whole.

We can't let this phony deal go down without a struggle, is all I'm trying to say, because it's important that we protect the few places we do have access to in large numbers, and if we don't protect them now we won't be *able* to get together like that in the future. We should embrace Richard Songer as a partner in crime, and we should organize around his trial and around the whole question of whether he will be permitted to put on any more rock & roll festivals at Goose Lake next year. We should give Songer the people's full support and demonstrate to the state that we are not going to submit to their "legal" fascism so easily. Because this is not an isolated incident—this is part of the pig's overall plan to snuff out our culture and keep us from developing as a powerful political force.

The main strategy of the reactionaries in power is to keep us separated, to keep us from coming together and realizing how powerful we are, how many of us there are, and what we might be able to accomplish if we really organize ourselves and move together to bring about the necessary changes which spell death to the death culture and life to the life culture. The attack on Goose Lake and now on Richard Songer personally is an attack on all of us, whether we relate to Goose Lake or to Songer or not. That's what we have to understand right now, and once we understand the nature of this foul attack we will be able to protect not only Songer but all of our people against this shit.

At the same time we can't pretend that Goose Lake was or will be the ideal thing we need it to be, because it won't—we won't have exactly what we need until we create and control it *ourselves*, through our own energy, our own work, our own capital, and our own total unity behind an active program of national construction. *But,* until we *can* obtain and develop and defend our own land where all our people can gather together whenever we want to, we have to rely on people like Richard Songer and places like Goose Lake Park, or we won't be able to set together at all. That's what our choice is.

And while we have to rely on these things for the time being, we *don't* have to let them remain the same—in fact we have to transform them as much as we can, from the inadequate Hollywood entertainment palaces and hip Disneylands they are now, into genuine people's cultural centers which will display and promote the people's revolutionary culture and which will serve as models for the social order of the future so people can see what their future will be in the New World.

With people like Songer we have the opportunity to exert a great influence on the *content* of these festivals even if we can't control them from a financial standpoint. It's up to us to take the initiative and force certain procedural changes in the way these things are put together, not just in terms of the facilities that will be provided (free food, free medical care, free passes for people who will work on clean-up and in the service centers inside the grounds) as we did this time, but also in terms of the kind of music that is scheduled and the way it will be performed.

The primary problem of this nature which we can affect right now is the Pop-Star Band Rip-Off scene, the way the promoters let themselves be manipulated by the big mother-country booking agents into buying the most expensive acts in the business (Joe Cocker, before he decided he was already rich enough to take a vacation from playing music, was contracted to play one day for $45,000!) instead of engaging the best bands from the people's own community and only very special bands from outside. This keeps the money from going back into our own community to our own bands, and it contributes heavily to the ridiculous admission prices that are charged at these festivals.

We can insist on people's control over the bookings for these festivals when they do occur in the future by setting up a collective program committee made up of people from the community who know what the deal is and who would have final say over who is contracted to play. We can make sure that the bulk of the money stays within our community, goes to our bands, and is used to build up our own local culture (including grants from the profits, at a fixed percentage of the total gate which would go to finance projects like people's ballrooms and community centers and other service programs for the people who pay to get in these events) instead of being taken back to banks in Los Angeles and New York and London to buy Rolls-Royces and shit with, for the B*I*G*S*TA*R*S. That's one thing we can and must do, and I know that steps were taken by STP to correct this problem to a certain extent, but only after the preliminary booking arrangements had already been made. In the future we have to make sure that the Tribal Councils are involved in the planning all the way through the preparations for these events, particularly in the booking arrangements.

Another thing we can do is make sure that there is more to the festival than just a bunch of pop bands getting up on stage for half an hour or forty-five minutes and playing their jukebox hits. We have to make sure that a real *festival* takes place, that steps are taken to break down the whole Hollywood ruse that these promoters run on the people more from ignorance than anything else. We should also make sure that blatantly sexist bands are excluded from the programs, that women's bands are engaged wherever possible, and that more black performers—blues groups, jazz performers, people like the Parliaments—are brought in to play and are paid on a scale with the big POP bands. There's a whole lot more to music than Ten Years After and John B. Sebastian and Grand Funk Railroad, and it's criminal for these promoters to keep denying the people access to other forms of music than those which they already know about—especially to deny people access to music like Sun Ra's, or Howlin Wolf's, or Archie Shepp's, or Doctor Ross and blues people like that. The only way the people can hear and feel and relate to this music is if the promoters bring it before them and make sure they hear it—and it's our responsibility to make sure that happens.

Some other possibilities are that a number of different stages could be set up in different areas of the land, so that more people can become more intimately involved with the music instead of being forced to relate to it like it's a big TV variety show and they're the studio audience; that workshops and jams and raps with the musicians could be arranged, which would also bring the whole thing onto a more human level and help break down the Hollywood separation ruse; that the strongest possible line-up of Michigan bands be arranged and juxtaposed to the All-Star lineup so the people can see and hear how powerful their own local culture is compared with the stuff the music industry pushes on us and that generally the people responsible for booking and staging the "show" be more responsive to the cultural and educational needs of the people instead of just sticking S*T*A*R*S up there on a stage and "giving the people what they want" in the most abusive, the most narrow sense of the term. The people can't *really* know what they want unless they have a chance to choose from the broadest possible spectrum of possibilities, unless they have full access to all available information, and they don't have that access under the present set-up.

Another major problem which absolutely has to be dealt with is the dope problem and the dopes who are involved in exploiting their sisters and brothers by selling them adulterated sacraments and outright pig drugs (heroin, speed, downers of all kinds). We have to take more active and more stringent measures to *make sure* that:

(1) *no smack* is allowed on the grounds at all;

(2) no bogus sacraments—adulterated LSD and mescaline, etc.—are allowed to be sold by avaricious pig hippies who don't have any community consciousness and are just out to make a big profit for themselves at the expense of the health of their brothers and sisters who are forced to cop from

them. It's too dangerous for us to set up weed and psychedelic-dealing collectives on a non-profit basis at this time, but we *can* exercise some control over the established dealers and make sure they aren't poisoning the people;

(3) dealers must cool themselves out and submit to some form of regulation by the people's health committees so the people won't be fronted off so bad by the pigs and the press, and so the people won't be subjected to shit like strychnine, dog tranquilizers, belladonna, speed-acid, barbiturates, and other pig-oriented drugs.

In other words, we have to start thinking about what we're doing and what effect it has—we have to start taking care of our own problems and not leaving the regulation of our affairs up to outsiders, and armed outsiders at that. *We* have to eliminate the Pig drugs from our communities, because in the first place the Pigs aren't going to do it for us—their actions (as opposed to their lying rhetoric) show us that they're much more interested in getting righteous weed and acid away from us than they are in dealing with smack and speed and all that shit. Our position must be that we will take care of the pig drug problem ourselves, we will eliminate that shit from our communities, but we must have the cooperation of the police in doing it, and that they must not be allowed to hassle or arrest people who are smoking or dealing weed.

This last point goes not only for the festivals, but all year around, throughout our nation—we have to get rid of the pig dope that's being pushed into our people's veins, and we have to do

226

it ourselves, and we have to do it *now*. People who shoot scag and speed aren't "doing their own thing"—they're helping destroy our national life as well as themselves, and they're playing right into the pig's hands in the process. All that shit does is turn people into Mr. Jones replicas—that's why Jones is such a perfect name for it—and all smack freaks are doing is keeping up with the Joneses just like the pigs want them to. Death to Jones—no more smack in our community!

Back to the festivals—there will have to be better arrangements made to provide for the people's nutritional needs, and I would suggest that we force the promoters to provide *free food* for all the participants—and not hot dogs and shit like that, but good healthful food prepared by the people and made available to everyone as part of the festival. Hot dog concessions and similar pig stands should be barred from the grounds, and plenty of good food and good juices should be made available for free. If the bands' profits are cut down this food could be paid for out of the gate receipts, figured into the cost of tickets, and provided in ample quantities for the people.

That should be enough to get us thinking about what to do and how we can do it—it's important that *everyone* concerned, from the bands to the listeners and groovers, have an active role in planning, promoting, producing and participating in our cultural affairs instead of just sitting around and sucking in the music or the money like it's a big TV show or something. Our culture must be a *participatory* culture, the opposite of the death culture where all you are allowed to do is pay your money and eat up the shit the pigs dish out on their plastic platters. The more active each one of us becomes in shaping and developing our own culture, the farther out we (and it) become. And the farther out we get, the closer we get to the future, where everybody can get as far out as they want to!

So I'll say it again in closing—we should all unite behind Richard Songer in his court battle against the forces of repression-we should take an active supporting role in his struggle to re-open his park, we should organize our people around the issues brought out by the pigs in this matter, we should demand that mass gatherings like the Goose Lake Festival must be allowed to continue without police and state interference, we should take charge of our culture and stop letting the pigs define its limits for us, we should start thinking and planning next summer now so we'll be prepared to carry through on our demands and we should definitely move to take an active role in planning and shaping any future festivals of this nature so we can transform them into stomp-down people's celebrations instead of honkoid entertainment scenes. But the main thing is to stand up to the pigs in every instance of cultural and political repression of our people and our culture and let the state know that we will not submit to fascism, now or any time, in whatever form. Defend Richard Songer! Self-Determination for Our Nation—Long Live the People's Revolutionary Culture!!

Guitar Army martyr Sandy Lee Scheuer

"We are just like millions of parents and Sandy was just like millions of daughters growing up."
—Martha Garland, speaking of her daughter Sandy

SLAUGHTER AT STONEHEAD MANOR

"There were only a few of us at school. The other kids called us hippies and freaks but we were the first ones. Now they all are into it."
—Donna Potts, speaking of Sandy Garland & herself

NOVEMBER 5, 1970

Three days after Allison Krause, Jeffrey Miller, Bill Schroeder and Sandy Lee Scheuer were murdered by National Guard troops at Kent State, three young brothers and a young sister were gunned down in their sleep on Lincoln Street in Detroit. They weren't demonstrating or burning down ROTC buildings or even woofing at the National Guard, but they were killed by the same thing that took the lives of their brothers and sisters in Ohio: they were killed because they were part of a culture, part of a people that is hated and feared by the dominant forces in Amerikan society.

They were sleeping in their room in Stonehead Manor, a "hippie commune" in Detroit's youth enclave situated in the middle of a half-black, half-Appalachian inner-city neighborhood, it was 2:30 in the morning of May 8, 1970, and Sandy Garland's father Arville charged through the door with a gun in each hand and blew his daughter, her partner Scott Kabran, his close brother Greg Walls, and Tony Brown, a 16-year-old escapee from the youth concentration camp at Whitmore Lake Michigan, blew them all right off the set.

Arville Garland faces trial in Detroit's Recorder's Court next week on three counts of first-degree murder (Sandy, Scott, Greg) and one count of murder in the second degree (young Tony Brown).* He was held in the nut ward of the Wayne County Jail for some time, but Judge Joseph Gillis felt sorry for him and cut him loose on $30,000 personal bond. Gillis sympathizes with Arville Garland because he's the same way himself, only his own brand of genocide is more subtle than Garland's and it's carried out under the guise of the law. Gillis sends people like Tony Brown to prison every day, people like Scott Kabran and Gregory Walls and Sandy Garland, he kills them off little by little with prison-death because they get high and fuck without a license and refuse to go along with the death-program of honkie Amerika.

"Many people say that Sandy and Scott and Greg and Tony deserved to be punished for the way they lived. For their long hair and their unconventional life-styles. For their hard rock music, for their dope. People say they might even have done what Garland did, if they had walked in on their daughter naked in bed, asleep with a hippie, a black boy in another bed in the same room."
—from the *Detroit Free Press* account

Amerika is writhing in the first throes of a civil war, a genocidal war being waged by the merchants of death against all those people who refuse to go along with their program of fear, greed, insanity and total control. This is a war of cultures, a desperate last-ditch attempt by the last generation of Euro-Amerikan people to retain their control over the rest of the people in the world, and the civil war in Amerika is just one front in the world-wide struggle between the West and the non-West, between Euro-Amerika on the one hand and all pre- and post-western peoples on the other.

The Battle of Chicago in which Dean Johnson was murdered, the Battle of People's Park where James Rector was murdered, the Kent State Massacre and the Slaughter at Stonehead Manor on Lincoln Street in Detroit are opening shots in a war that will be fought to the finish, a war which could not have been predicted five or ten years ago (as the rest of the current wars could have been) simply because the people who are fighting it, the people who are on the side of freedom and self-determination in this war against the Euro-Amerikan monster, didn't even exist as a people, ten years ago. Many of them don't even realize yet that they are part of a national liberation struggle, part of an international revolutionary movement which is destined to win this world-wide war and secure the future of the planet and its people from the Death merchants of the West. But as

---

*Arville Garland was convicted by a Recorder's Court jury on December 31, 1970, on three counts of 2nd-degree murder and one count manslaughter. He was sentenced to 10-40 years in prison at Jackson, where he is now.

"Children have no freedom. They are property just like a book. She's my property and I can do whatever I want with her."
—Arville Garland, speaking of his daughter Sandy

the repression, as the genocide campaign is stepped up against us as it has been stepped up against black people and other oppressed peoples all over the world, millions of post-western young people will awaken, arm themselves with weapons and with revolutionary consciousness, rise up together and join with their rising brothers and sisters within the mother country and throughout the world to smash the Euro-Amerikan beast once and for all.

Let me back off a little and come at this from another direction, because it's important that all of us understand what I'm talking about, and I don't want just to run a bunch of violent rhetoric and make everybody feel better about this shit. I want you to understand why and how *we are a people,* what it means to be a people, and what the murder of Sandy Garland and Scott Kabran and Greg Walls and Tony Brown has to do with our peoplehood and our struggle. And I'll start again with the last question, because their deaths and the circumstances under which they died may provide an opening for the rest of us into the kind of consciousness we need if we are going to prepare ourselves for and protect ourselves against further assaults of this kind.

These four people died not as individuals—Arville Garland didn't even know the three brothers he shot—but as part of a people, a people which is alien to Arville Garland and the culture he is representative of. They died as a result of a political act, they are casualties in a war which as all wars is a political action, and their death came as a political consequence of the way they lived their lives. They may

not have been "radicals" or "political;" people, but they lived as part of a people which in itself is a political entity, a people which is defined as a people by its own national culture and by that culture's opposition and resistance to the dominant culture of Euro-Amerika from which it has declared its independence.

I know it's hard for some people to relate to this slaughter as a Political event, because we tend to have such a narrow view of Politics as something separate and apart from everyday life, some kind of abstract activity in the sense that one day you decide you're going to be "political" and go to a demonstration or throw some rocks through a classroom window or something, but that's precisely the sense we have to expand. And we have to expand it until we can sense that our lives themselves, whatever we do with them (or them with us), are political in the most functional term—that we *live* our politics, and that the question is not, are you or is he or she "political," but, what kind of politics do you (or does he or she) *practice?* Can you dig that?

It is in western society that politics are most purposefully separated from daily life and treated as something superfluous to it—the average westerner is brought up to believe that politics is that activity which is carried on by professional politicians and which has very little to do with his or her life except for a few brief months every two or four years when the politicians are "running" for office. And in the past few years another sense of "political" has emerged which would appear to be different from this one, but which is really not different at all: young people who concern themselves with the condition of their world and act in a more or less organized fashion to change it are considered "political," and consider themselves "political," while the masses of their brothers and sisters who do not organize themselves are considered as "not political" at all.

Thus this new sense still perpetuates the separation of the political from the rest of life, and one chooses either to "be political" or not to "be political" depending on one's desire to take part in demonstrations, go to SDS meetings, join the Student Mobilization Committee, etc. And even with the "political" people there is still a great gap between their "politics" and their daily lives; that is, unless they become full-time politicos and spend all their time going to meetings, planning demonstrations, reading political literature, etc.

But what I'm talking about is a way of life in which the "political" is fully integrated with all other areas of human experience so that one's politics can be seen in one's total life-style, a way of life in which one's every act is a political act, and consciously so—or a way of life in which, if one isn't consciously political, then the *effects* of that way of life are thoroughly political in the sense that radicals relate to, that is, in the sense that one's whole life is a blow against the established order, a continuous blow which has tremendous force and which strikes fear into the hearts of the pigs in power—so much fear, in fact, that they do not hesitate to shoot down, or to have shot down,

their own sons and daughters.

I'm talking about James Rector and the Kent State brothers and sisters when I say it that way, and not about Sandy Garland and Scott Kabran and Greg Walls and Tony Brown who were murdered by Sandy's father acting not as part of an organized force like the National Guard or the Alameda County Sheriff's Dept. Yet it's all part of the same thing, because Arville Garland is just a powerless version of Richard Nixon or Ronald Reagan or David Rockefeller, they share the same culture and the same political beliefs, and Arville Garland (and the "millions of parents" like him) are taught that their interests are the same as those of the pigs who do have the power, that what affects the pigs adversely also affects them in the same term, they are literally given to believe that, as Engine Charlie Wilson said back in the good old Ike Eisenhower days, "what's good for General Motors is good for the country." They believe that, and they act accordingly, they do what is prescribed for keeping General Motors and its accomplices in control of their society, and when the National Guard, acting under orders, shoots down four young people at Kent State University their example is immediately followed by a man like Arville Garland, a member of the Detroit Police Emergency Reserves, who picks up his guns and drills his own daughter and her "hippie friends."

It's all part of the same thing, that's all I'm trying to say. Sandy and Scott and Greg and Tony weren't what radicals would call "political," they were hippies and poets and weedheads and rock &

roll fiends who loved to get high and fuck and hang out with their friends, who had a pile of Woodstock buttons on the table by the bed and Jimi Hendrix playing on the record player and a dartboard with Lyndon Johnson's ugly face on it and a poster of John Sinclair on the wall, who worked for Open City when they could and who were planning to march the next day in a demonstration against the massacre at Kent State—they were stone freeks who lived in Stonehead Manor and probably never read Mao or Lenin or Kim II Sung, but the sum of their lives was thoroughly political and their deaths are now as political as anything I know. They were murdered because they were part of a despised people, a people as despised by Euro-Amerikans as black people or yellow or brown or red people are.

What I'm trying to say is that we are attacked because we are what we *are*, because we *live* our beliefs and not just mouth them as part of a political philosophy, because we are part of a people that is developing as something essentially different from Euro-Amerikan people—that we are assaulted and jailed and gunned down not because of our "politics" as radicals understand that term but because we represent, *as a people* we represent a threat to the dominant culture in this country, in the west as a whole, and the people who are part of that dominant culture feel every bit as threatened by the most "non-violent," peace/love hippie on the street or at the pop festival as they are the "violence-prone Weatherman faction."

That's what we have to understand, that we are *all* seen as a threat by the pig power structure and the people it controls, no matter what our individual differences. Just as a black nuclear scientist, as the old honkie joke goes, is still considered merely a nigger by the average Euro-Amerikan, so is the innocent hippie seen as a dangerous degenerate who must be stomped off the set every bit as quickly and viciously as the protesters and bomb-throwers of the "radical left." The pigs know we are a people, even if we refuse to see it ourselves, and they are determined to give all of us the same inhuman treatment they give to other non-western peoples.

Sandy Garland and Scott Kabran and Greg Walls and Tony Brown were murdered because they were part of an alien people because they shared an alien culture which to Euro-Amerikans is only deserving of extermination and oblivion. Their deaths, as their lives, link them with slaughtered black people, with slaughtered Vietnamese people, with slaughtered American aborigines whose land was ripped off and whose culture was all but eradicated by Arville Garland's ancestors. Arville Garland gunned down his daughter and her three brothers for the same reason that the National Guard troops in Ohio gunned down Bill Schroeder and Sandy Lee Scheuer and Allison Krause and Jeff Miller, because they were part of a people that rejected the Amerikan death-style, that could not support the repression and slaughter of black and brown and red and yellow people just so Euro-Amerikans can buy more television sets and more cars and more electric toothbrushes and shit like that.

It comes down to that. The distinction can be that clearly drawn. Sandy Garland and Scott Kabran and Greg Walls were together because they loved each other; Arville and Martha Garland stormed into their room and killed them, and Tony Brown who happened to be sleeping on the couch in the other room because he didn't have anyplace else to stay and his brothers and his sister took him in because they loved him too, Arville Garland killed these people because he "loved" his daughter too much to see her consorting and living and sleeping with hippies and niggers. One love—our love for each other, our love for our brothers and sisters given without demands and controls and promises and threats—measured against the hate-love of the honkies, which says I love you if you fulfill all these insane conditions, and if you refuse I'll blow you away. It comes down to that.

But Arville Garland is a dupe, just as the National Guard troops are dupes, just as our brothers in the U.S. Armed Forces are dupes of the pigs who run this country for their own gain. These people are every bit as much victims of western culture as are the non-westerners this culture, this society, oppresses and murders to keep its own people "happy" with the shoddy consumer goods it gets thereby. That's something we also have to understand. Western culture is formed and propagated by the pig owners as a precise means of reinforcing their economic and political control over the masses of Euro-

Amerikans under their influence, and they use that culture to instill their vile principles of greed, fear, insanity and control in the people who are within their reach. It is the perpetrators and benefactors of this culture—the pigs in control—who are our enemies, and not their dupes.

What we have to overcome if we are to avert the worst, if we are to have our freedom without an all-out civil war between the people of Euro-Amerika and the non-westerners who they see as their enemies, what we have to overcome is the vicious propaganda put out about us by the pigs. We have to remember that the Arville and Martha Garlands of Euro-Amerika are not our enemies unless they insist on being that, and we have to remember that they attack us only because they have been made so crazed by the pigs who control their consciousness by manipulating their economic possibilities and the information on which they base their beliefs. We have to make these people see, somehow, that the world we are determined to bring into being is *their* world too, if they will only accept it—and accepting it doesn't mean giving up their own culture except insofar as that culture poisons them against people who are different from them.

They don't know this, they're afraid of us, they don't understand us and they think—they've been told again and again by the pigs—they think we're trying to take everything they've worked and slaved for all these years away from them. We have to understand how far they've been twisted by the pigs in power, and we have to try to untwist them somehow so they can regain (or gain for once) their own humanity at last. They are not the enemy, we have to remember that, but they are the enemy's pawns and they will carry out the enemy's bidding unless and until we can teach them differently, and if they continue to move against us we will have to kill them. We have to protect ourselves, and we will protect ourselves, and there is a great number of Euro-Amerikans who will have to die before the people of the rainbow colony and all oppressed people win their freedom. The point make it be as few of them as possible who die, or as I wrote in a poem some years ago, "how to get out / & dance, without stepping on any more heads / than we have to."

The slaughter at Stonehead Manor is finally and perfectly metaphor for the larger struggle going on throughout the western world, as the children of the last generation of westerners develop a whole new way of life for themselves, a way of life that prepares them to live in the New World, in the New Age which begins with the final collapse of the West. It is a grim struggle already and will get even grimmer as its internal dynamic develops—parents will be moved to murder their own children and their children will rise up against the parents and strike them down if they have to. That isn't what we want to do—our culture is based on openness and free expression and love and sharing not on repression and fear and greed and control, and we want to make it available to everyone without exception—but that's what we'll do if we have to, because we will defend our people against aggression and we will destroy the domination of the West, and we'll do it by any means necessary even if it means all-out war. We'll do it because we have no choice, but we'll do it.

We have to build up our sense of peoplehood, our sense of nationhood, our sense of being something bigger than just ourselves and our close friends—we have to realize that we really *are* a people, that we must defend ourselves as a people, that we must move together as a people in all ways if we are going to have the world all of us, from the most militant radicals to the most spaced out hippies, talk about all the time. It's not going to come about by magic, it's not going to happen the way we wish it would happen, it's going to happen the way it's happening now, through struggle and bloodshed and war—not because we want it that way, but because that's what's being forced on us, and we either submit to the perverted demands of the Arville Garlands and Spiro P. Agnews and Henry Fords, we either submit to fascism and give up our culture and our dreams of new life for the planet, or else we defend ourselves and our people against it, we unite with each other and with our natural allies, our natural brothers and sisters in the black colony, in the other oppressed colonies within the mother country and throughout the world, we unite and fight to preserve ourselves and our culture, to win self-determination for ourselves and for all people (including the Euro-Amerikan masses), we unite in every way possible and do everything we have to do to eliminate the imperialist beast that is oppressing all of us. Otherwise we can join these martyred brothers and sisters in the paradise of the death culture, which is to say, the graveyard.

That's what it comes down to, like it or not, and we'd better wake up and get ourselves together before we wake up like Scott and Sandy did, with a gun at our heads. I referred to these dead brothers and sisters as martyrs, but before I stop I'd better clarify that at a little: if their deaths can inspire us and move us to recognize our common bond, our peoplehood—if their deaths can move us to that, and inspire us in our struggle for freedom and self-determination as a people, then they are truly our martyrs. Otherwise they're just dead, and the thing they lived for and as a vital part of dead too, dead and buried like the are now.

The last thing I'll say is this poem by Scott Kabran which is part of a book of his poems printed after his death by his father Stanley Kabran in cooperation with The Alternative Press. The book is called *Motionless/Lest It Fall.* the poem is about our people:

too many
a friend
i've had and lost
but now i think, now i know
amongst these beautiful
people is a bond
of friendship
a feeling of love
a lasting hope
an eternal bondage
of love.

VIETNAM PARKING LOT BLUES

MAY 1971

It doesn't seem to be any kind of exaggeration anymore to say that the overwhelming majority of the people in this country, and especially the people of the rainbow colony, are "against the war" in Indochina now—the tide of feeling about the war has certainly turned in the past six years since the time when only crazy beatniks and commies and militants and dope fiends were saying "Hell No We Won't Go" and protesting against the escalation of murder and terror by Lyndon Johnson and his goons in the Pentagon. Now the daily newspapers run editorials against the war which are farther out than the rants in the underground press, senators and congressmen/women speak out in terms which got Dr. Spock and some other people charged with criminal conspiracy a few years back, and even the mayor of Ann Arbor takes part in peace marches and rallies with no fear of the kind of repression which came down on people back in 1966 and '67 and '68 (remember that the protest in Chicago which touched off a massive police assault on thousands of unarmed people was primarily intended to be a demonstration against the war in Vietnam). The president himself says that he wants peace and that he is bringing peace by withdrawing a few thousand troops from month to month.

John Sinclair burning a draft card, photo by Leni Sinclair

What seemed really far out a few years ago is now commonplace—ideas which were regarded as either treasonous or completely insane are now embraced by whole legions of straight people and held up like banners in the wind, drawing more and more people to their beauty and brilliance. Honkoid newspapers which used to run every CIA, Pentagon, FBI and Narcotics Bureau press release as fact are now questioning almost every phony statement made by these goons, and instead of the whole power structure (in which the mass media plays an enormous role) being united against a tiny group of obviously communist-inspired outside agitators and dissenters we can now see that there are great splits and antagonisms within the power structure itself—Agnew attacking the media barons, senators attacking the FBI, CBS exposing the Pentagon, the Detroit Free Press calling for the legalization of marijuana, former attorney generals defending radicals and enemies of the state—all of which is certainly a step forward for the rest of us.

The point is that we have come a long way in the past few years, even though it may not seem like it all the time, and even though we've got an awfully long way to go before we get what we need. But the beginnings of a mass movement against the dinosaur state and the social system which supports it have been made, and now what we need to do is give that movement some creative direction so people can be able to identify the real enemy and move to defeat it. Millions of people are already turned off by the system and know that it's not being operated in their best interests, but they still don't know *how* and *why* it's so messed up. The newspapers and the more liberal politicians talk about what's wrong, but they never explain *why* because that would expose the whole Amerikan ruse and they're too much a part of it to contribute that directly to their own defeat.

Take the war—now, you hear all the time that it was a "mistake" to get involved in Vietnam in the first place, that it's a "mistake" that "we're" still involved in it, that "we" should just pull out now and bring all the troops home, stop all the bombing missions, and remove all U.S. forces, advisors, supply bases and every bit of the "Amerikan presence" from Vietnam. Right on, that's exactly what has to be done, and I'm sure no one would be happier to be able to do that than Richard M. Nixon, because it would sure make it a lot easier for him to get re-elected and all. But the point is that he *can't* just do that, not without causing an even greater economic crisis here in Babylon than he's already got on his hands, and he's being paid to stop such crises from developing. That's Nixon's job, to keep the economy under control so the big capitalists who own him can continue to make their profits and exercise their control over the people of the world the best way they see fit, and if a chump or two in the White House has to be sacrificed the big owners don't mind at all—they can always find another sucker to front for them, but if they lose control of the economic system they can't ever get *that* back.

That's why it's so stupid for people to always be talking about "Johnson's War" or "Nixon's War" like those individuals have a vested interest in being evil and making war against one or more of the communities of the earth—there's nothing they'd like better than to be able to play President without any risk to their own personal ambition, but being fronted off by the pigs (or I should say, the vampires) who control them is the price they have to pay for getting the chance to strut around on the stage of history for a while. And if we've learned *any-thing* about pig-time politics by now we should be able to see that this war probably more than any other is *not* to be attributed to any specific political figure—because the whole point is that it's a *corporate* war, waged in the interest of the big monopoly corporations, and it has almost nothing to do with who's president or even what party is in office. The war started with Truman's support of the French after World War II, continued through Eisenhower's regime, got bigger under Kennedy and then Johnson and still continues with Nixon in the presidency. Democrats, Republicans, Democrats and Republicans again—Amerikan "foreign policy" is constant, and its purpose is to make the world safe for imperialism and the cancerous spread of western civilization which follows its armies across the face of the earth.

Dig it—they talk about "fighting communism," and that's exactly what they're doing, that's exactly what this war is about no matter what anybody tries to tell you. Only it isn't communism as a political form they're fight-ing so much as communism as an *economic* system in which the *people* control the means of production and the big monopoly pigs are put out to pasture where they can't exploit anybody any more. And by extension it's communist *culture* which is also being attacked, because the collateral aim of imperialist foreign policy is to smear the planet with imperialist culture, that is, *western* culture, which is what we're struggling against here in Babylon ourselves.

The Amerikan ruling class wants to build highways all over Indochina, and it wants to fill those highways with billboards and millions of greedy automobiles and parking lots and killer death factories, Ed Sullivan television sets and electric toothbrushes, all the shit that we're trying to get away from our ownselves. The Purpose of the war in Vietnam is to turn our Vietnamese brothers and sisters into plastic replicas of our parents, to sell them hamburgers and suits and ties and life insurance, to turn them into mindless consumers who can be manipulated by the same corporations and brainwashing machines and secret police that are pushing *us* around right now.

And while the war's going on these same corporations are taking tons of money by manufacturing bombs and airplanes and other weaponry, the incredible technology of death and destruction which keeps the workers in line in the factories of Babylon and the profits pouring into the banks and holding companies of the super-rich vampires of monopoly capitalism

Brother Jay C. Crawford before an MC5 concert, photo by Leni Sinclair

Liberals and other wimps are always talking about all the money that's being "wasted" on the war, but don't let them fool you—that money isn't being wasted at all, it's going straight into the pockets of the owners of the big corporations, General Motors and General Dynamics, Lockheed and Boeing, North Amerikan Rockwell and ITT, all the vampire institutions of Amerikan imperialism which sell death in one form or another for a living—CBS and RCA, TransAmerika and the Bank of Amerika, the same corporations which exploit the rainbow colony and the broad masses of the Babylonian people by ripping off our natural wealth, adulterating it and selling it back to us, are also ripping off the other oppressed peoples of the world too, and killing them in cold blood if they won't stand still for the rip-off.

So it's right on to demand that the vampires end the war in Vietnam, because that's got to happen, but at the same time we've got to get hip to the real reasons for the war and why rats and snakes in Washington drag it out so far even though the people are increasingly opposed to their tricks—it's *gotta* be that way because their whole system depends on it, their economy is based on war, and the octopus won't stop breeding death until we cut its head off once and for all—*for all*, meaning all the people in the world. If they pull out of Vietnam they'll just send all those troops and bombs and shit somewhere else, to kick some other peoples back in line, and they won't stop until we stop them right here in the belly of the beast itself. While our brothers and sisters around the world are trying to free themselves from the tentacles of the octopus, they can't really be free—and *we* can't really be free either—until we ourselves take off the monster's head. That's the *only* way to "end the war," and it's up to us to do it. All Power to the People! Life to the Life Culture/Death to the Death Culture! Revolution Is the Way to Life!!

IT JUST CAN'T BE

Janis
with tracks in her arms
dead
2 weeks before
Jimi too
the same way
before that Al "Blind Owl"
Wilson and the Canned Heat is no more
and it was a "trade secret" that Brian Jones was a
junkie
but there ain't no secrets no
more with the hip conversation turning to "whose
next?"
and Ginger Baker in serious condition in a London hospital
will he
make it?
no it ain't no secret no more the
Plague ain't no secret it's all
over now with suburbia
full of THC and smack and downers and
speed
and it ain't no secret at the Eastown
where it's the
hip thing to do
no it
ain't no secret either that we
loved you Janis we only
wished that you had loved
life more
because we
all need you
all

OPERATION JONES

MAY 1971

When I was still on the streets, up to July of 1969, Jones still hadn't gotten very far into the bloodstream of our community—there was a lot of speed around, and a lot of obnoxious speedfreaks running around ripping people off and babbling hours on end, but then it wasn't really "a lot" in terms of everybody else who was on the scene. I mean it was more or less of a minor thing that I didn't worry about very much, because it just didn't seem to me that it could spread very far. And as far as smack was concerned, there just wasn't any—of course there was as much as there'd ever been, but that was never very much at all, and the people who were shooting scag were almost universally despised as creeps and fools who were to be avoided at all costs.

After I got locked up I started hearing about the plague which seemed to be spreading all across the rainbow colony, and particularly in Ann Arbor where my letters came from. I was up in Marquette and it just didn't seem very real to me at the time—I thought my people were exaggerating, and it was a few months before I even discussed it with them when they could come to see roe. They said it was like an epidemic, a raging sickness which was affecting more people every day, and they were desperate to do something about it, but they didn't really know how to deal with it because they couldn't really understand why people were getting into such a bogus trip.

So I thought about it for a long time, and then I got sent back down here to Jackson where I talked with a lot of brothers who had been smack freaks on the street, and finally I was shipped down to the Wayne County Jail where I spent 3-1/2 months on a ward in which almost every prisoner had been using jones before they got locked up. I don't know how together my ideas on it might be because I can't be out there to check things out for Myself, but let me try to run a few things down and you tell me if I'm right or wrong, ok?

I haven't ever had any trouble understanding *why* people start using scag—I've watched enough people squeeze that garbage into their veins to know what effect it has, and I don't really blame people for wanting to get that way, especially as bogue as things get out there sometimes. What got me was why so *many* people were doing it, and particularly the kind of people who were smoking weed and dropping acid and really getting turned on to what was happening all around them. Jones had always been an escape for people who were hopelessly oppressed, who didn't have anything to *do* and no hope of *ever* being able to get anything together for themselves—that's why it was so weird to hear about so many *kids* shooting dope, because there was so much happening and so many things to do that it just didn't make any sense for scag to be so popular, right?

Then I started putting this thing together with a lot of other things I'd been thinking about, and it all started to make a lot more sense. The fact is that the epidemic of heroin addiction has spread in direct proportion to the increased oppression of young people here in Babylon, that heroin has been used as a weapon of imperialism here in the rainbow colony just as it has been used in the black colony and among colonized peoples throughout the history of western imperialism (check out the Opium Wars in China in the 19th Century—the British and to a lesser extent the Amerikan imperialists *imported* opium into China and used it to enslave and exploit the masses of the Chinese people for years; the Opium Wars were incipient national liberation struggles fought in support of the demand that opium be outlawed from China).

The rising addiction rate in the rainbow colony paralleled the increasing political and cultural repression of young people—it went along with the gradual de-energizing of rock & roll music, the increasing monopolization of our culture by the rock & roll imperialists of the mother country music industry, the disappearance of the dance/concert and the local rock & roll clubs in favor of big sit-down concerts and mammoth so-called "pop festivals," the steady rise of marijuana persecution, campus repression, and general police harassment directed against freeks and all kinds of young people all over Babylon.

The grimmer things got on the street, the more kids started shooting scag and running up big dope habits. Instead of there being all kinds of things for freeks to do, it got so that people were afraid to go out in the streets or to a dance (if there *were* any) or to the park (if the police hadn't shut them down) or even to a pop festival, because the pigs were everywhere and they were getting more and more vicious by the day. Besides that, the alternatives they had been promised for so long by people like me weren't to be had, and instead of things getting better everything was just getting worse, with no relief in sight. The "political" freaks who were supposed to get things going and create alternatives like People's Ballrooms and Defense Committees and everything else we talked about were still just running around babbling about "revolution" and "off the pig" and all kinds of useless talk like that instead of building an alternative social order, so the people on the streets who we had expected to join us got turned off to everything we were saying and got so they didn't want to *hear* it any more. And I don't blame them one bit—that part of it was our fault, and will continue to be our fault until we start *doing* some of the things we've been talking about for so long.

Even when we *did* try to "do something about the plague" we did the wrong thing, saying that dope addicts were the enemies of the people and threatening to turn them in to the police, which was just stupid to begin with. But we were desperate and couldn't think of anything else, having forgotten that the *only* solution to problems like this is to create positive alternatives and work with the people to put them into practice. We weren't capable of doing that so we turned on the most oppressed people in our community and called them names, which was a really dumb thing to do. I think we know better by now, but you'll be able to tell by watching what we do in the future, ok?

Anyway, all of this was happening, and to top it off the Nixon administration, working closely with the CIA and the big vampire interests it fronts for, had engineered and was carrying out a long-range program designed to cut off the marijuana supply to the rainbow colony, *adult*erate the psychedelic sacraments, and get millions of kids strung out on scag so they wouldn't pose any kind of threat to the established order. Actually I shouldn't say the Nixon administration, because this plan originated under the Johnson regime and only became obvious after Nixon and his goons stepped into office. So what I should say is that it is an imperialist plan, a program designed by the *real* Amerikan government (i.e. the CIA and its backers) which uses it in whatever colony it can according to the dictates of imperialist "foreign policy."

For example, the same plan was being executed at the same time in the black colony of Babylon, except it was more extensive and more intensive at the same time because things looked even worse for the forces of imperialism in the black colony than in the youth colony, especially after the wave of uprisings in the summer of 1967. With the revolutionary spirit rising in the black ghettos and hundreds of thousands of young white kids dropping out of the Amerikan madness in the suburbs and cities of Babylon, blowing their minds (and all their illusions about the possibility of living within the confines of the Amerikan dream) on LSD and looking to black people for a new way to live, the octopus power structure got panicky and started scheming. Either one of these new problems of a dying colonialism would've been enough, but it was their intersection during the Summer of Love/Summer of Rebellion that struck the cold hearts of the vampires of Babylon with fear. Niggers *and* diggers just weren't staying in their place anymore, and they had to be stopped by any means necessary.

So the government launched a domestic chemical warfare campaign designed to suck the life out of the black colony and the heart out of the emerging rainbow colony and put those upstarts back where they belonged, nodding out in the corners and ripping each other off to feed their habits—*anywhere* but in the streets, fighting and loving together, getting high and exploding together, striking out at the instruments of colonialism which were the omnipresent racist thug police in the black colony, and the plastic brainwash conditioning used on kids—the brain police—which kept young rainbow natives from getting out of hand. Operation Jones was just one phase of Operation Total Control, but it was an important one. Vampire fangs in the necks of the people!

In the earlier part of 1967 there was a whole lot of righteous weed and even more righteous acid floating around the rainbow colony working its magic on thousands of virgin minds, opening them up to new vistas of post-western possibility and giving them a whole new direction in life. Acid cut through the plastic conditioning within which kids' mental/spiritual/physical energy

had been imprisoned and broke that energy free to search out new ways of living with other people in the universe here on earth. LSD was the irreplaceable catalyst in the post-western experiment: it was the spiritual equivalent of the atom bomb, and it blasted a hole in industrial consciousness big enough for millions of young mutants to run through into the future, laughing and dancing and flashing on visions of a whole new world which would be big enough for *everybody* to live together without exploitation and greed and fear.

Well, it was bad enough when a few crazies were taking the stuff in their filthy communes and enclaves, but by the spring of 1967 rock & roll bands were singing about it on the radio and the suburbs and high schools were full of maniacs tripping around the halls and barely waiting to get out of school for the summer so they could go to San Francisco and see what this new life was all about. And by the time the first wave of psychedelic Pilgrims hit the Haight the vampires in New York and Washington were already plotting their evil programs and setting up the apparatus which would eventually put a stop to this madness—or so they promised one another, sweat pouring off their immaculate brows, as they mapped out their final solution to the Problem of freedom: OPERATION JONES, or, crystallized death in a dropper.

Meanwhile, in the black colony of Babylon the suppressed spirit of liberation which had barely been contained since Watts had exploded against the sky two summers before was rising high in the blood of the black masses, and by the time San Francisco was reaping its first harvest of wandering flower children the Black Spirit had burst into life in Newark, then Detroit, Cleveland city after city feeling the spontaneous destructive power of centuries of repressed feeling blasted free at last into the streets of capitalism, screaming to be heard and felt finally and for all time. The very foundations of imperialism were shaken by this blast, and its whole edifice shuddered and trembled caught in the hurricane of change. Its armed forces, sent in to put out the raging flames of black liberation, ripped away the mask of colonialism once and for all, and the vampire strategists were hard pressed to manufacture a new plan for keeping the black masses in their place. Naked military suppression was just too blatant and too destructive of the necessary conditions for commerce, but nothing else seemed to work and things were looking exceedingly grim for the terrified octopus.

OPERATION JONES! someone screamed, that'll do it! We've already experimented with it among those savages, and it's the best thing since television for keeping people down. All we have to do is INCREASE THE DOSAGE, make the stuff stronger and easier to get, and we'll have those niggers eating out of our hand. Shoot enough schmeck into them and they won't even *think* of burning and looting—instead of ripping off our stores and businesses they'll rip each other off, and if they get any stores it'll be the little ones they'll put out of business, and we've been trying to do that ourselves for a long time anyway. What a solution! It'll deaden their spirit and keep them turned against each other at the same time, and it'll start a wave of crime in the streets that we can use to build up our police forces so we can have all those militants under control if they ever try to stir up the people like that again. Brilliant!

So the program got under way— each situation required slightly different tactics, but the strategy was the same: get 'em hooked on heroin, and we'll have 'em where we want 'em. The black colony was flooded with a new, much stronger grade of junk called "P" (for "pure" heroin) and tons of reds and yellows to take care of the ones who didn't use a needle yet. In the rainbow colony where needles were almost unheard of they used a different tactic: the ADULTeration of LSD under the 3-year plan, easing speed onto the scene and then replacing it with smack and elephant tranquilizers in order to deaden everyone out.

You think this is far out? Just check it out for a minute: before the Summer of Love there was hardly any speed around at all, and the kids who were just starting to smoke weed and drop acid had never even heard of it for the most part. The acid was truly dynamite, and it was all over the place, so the first step was to start cutting the LSD with amphetamine and market it as some kind of powerful new trip: STP! Wow, man, STP! You trip for three whole days! FAR out! And within a couple weeks STP was the hottest thing on the psychedelic market—it debuted in San Francisco and spread back across the country like white lightning, which was the next phase after STP. All these were acid or synthetic mescaline mixed with amphetamine, and the speed gradually replaced the acid almost entirely. By 1968 just about every hit of acid on the set was 80 or 90% speed with just a tinge of LSD to make it seem weird and scary enough to pass as a psychedelic. It got so there were thousands of freeks dropping "acid" every day who had never really *had* any genuine LSD but thought that's what they were getting—they became habituated to speed without even knowing they were taking it.

The next step was to slide a few tons of amphetamine crystal onto the scene, and to get people *shooting* it so they could get a *real* flash. Kids who had been dropping a lot of adulterated acid could really dig this new trip—pure speed—because it was like the "acid" they had been taking only without the "scary" side-effects. Crystal got to be real popular, and more and more people started shooting it to get the flash all the super-hip creeps were talking about. Once they started running speed it was just a hot minute until smack creeped onto the scene, and it got to be popular at first as an antidote for the jangley after effects of speed runs—you could shoot the scag with the same works you used for speed, and it would really cool you out. And besides, everybody thought they could use it without it using them—"yeah, only fools get addicted ... me, I'll just run some of this jones once in awhile and won't get strung out like them nasty junkies." Sure. Only it just didn't seem to work that way.

Then the government surfaced its "Operation Intercept" program, which was actually just a minor phase of the secret campaign that'd been carried out since 1967. "Operation Intercept" was meant to cut off the marijuana supply from Mexico and drive the price of weed up so high that kids just couldn't afford it, and so it'd be cheaper and easier just to cop some smack. As weed got scarcer and scarcer the smack supply got bigger and bigger—it was killer hard to cop some reefer, but jones was everywhere, and "everybody's doin' it, man" led a whole lot of kids into Nod-Out Corners. Bogus rock & roll stars added to the mystique about smack too—it wasn't enough that they were shooting dope themselves, but their example allowed them to be used by the vampires to get thousands of kids strung out on death drugs so they could be more easily controlled. Pretty soon smack was the biggest thing around, and "hip" began to mean what it had meant back in 1945—super-cool, cold as ice, and twice as deadly.

Isn't it *perfect* the way heroin works to destroy people and their sense of *community?* Isn't it even more perfect than television or schools or factories or prisons in separating people from each other and keeping them locked up in their own little egos? William Burroughs described heroin as "a shot of cooked-down image," and that goes right back to the root of the word heroin, which comes from "hero," you dig? It gives everybody the chance to feel like

250

a "hero" or a star, to feel as real as Paul McCartney or James Taylor without having to do anything more than shoot some powder into your arm, like buying a ticket to a pop concert and even the price is the same. Burroughs also said that junk is the "perfect commodity"—it degrades the consumer and makes him or her utterly dependent on the product—and there's no better way to put it than that. It's even better than television, because it puts you out and keeps you out, and you can't even change the channel or shut the set off without going through a whole lot of physical agony.

That's what it's all about, keeping people strung out on commodities, keeping their minds on getting the next do —whether it's a shot of dope or a newer and bigger car—and never on anything more than that. Cars and things are ok as products, but heroin is the ultimate commodity of all time, and the ironic thing is that the kids who called themselves getting away from the slavery their parents were trapped in have been turned into even bigger slaves, with even less to show for it than the most brainwashed honky. Jones has simply perverted everything we started out to do, and if we're ever gonna get back to where we were going when we started out we're gonna have to eliminate this poison from our communities. Jones is just cooked-down imperialism, and if we want to be free we have to fight back against this vicious genocidal weapon with everything we've got. Scag ain't dope/it's death! Death to the Death Drugs! Life to the Life Culture! Rainbow Power!!

RAINBOW POWER!

AUGUST 1971

I want to take this space in my column this time to thank everybody who's been working on the *Free John Now!* campaign, all the people in the community who have supported it with their energies and their money and their beautiful selves, all the people who signed the ad in the *Detroit Free Press* or sent postcards and letters to the governor, all the people who've gone to the benefits and helped us raise the money we need to carry on our struggle against the anti-marijuana laws, and especially all the dynamite people's bands who have contributed their time and their powerful music over the past two or three months so we could have these benefits—there isn't anything I can possibly say that could express the gratitude I feel. I'm overwhelmed, that's all, and I just hope this thing works so I can be with you all again and tell you how I feel about it in person.

Genie, Skip and Sunny

I want to thank all the people who helped on the radio special, especially Bud Spangler and Jerry Lubin and Jim Dulzo, and the radio stations that played it for people to hear—WABX, WRIF, and WDET in Detroit, and WNRZ in Ann Arbor. All of this stuff is really important, and we have to understand that it goes far beyond being an individual thing—I'm not in here as an individual "criminal" in the first place, I think everybody knows that already, and if I *am* cut loose it won't be because the so-called "legal" system wants to rehabilitate itself by finally following its own laws. It'll be because the people have shown that they're hip to the separation/isolation ruse and refuse to let the state divide us and break us down into isolated individuals like it has to do if it wants to keep us in our place. That's what it's all about, and I'm just totally wiped out behind this campaign because it represents a real victory over the rock & roll imperialists and their running dogs in the courts and legislatures of Babylon.

See, even if I have to stay here in this penitentiary for a while longer, that is, even if the Supreme Court continues to violate the obvious will of the people and the terms of its own sacred "laws," we've still handed these creeps a tremendous defeat, we've still won a killer victory in our struggle for self-determination and freedom *as a people,* because instead of being divided and separated and reduced to pitiful little individuals interested only in our own security so we can be isolated and picked off one at a time as the rulers see fit, we're more together now, and stronger, and more unified than ever before, and we've really begun to learn just how much power we have when we all move together and work with each other to deal with our own needs.

It's the benefits which are the most exciting indication of how much progress we're making, though, because it's precisely in the rock & roll bizness that the imperialists have been exerting the strongest pressure on our new communality, in a desperate attempt to keep us from building up any real self-determination power. Our bands are the strongest economic force in the rainbow colony, they represent our national wealth as well as our national spirit, and as long as the mother-country rock & roll imperialists can control the destinies of our bands they can control our national destiny as well. They use our bands against us most of the time, turning them and their music into commodities and the people into consumers, and they use the decrepit Hollywood s*t*a*r system to keep the bands separated from the people, and the people—who would otherwise come together in the music as natural brothers and sisters—separated from each other. The dual force of the music is thus doubly perverted—its potential as a powerful unifying factor (its political/spiritual force) is undermined, and its potential as the basis of our national economic development is almost completely destroyed.

But these benefits turn all that around—the bands return their music to the community and bring the people together, and they put their economic power directly in the service of the community, making it possible for us to begin to raise the sums of money we need to defend ourselves and to

Next page: Free John Sinclair concert, photo by David Fenton

start moving on our own to create the alternative institutions we need for our communal growth. The bands are *our own people* first of all, they've been ripped off from us and used against us in the past and they'll continue to be used against us until our community grows strong enough to be able to support them ourselves, but with the bands' killer participation in these benefits we've made a big step forward, a *huge* step forward, which will have an increasingly greater effect on our immediate future as a people. Because we've begun to reclaim our national resources from the tentacles of the octopus, we've really started *bringin it all back home,* we're laying the foundation right now for a whole new communalist social order, and the closer the bands get with the people the faster we can grow into this beautiful thing we've all dreamed about so long.

Let me try to go into this a little bit deeper before I move on: as Frank Bach pointed out so beautifully in his Rock & Roll Dope column last issue, there is a very basic contradiction between our rainbow culture and the imperialist culture which envelopes us—our culture is about *unity,* while imperialist culture is about *separation,* and the only way the imperialist system can survive here in Babylon is by keeping us separated from each other. Once we start getting *together* with all the people who share a common interest in self-determination and freedom, starting with all our own people in the rainbow colony and eventually extending to all the people in the world who are oppressed by the imperialist system, we begin to develop the economic and political power which will enable us to determine our own destinies and put an end to the imperialists' control over our lives. If we live as individuals or as fragmented little groups, each concerned only with its own immediate interests, we don't have any power at all, and the imperialist vampires and the snakes, rats and pigs who work with them can manipulate us at will. So their strategy at all times and on all levels is to keep us apart by any means necessary—even if it means putting some of us in cages like they keep me—and they've been doing a pretty good job of it ever since they began to realize that we really *were* getting it together.

This is particularly true in the rock & roll sector, because they realize how great a part the music plays in our lives and how powerful we would be if we could control all the aspects of our national music scene. They realize that the music is truly dangerous when it is an integral part of our communal life, when the musicians work for the people instead of for the mother-country middle-men, when the music comes directly out of the People and goes directly back to the people without anybody standing in between the bands and the people to rip off the Profits and carry them out of our community altogether. That's why they hate benefits and free concerts so much, because those forms show the people *and* the bands that the rock & roll imperialists are *not necessary,* and because benefits in particular enable the people to begin to amass enough capital to create institutions of their own which will put the outside exploiters right out of business.

They can see that if we were totally united with our bands—to the extent that *all* our musicians would play as many benefits for people's causes as the Up does, for example, we would be able to raise money for every project we decide to undertake—we could buy land and buildings, we could build recording studios and pressing plants and huge printing operations so we could produce ail our own records, we could set up distribution networks and booking agencies and every thing else we need in order to gain complete control of our own culture, and there wouldn't be any more room for the rock & roll imperialists *at all.*

And if we had that kind of control over our music, that is, if we controlled every aspect of the music production business, we could develop the music and the whole culture which is based on the music along its highest and purest lines, so that rock & roll would be able to realize its full potential as a revolutionary form. We could do away completely with sit-down concerts which sap the people's energy and reduce them to consumers instead of raising their energy level and making them full participants in the process of creation. We could do away with the ridiculous prices which are charged for these concerts and for the records we live on—the bands wouldn't charge such exorbitant fees because the antagonism between the productive forces (the musicians) and the "owners" would disappear and the whole profit factor would be eliminated. The musicians wouldn't feel the need to "get rich" because they would be one with their people and would feel good living the way the rest of us live—

their needs would be taken care of, they would be full functioning members of their communities, and they would be free to play as much music for their people as they possibly could.

For the time being our bands will have to continue to work within the imperialist music industry in order to survive, because we can't provide for their needs yet by any means, but at the same time the bands can contribute their time, energy and genius to the rainbow self-determination movement, like they've been doing here in Ann Arbor and Detroit, to help us create the alternative institutions which will eventually bring about the kind of situation we all need in order to survive and grow. Once our bands realize, as so many of them are starting to realize now, that their interests are identical with the people's interests and not with those of the rock & roll imperialists, they'll find a lot more time to play benefits and free concerts whenever they don't have paying gigs, and they'll be able to contribute a lot more to the growth of our new society. Their music will get a lot purer, the people will get a lot farther out, our community will grow stronger and stronger, and all of us will be a lot better off. The only people who can possibly suffer from it are the vampires of Babylon, and they'll only get what they deserve.

None of this is going to happen overnight, and it might seem a bit ridiculous for me to be so excited about five or six successful benefits for my own Freedom Fund, where the money doesn't even go back into the community at all, but the point is, people, that

HELP END MARIJUANA PROHIBITION
FREE JOHN SINCLAIR
SAT JAN 24
SUN JAN 25
GRANDE BALLROOM
GRAND RIVER AT BEVERLY
GRANDE BALLROOM
EASTOWN BALLROOM
HARPER AND VAN DYKE
SRC - MC5
UP - STOOGES
SCORPION
COMMANDER CODY
AMBOY DUKES
BOB SEGER SYSTEM - MITCH RYDER AND THE DETROIT WHEELS
VIRGIN DAWN - WILSON MOWER PURSUIT - RATIONALS - JAGGED EDGE
RICHMOND - ALL THE LONELY PEOPLE - SKY - BROWNSVILLE STATION
FLOATING CIRCUS - SUNDAY FUNNIES - SHAKY JAKE - BLUES TRAIN - 3RD POWER
speakers ABBIE HOFFMAN - KEN COCKRELL - SKIP TAUBE - ED SANDERS
COALITION TO
STP
SERVE THE PEOPLE

Left: David Sinclair, photo by Charles Auringer; right: Ed Sanders, photo by David Fenton

we've made a real breakthrough with these dances, we've started to bring our musicians back with our people and the people back together with each other in the music, and we've shown each other what we can do if we all work together like this. And all of this has happened after almost two years of the total douce, at a time when the established capitalist-run rock & roll institutions are collapsing all over the place, in the face of a general atmosphere of pessimism and frustration on the part of almost everybody in the whole community, and it just shows how much potential power we have even when things look worse than they've ever looked for us. That's why it's so beautiful to me, because it proves that all that pessimism is *wrong* and it teaches us that we really *can* get what

we need for ourselves if we use our own resources and put all our faith in the people. That's what it's all about finally—All Power to the People! Long Live Rock & Roll! Rainbow Power!!

Special thanks to the people's bands of Ann Arbor and Detroit: the Up, the Brat, Detroit with brother Mitch Ryder, Guardian Angel, Carnal Kitchen, Bob Seger, Teegarden & Van Winkle, Commander Cody & His Lost Planet Airmen, SRC (Blue Scepter), Amboy Dukes, MC5, Frut, Harvey Khek, Assemblage, Third Power, Salvage, Rumor, Iron Horse Exchange, Bad Luck & Trouble, the Bad Foot Blues Band, Pride of Women, Barbara Holliday, and all the other bands and musicians who have played in the benefit/free concert series this summer. Self-Determination Music!

John Sinclair with mother and daughter after release, photo by Andrew Sachs

FREE AT LAST!

hew! It sure is *nice* out here! It's such a shock though, that it's gonna take me a few weeks even to get *used* to it, right? I'm just so *blasted* right now that I can't get very much together to say to you in this space, but there's no way I would let this issue go by without saying *something* to let you know how great it is to see all of *you* again out here on the streets—whew! And to know that it's *you* who got me out of that place—you and nobody else!

Before I go any further I want to say thank you and power to ya everybody who's supported the Free John campaign for the past five years, everybody who's contributed in any way to this tremendous victory for all of us—because it *is* a people's victory, it's no kind of individual thing now and it never *has* been, ever since the bust came down five years ago it's always been about the dinosaurs trying to stomp the rest of us out any way they can, and it's been about them trying to keep us separated from each other, isolated, powerless and alone, so we can't do anything together to solve our collective problems, right? Like getting the marijuana laws changed was a collective problem, and we all dealt with it in a collective fashion, and when the solution, or part of the solution anyway, when the change came down it affected all of us who smoke weed, or it will affect us as soon as the new marijuana bill goes into effect. That was something we accomplished collectively, something we worked out together, just like the Free John problem was something we worked out together and solved together, and which affects all of us finally, not just me.

John Sinclair, Peter Andrews and David Sinclair, photo by David Fenton

Because what we did was to show the dinosaurs that we *can't* be separated off and apart from each other, that we really *are* a whole thing which cannot be broken, that we can come together and move together to force changes where the control addicts think they've got us safely in our places, right? I mean, it's so killer, people, we really DID IT! WHEW! I still can't believe it, like I guess I still expect a guard to come up and say "the visit's over" or something, and take me back to my cell, you know? But if they come with that again, and we have to be looking for them to be trying all kinds of ridiculous shit like that at any time, if they come with that shit again then we'll just have to deal

with it like we dealt with it this time, and it won't take no two and a half years either!

I'm sorry I'm just babbling so much, but I'm still so excited to be home and back on the streets that I can't even think straight yet, you know? Everything looks so *beautiful* out here—freeks are *everywhere!* I've never seen so many freeks before in my *life!* And it keeps turning me around because everything I've been able to read and everything I've heard from other people for so long is that the movement is dead, people are messed up and apathetic, everybody's downed out, all kinds of negativistic shit like that, and it's just not *true!* It's probably a lot different for people who've been on the street all this time going through all the changes that have come down in 1970 and 1971, but for me it's like coming out into a whole different world from the one I left in 1969, a world where all the stuff we were talking about and trying to bring about has all come true and now there are thousands and thousands of brothers and sisters sitting around waiting for something to happen like we used to say it would, ready to support any kind of programs and projects that are brought forth to deal with the people's needs. There's so many of us that we can do goddamn near anything we set out to do now, and it's really blowing my mind!

It's like when I was on the street before, and especially in 1968 and the first part of 1969, all we were doing was running around trying to turn people on to being freeks and smoking weed and digging high-energy jams and growing their hair long and eating good food and everything else everybody's doing now, you dig? We had to have a mass movement of freeks in order to support self-determination programs and community control programs for the people, and before we could really get the programs together we had to try to help prepare people to relate to these programs so the programs would *work* when we got them together. I don't know if that makes any sense to you, but what I'm trying to say is that we can concentrate on creating and building up the *programs* themselves now, because any kind of programs which will serve the people will be successful now, because there's

so many people to participate in them and make them real!

Everything happens step by step, it's a process, sometimes we have to have a few steps back in order to go forward again, but the point is that we're always moving *forward,* we're steadily advancing, and we have to see that we're really a whole lot more powerful than we are made to think we are. You know what I mean? To me, we're dealing from a position of strength right now, we're not weak at all, we've begun to tap our collective potential and we're just beginning to see how well it *works* when we all move together along the lines of self-reliance and self-determination to get what we need. The dinosaurs don't want us to realize how strong we are, or how together we are, and they go to great extremes to keep us from finding that out—like what is more extreme than a segregation cell in the penitentiary, right? where you're all by yourself, no one to talk to, no freeks around at all, nothing but desperation and gloom day after day after day, they want you to think you're all alone, everyone has deserted you, they want to break you down and make you give up on everything you dreamed about doing, right? That's what the penitentiary's all about, breaking people down into individual units that can easily be manipulated and controlled, and it's really the same thing out here on the street when you get down to it, you dig? Breaking people down, separating us from each other, getting us downed out and discouraged and thinking we're just absolutely powerless when in reality

Judge Columbo with Gary Grimshaw's original crop marks

we're the strongest thing on the planet, we're a powerful rising young force in the world, our culture and our spirit are spreading higher and farther every day, we've accomplished a lot already and we're just *starting* to move really—I mean, wait'll we get all this shit *together,* right? Wait'll *all* of us start getting together *all the time* and start organizing and utilizing our tremendous energy and genius and brilliance! Whew! *That's* what *I'm* talking about, and if you all think it's weird then just stick around and see what happens, because we're gonna *do it* this time!

I won't babble on any longer today, but I'll try to get myself together so in the next issue of the paper we can tell you about our immediate plans and the programs we want to get going, ok? Right now I just want to say THANK YOU again, to everybody who's helped get me out and everybody I've seen on the street in the past week since I've been home—whew! That's all I can say on paper, but we'll be talking about it sooner than you think. And I want to say, right here, THANK YOU to everybody who Participated in the planning, organizing and production of all the Free John events, starting with the people who have pushed everything from their position on the Committee to Free JS: Representative Jackie Vaughn III, Zoltan Ferenczy, Dr. Paul Lowinger, Allen Ginsberg, sister Jane Fonda, Attorney Bill Kunstler, sister Nadine Brown (thank you sister!), brother Mitch Ryder (whew!), brother Peter Werbe and comrade Buck Davis of the National Lawyers Guild—and Leni and David and the party workers who have given *everything they had* to bring this about, and Chairman Bobby Seale, and John and Yoko, and comrade Jerry Rubin, and Peter Andrews and all the people who work with him, Denny Hayes, Phil Ochs, Ed Sanders, brother Archie Shepp and brother Roswell Rudd, CHARLES MOORE and the CJQ and Danny Spencer and Bud Spangler and Ron Brooks and Kenny Cox, the Commander and his boys, Billy C, Billy Kerchen, dynamite Bob Seger, Skip & Dave, Stevie Wonder the genius surprise of all time, David Peel and the lower east side, Jim Fouratt, Fr. Groppi, sister Jonnie Lee Tillman, brother Dave Dellinger, Rennie (Rennie! thank you!), sister Marge Tobankin, everybody everybody and especially righteous Rudnick and sister Anne LaVasseur and the Jamaican Flash Brother Jesse Crawford, my mother Elsie, and Jerry Wexler and Danny Fields and Steve Roday and and and and and ...

THANK YOU! SEE YOU ALL ON THE STREETS! ALL POWER TO THE PEOPLE!
　　　　—John Sinclair, Chairman, RPP

LONG LIVE THE BLACK PANTHER PARTY

JUNE 1, 1971

There seems to be a lot of confusion in the rainbow colony about the recent turmoil within the ranks of the Black Panther Party, and also about the position of the Rainbow People's Party *vis a vis* that situation. We want to make it clear that the Rainbow People's Party stands in solidarity with the Central Committee of the Black Panther Party, its Chairman Bobby Seale, its Minister of Defense Huey P. Newton, and all dedicated members and cadres of the BPP. We recognize that there is only one Black Panther Party—the organization founded in October 1966 by Huey P. Newton and Bobby Seale—and that Eldridge Cleaver, Kathleen Cleaver, Michael Cetawayo Tabor, Connie Mathews Tabor, Richard Dharuba Moore, and other former party members have defected from the ranks of the Black Panther Party to pursue their own interests.

We also want to make it clear that the Rainbow People's Party, in adopting our new name and structure, has not abandoned or repudiated the Black Panther Party, which inspired us to organize ourselves in 1968 as the White Panther Party. To the contrary, we feel that with our new name and our new organizational structure we are even better equipped to support and to further the goals of the Black Panther Party, and of the black liberation struggle as a whole, because we will be better equipped to serve the people of the rainbow colony and to help organize our people into a powerful united force against fascism and for the liberation of *all* peoples.

We realize that slogans, rhetoric, and simple statements of support will not bring about the liberation of the people; that the forces of fascism and imperialism which oppress *all* non-western struggling peoples can only be defeated through a protracted struggle waged on all fronts by a united liberation front of all the oppressed peoples, including the people of the rainbow colony; and that the best way we in the rainbow colony can contribute to the liberation of our natural brothers and sisters in the black colony—and all oppressed peoples—is by organizing ourselves in our own communities and moving in an organized fashion against our common oppressor, dealing with our own survival needs through community self-determination programs and constructing an alternative social order within the shell of the old.

We see the recent turmoil in the Black Panther Party, which culminated in the defection of Eldridge Cleaver and his followers, as a result of the basic contradiction between the two lines of "protracted struggle" and "eve-of-the-revolutionism" which has also developed to a decisive point within the rainbow colony and within the mother-country revolutionary movement as well. In the Black Panther Party the "eve-of-the-revolution" view was held by Eldridge Cleaver and his followers, who believe that the immediate task of revolutionaries in this country now is to go out into the streets and begin the armed struggle against the oppressor, even though the masses of the people are not yet ready to participate in or even to support such an advanced form of struggle. They believe that any-

one who is not ready to join the armed struggle now is counter-revolutionary and should be treated as the enemy.

The exponents of "protracted struggle," on the other hand, believe that revolutions are made by the broad masses of the people moving together in an organized fashion over a long period of time to determine their own destinies; that the forms of struggle at a certain time and in a certain place are determined by the level of consciousness and support of the people; and that to move to begin an armed struggle against the concentrated military might of the Amerikan Empire without the support and participation of the broad masses of the people is not only suicidal but is also against the best interests of the people.

Since this contradiction emerged within the Black Panther Party it has been resolved by the defection of Eldridge Cleaver and his followers on the one hand, and by the definitive stand in favor of protracted struggle and "survival pending revolution" taken by Huey P. Newton and the Central Committee of the BPP on the other. We are sorry that this contradiction had to be resolved in such a public and antagonistic fashion, but we feel that it was a good thing and not a bad thing that it was brought out into the open and resolved.

We mentioned that we were originally inspired to form our party by the example of the Black Panther Party; we have learned almost everything we know about political struggle and political organization from the BPP. The most important lesson we learned was that revolutions are not spontaneous upheavals generated by simple anger and oppression, that in order for there to be revolution there must be an organized, disciplined, class-conscious revolutionary party which works closely with the people to organize the mass struggle and to inform it with a revolutionary content. This was a difficult lesson for us to assimilate because our people—the people of the rainbow colony—have a general, widespread distaste for organizational forms of all kinds and an overwhelming aversion to any kind of discipline and structure, even when they can see that their needs cannot be met otherwise.

When we first started relating to the Black Panther Party, in 1968, we were exponents of the "eve-of-the-revolution" point of view, and we saw no need to organize ourselves and our people in other than spontaneous, emotionally-derived forms. But through observing and absorbing the example of the Black Panther Party and following the course of political study it laid out for us, we learned to organize ourselves along democratic-centralist lines, to give our community service programs an explicit revolutionary content, and to practice the method of criticism-self-criticism which has been the moving force in the development of our party to its new level of existence.

We see the recent changes in our party as paralleling those in the Black Panther Party, and we feel that we can now move forward in solidarity with the Black Panther Party and all revolutionary organizations which are making the protracted struggle against the Amerikan Empire and its deathly imperialist culture. We feel that we can best support the struggle of black people, led by the Black Panther Party and other black liberation groups, as well as the struggles of all oppressed peoples, by working in our own communities in the rainbow colony to unite our people and help them organize themselves into a powerful force for revolutionary change. We believe, as Malcolm X said, that there can be no black-white unity until there is first black unity—and rainbow unity. Once the oppressed colonies in Amerika and throughout the imperialist empire achieve internal unity, we can unite with each other as *whole peoples* in a New World Liberation Front to bring about the end of imperialist exploitation and control and the beginning of a whole new era in human history—the creation of an inter-communal Rainbow society based on self-determination for all peoples and the total interdependence of the whole of humanity on this planet.

All Power to the People!

Rainbow Power to the People of the Future!

Long Live the Black Panther Party and its Central Committee!

Let It Crow! Let It Grow!

—*Central Committee, Rainbow People's Party, June 1, 1971*

THE LESSONS OF JULY 23: THE TRANSFORMATION OF A REVOLUTIONARY CULTURE

A year ago today Pun Plamondon, Skip Taube, and Jack Forrest were captured by the mother-country police forces outside of St. Ignace, Michigan, on their way to an Upper Peninsula hideout where Pun had planned to secrete himself from the FBI. At that time brother Pun, Minister of Defense of the White Panther Party, had been underground for over nine months as a fugitive from U.S. just-us after being indicted by a Detroit grand jury on October 8, 1969 and charged with bombing the CIA's Ann Arbor recruiting office the previous year. He was also charged with "conspiring" with Chairman John Sinclair and brother Jack Forrest to bomb the CIA office. Pun has been held in various county jails—including nine months on the maximum security ward of the Wayne County Jail—under $100,000 bond (recently reduced to $50,000 after the U.S. government postponed the CIA Conspiracy Trial indefinitely), and Skip and Jack have been sentenced to 5-year sentences in the federal penitentiary system for "aiding and abetting a federal fugitive." Skip is in the federal prison at Sandstone, Minnesota; Jack is in another prison in El Reno, Oklahoma.

Up!, photo by David Fenton

The July 23rd debacle was a major turning point in the history of our party—it marked the end of one stage of our development and the beginning of our present era, which was given further definition by the dissolution of the White Panther Party and the founding of the Rainbow People's Party on May 1, 1971. Since this event had such a profound effect on us, we want to try to explain the changes it put us through and what we understand as the significance of those changes in terms of the future of our struggle for the liberation of the rainbow colony and the triumph of the life culture over the death culture. In order to do this we have to go back to the beginning of our history as an organization to put the events of the past year in their proper context.

ARTISTS' WORKSHOP

We were first organized as the Artists' Workshop on November 1, 1964 when John Sinclair, Magdalene Arndt (Leni Sinclair), and 14 other poets, musicians, photographers, filmmakers, painters, actors, composers and heads came together to deal with their problems collectively. The Workshop was established as a community center for the small hip community in Detroit, and for two years we produced our own free concerts and poetry readings, exhibitions, film screenings, books and magazines; we organized a free school (later the Free University of Detroit) and a cooperative housing project through which we controlled six houses and two storefronts for the people who worked in the Artists' Workshop community. Our basic principle was self-reliance and self-determination for hip people, and the Workshop community was no more than our theory of self-reliance put into active practice.

During this first stage of our development we wrongly believed that we could "drop out" of Amerikan society and "do our own thing" without bothering anyone else. We felt that the death culture was already dying and would soon collapse under the weight of its own contradictions, and we saw ourselves as building the new order which would replace the death culture within the very shell of the dying system. But even from the beginning we were faced with a contradiction of our own: even though we didn't want to have anything to do with the established order, it wouldn't leave us alone. Police agents were sent in to infiltrate and cripple our tiny movement for self-determination by ripping off its prime mover—John Sinclair—and terrorizing the rest of our people. These agents took advantage of our openness and idealism by begging to be turned on to our sacraments, marijuana in particular, and then arresting us for violations of the state narcotics laws.

Our failure during that period to create true collective organizational forms for ourselves resulted in the disintegration of the Artists' Workshop when John Sinclair was imprisoned in the Detroit House of Correction on February 24, 1966; Leni Sinclair was left with the whole burden of maintaining the Workshop's shaky economic foundation, most of the people who had been involved in the project left Detroit in pursuit of their own individual inter-

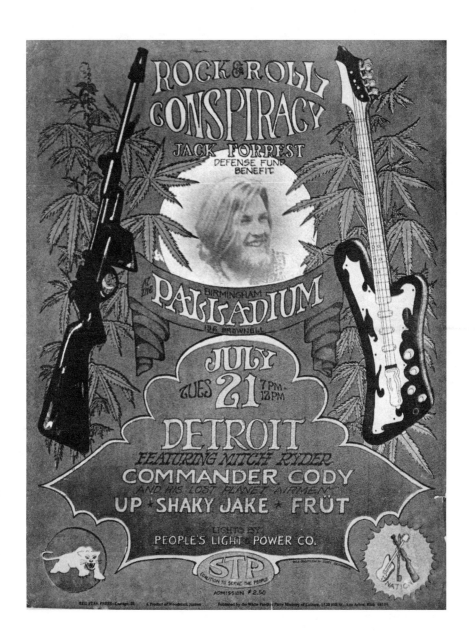

Citizen Sinclair and squares with White Panther donation

ests, and the blossoming operation shrunk back to the Artists' Workshop Press and the two storefronts in which it was housed.

When John got out of jail in August of 1966 he and Leni started all over again, drawing new people into the hip self-determination movement and expanding its scope to try to deal with the needs of the hordes of teenage "hippies" who were exploding onto the scene in greater numbers every week. The hip community was still minuscule—the first year's dances at the Grande Ballroom, which replaced the Artists' Workshop as the focal point of the community, averaged maybe 300 people a night—but it was constantly growing as more young brothers and sisters dug how beautiful it was and started deserting the suburban wastelands they had been trapped in. By this time the nucleus of an alternative social order which had been previously formalized only by the Artists' Workshop had grown to include the Grande Ballroom, the *Fifth Estate* newspaper, Mixed Media, the complex of stores and services on Plum Street, a growing number of high-energy rock & roll bands and light shows, and a proliferation of communes of spaced-out freeks. None of this had existed back in 1964, and the established power structure was flipping out—something had to be done to stop this epidemic of long-haired dope-smoking rock & roll maniacs before the hippies could organize themselves and realize their collective power.

GREAT DOPE RAID

On January 24, 1967 the police, under the direction of Mayor Jerome Cavanaugh and Police Commissioner Ray Girardin (who both made personal appearances at the scene of the crime), mounted a desperate full-scale attack on the hip community in Detroit with a massive "dope raid" aimed specifically at the Artists' Workshop and the people who were working to build it back up. This time both John and Leni Sinclair were arrested, along with 54 other brothers and sisters in the Warren-Forest neighborhood—including a rock & roll band, a number of poets and musicians, the Magic Veil Light Show, most of the staff of LEMAR (Legalize Marijuana) and *Guerrilla* newspaper, and several hip crafts-people who had shops on Plum Street. It wasn't just a bunch of freeks rounded up at random—the "Great Dope Raid" was aimed precisely at the people who worked at the center of the hip community, and it was staged precisely as an act of terrorism rather than as an attempt at "curbing the drug traffic" in the city. Of the 56 people who were arrested that night at the Workshop, the Castle (a great old housing center which had been the center of the Workshop's cooperative housing project and which was at the time a headquarters for four separate communes of freeks), and two or three other communes in the neighborhood, 43 were released in the morning without charges and the rest of the victims—with the exception of John Sinclair—were eventually released on probation. Leni Sinclair fought her case and beat it in court, Ralph Greenwood jumped bond, went underground, and eventually committed suicide, and Ron Frankenburger of the Magic Veil Light Show fled to California, while John Sinclair took this opportunity to challenge the constitu-

tionality of the Michigan marijuana statutes and ended up in the penitentiary two and a half years later.

The January 24th raid was another major turning point for the Workshop and the whole community—a lot of people were completely terrified and went back to their safer former life in the suburbs, but the people who held fast, after a shaky period of total paranoia, began to understand that the only solution was to organize ourselves so we could deal with shit like this while continuing to build up our alternative social order. The growing repression only strengthened our will to resist and to fight back more effectively, and it forced us to begin to re-examine the premises upon which our movement had been based. We saw that it would be impossible to simply "drop out" without protecting our rear at the same time, and we started the first organized Legal Self-Defense group, under the auspices of LEMAR, after the January 24th raid.

TRANS-LOVE ENERGIES

The major result of the raid, however, was the formation of Trans-Love Energies, which was an extension of the Artists' Workshop and the interim group called the 1967 Steering Committee, formed at the beginning of January by John Sinclair and Gary Grimshaw, Emil Bacilla, Rob Tyner of the MC-5, Allen Van Newkirk of *Guerrilla* newspaper, and Jim Semark of the Workshop. Trans-Love began as an umbrella coalition of all the active elements in the hip community—the

Workshop, LEMAR, *Guerrilla*, the *Fifth Estate*, Mixed Media, the Magic Veil Light Show, people from the Plum Street stores, the MC-5, Billy C. and the Sunshine, and individual poster artists, musicians, poets, filmmakers, photographers, printers, craftspeople and artisans from the community. There was no organizational structure whatsoever—the Workshop people provided headquarters and staff for the collective, meetings were held from time to time to plan specific community activities, and a Trans-Love newspaper (the *Warren-Forest Sun*, forerunner of this newspaper) was started by Sinclair and Grimshaw to promote the work of the organization and pull the community closer together, but once more the same mistake was made as had been committed by the Artists' Workshop's organizers: no permanent structural form was created to make sure that the organization could grow into a real alternative social institution capable of serving the long-range as well as the immediate needs of our people. A small minority of the "members" of Trans-Love Energies made all the decisions and tried to execute them without drawing everyone else into the process and making servants of the people out of all the brothers and sisters who wanted to work in the interest of the community.

Still, Trans-Love was a great step forward, and the staff collective carried out a lot of important programs under the Trans-Love banner during the spring and summer of 1967. We put out the *Sun*, tried to put together a cooperative booking agency for the bands that related to what was happening, started a phone message center, put out a daily mimeographed news bulletin for a while, turned the Workshop into a 24-hour-a-day community center and crashpad, started a free store, tried to organize a free ride service for people who had to get around town, provided rehearsal space for bands who didn't have a place to work out, sponsored benefits to raise money for the Bail Fund, directed people who got busted to attorneys and bondsmen and sometimes posted bond for them, started the Psychedelic Rangers as a "peace force" for free outdoor gatherings like the Belle Isle Love-In of April 30th which we sponsored and organized, and even tried to open a people's ballroom under the direct control of the community as an alternative to the Grande, which had begun to deteriorate into a big-name pop business showplace instead of a spaced-out community center. And during the Detroit Uprising which started July 23rd, 1967, we distributed free food and clothes to poor black and white people who didn't have anything to eat after all the neighborhood stores had been looted and burned down.

During this period Pun Plamondon, Genie Johnson (Plamondon), and Dave Sinclair joined the Trans-Love community workers. This was the famous "Summer of Love," and all of us were filled with great LSD-driven visions of the imminent spiritual rebirth of America and the collapse of the dying order. When the Detroit Uprising jumped off we thought the beginning of the end had arrived, and we were busy planning for the "post-revolutionary construction" which would start with the victory of the insurrection. But that

Federal building, Detroit, 1970

fantasy ended with the brutal suppression of the slave revolt in the streets and the gun-butts of the National Guard and U.S. Army troops who beat our door down and threatened to shoot all of us on the spot. The Summer of Love came to a premature end in Detroit on the 1st of August—the dynamite acid which had been blowing the minds of thousands of hippies started to turn into speed, our dreams of instant Utopia were smashed to smithereens, and the focal point of our work gradually shifted to the rock & roll arena when we took in the MC-5 and started building them into a powerful propaganda weapon for the "cultural revolution" in Michigan.

MC-5

By the fall of 1967 we were working full-time with the MC-5 and the Up (who had just got together then) and made another attempt to influence the direction of the Grande Ballroom

as a real community center, since our attempt at establishing an alternative to it had proved premature. The Trans-Love commune moved over to the corner of 2nd and Forest in Detroit, turning the old Workshop over to the 5 so they would have a place to practice regularly, and we opened a community information center in our new quarters. We also set up another center in the Grande itself and took over the light show there. We had seen that the "revolution" wasn't going to happen overnight, and our new plan was to commit ourselves to making the MC-5 into a major influence on young people as well as an economic power which would enable us to get enough seed capital so we could fund long-range self-determination programs under our own control. By building the bands into super-popular forces in the music industry we felt we could gain entrance into radio, television, the recording industry, and big entertainment palaces where we could reach more and more of our brothers and sisters with our "total assault on the culture" message while at the same time pulling in enough money eventually to create our own record company, buy printing presses and other means of production and even radio stations which we could operate collectively in the interests of the people. This program would also allow us to support ourselves and expand our operation so we could more effectively serve the people.

We put everything into this effort through the winter of 1967 and the spring and summer of 1968, when we began to run into heavy opposition from the police and other authorities.

We left Detroit for Ann Arbor in May of 1968 because the police harassment of our headquarters was threatening our continued existence there, and soon after that Pun and Grimshaw were arrested by Traverse City police on a phony marijuana charge. Pun was held in the Traverse County jail for almost three months under $20,000 bond, and Grimshaw fled the state to go underground for two years. At the same time the MC-5 started getting hassled by police at almost every gig they were playing around Detroit and Michigan, taking arrests for playing free music in West Park in Ann Arbor and for "assaulting a police officer" in Oakland County when John Sinclair and Fred Smith got beat up by a bunch of storm troopers at a teen club there. It was becoming clearer than ever that the established order was not going to stand by and let us carry out our program without a fight, and we found ourselves forced to fight back against the increasing repression of ourselves and our people every time we turned around. Our illusions of a "cultural revolution" without any need of armed struggle or other political measures were finally smashed completely when we went to Chicago in August to take part in the Festival of Life with the Yippies and just barely managed to escape from Lincoln Park without getting our heads—and more important, all our equipment—smashed by the Chicago police.

WHITE PANTHER PARTY

We had also come under the powerful influence of the Black Panther Party

Up! in studio, photo by David Fenton

during that summer, and when Pun was finally sprung from jail on bond he was excited about creating a similar organization for the youth community, which we would call the White Panther Party. The WPP was formed on November 1, 1968, the day after we recorded the MC-5's first album at the Grande Ballroom, with the primary purpose of trying to put the "cultural revolution" into an explicitly political context by merging the "total assault on the culture" program of rock & roll, dope, and fucking in the streets with armed self-defense and what Eldridge Cleaver and Huey P. Newton called the "mother-country radical movement." We still considered our major function to be mass propagandists for the "revolution," and with a major record album and a projected series of national tours for the MC-5 we were now able to multiply our effect tremendously.

Skip Taube and Jack Forrest entered our collective at this time, too, each of them bringing his movement experience and rhetoric to our total assault program and heightening the intensity of our rap, which had been raised to a whole new level of militancy by the anti-repression rants of John and Pun. Skip had been active in Ann Arbor SDS with Diana Oughton and Bill Ayres (later among the founders of Weatherman), and Jack had organized a Yippie collective in Detroit after working with SDS there (he was the first White Panther recruit in Detroit when we formed the WPP). Their movement background combined with the increasing influence of the Black Panther Party and the unprecedented police repression we were drawing to push

our whole approach farther and farther to the left, toward the general hysteria and frenzy which was driving the former civil-rights/peace movement into the streets with rocks and bottles instead of protest signs after the Chicago stomp scene.

The problem with this approach, which soon overshadowed the constructive work we had been doing, was that it was mounted out of simple frustration and rage without much thought for its consequences. We had been pushed to the point where we just *reacted* against the forces that were messing us over, and the harder they pushed the more frantic our reactions became. We started threatening the government with all kinds of ridiculous militant rhetoric which we could not possibly back up, and the government of course took us at our word: when we said we would "smash the state" and "off the pigs" they took us very seriously indeed and moved against us in ways that would insure our elimination as any sort of threat to their existence. This would only piss us off even more, and our rhetoric would heat up another notch, which would in turn increase the repression against us. We were caught up in a mindless spiral of empty threats and very real repression from which it seemed impossible to escape, and to add to the problem our constant woofing and screaming helped alienate our people from us, probably because they could easily see that we were just getting what we were asking for: plenty of trouble and unnecessary grief, which they didn't want any part of.

This spiral reached an early peak in the summer of 1969, when John

Sinclair was first convicted in Oakland County of assaulting a police officer after he blatantly challenged the police to lock him up in a television news interview. Then he went to trial on the January 24th marijuana ruse in July, 1969, and ended up being dragged out of the courtroom while hollering at the judge and making insane threats to narcotics officers which weren't even meant to be carried out—just plain woofing pure and simple. He was acting out of a warped sense of "politics" which said that it was "revolutionary" to talk real bad and come on super-defiant, expecting the power structure to run away in fear and trembling, but the real effect was of course just the opposite, and it cost him the opportunity to remain free on appeal bond while his conviction was being appealed.

THE CIA CONSPIRACY

The worst part about this kind of reactionary behavior was that it influenced not only the rest of us, but a lot of our sisters and brothers who related to what we were doing, and this only made matters worse instead of better. After John was locked up Pun, Skip, Jack, and most of the rest of us carried on the same approach in our public work, and those of us who didn't really feel right about it didn't speak up in opposition because we respected our brothers' judgment and had to back them up in the face of all the heat they were drawing. Pun took John's place as the major spokesman for the WPP, and his frustration at the ripoff of his ace comrade only increased the

intensity of his militancy, as it did to the rest of us.

On October 8, 1969, with John in Marquette Prison, Grimshaw still underground, Pun facing marijuana charges in three states, Genie and Leni with a marijuana charge in New Jersey (they got busted for possession on their way back from Woodstock), Skip with various misdemeanor beefs against him, and a general feeling of impending doom permeating our collective consciousness, a federal grand jury in Detroit handed down an indictment charging John, Pun and Jack Forrest with conspiring to blow up the Ann Arbor CIA office, and Pun with actually blowing the place up over a year before. Pun immediately split when he heard the news over the radio, choosing to "go underground" even though he could have stayed around to be arraigned and freed on bond. The underground mystique was very big at that time, and the government won another victory over us by virtue of our ignorance and our desire to be as "revolutionary" as everybody else. Weatherman had just been formed that summer, the Chicago Conspiracy Trial was going on, the Days of Rage started that same day, and it was like there was a big contest on the "left" to see who was the "most revolutionary." The Black Panther Party had contributed to this situation throughout 1969 by stressing that it was the "vanguard of the revolution" because so many of its members had been killed, forced into exile, or locked up in jails and penitentiaries, and the "mother country radicals" (including ourselves) seemed to feel that the way we could "prove

Top: Trans-Love Energies, photo by Leni Sinclair;
bottom: Leni Sinclair and Genie Plamondon

Top: CIA conspiracy defense team; bottom: Genie and Pun Plamondon, photos by Leni Sinclair

ourselves as revolutionaries" was to get beat up, killed, locked up, or indicted by the government for various forms of violent activity.

So Pun went underground and Skip took his place as the most prominent member of the party, continuing the policy of woofing and hollering at the "pigs" that had been established by John and Pun. Our positive community organizing and service programs all disintegrated as all of our energies were taken up with trying to get our comrades out of prison or back from underground and with trying to stay out of jail ourselves. Nothing seemed to be working out right—we could barely support ourselves and pay the rent on our house, we weren't having much success in gaining the support of the people we professed to be "serving" with our work, and we just got more and more frustrated. But we kept on following the same approach to "the revolution," pushing our super-militant line and even trying to spread what little "influence" we had into more and more areas of the country. John was dreaming up all kinds of grandiose schemes from prison for us to carry out, and Pun was constantly issuing statements from underground which exhorted people to "make the revolution" and "raise the level of the struggle in the mother country." He persistently flaunted the FBI with their inability to capture him, which they rewarded by putting him on their infamous "Ten Most Wanted List"—Pun was advertised by the government as "the first white radical" to gain that distinction, and we were all deeply honored by this achievement.

JULY 23 BUST

Pun had been safely in exile for a while, but he was desperate to come back to the "mother country" and "make the revolution in the belly of the beast." Without contacting anyone in advance he suddenly reappeared in the vicinity of Michigan and made contact with some people in the party, who started to make arrangements to "aid and abet" their closest comrade. During this whole period, from the beginning of the WPP to the summer of 1970, we had never managed to get ourselves together enough to build a collective leadership structure for our "party," and most if not all of the most important decisions of our "organization" were made individually and spontaneously with little or no thought of the consequences of those decisions. That went for John's behavior in the courtroom as well as Pun's decision to go underground, his decision to come back to Michigan, and his, Skip's and Jack's decision to pull what turned into the July 23rd caper. In effect we were all just running around like a bunch of maniacs running our mouths and begging for trouble, and we didn't take into regard the consequences of our actions on our sisters and brothers in the WPP or, more importantly, all our people in the community at large. We felt real "revolutionary," but we weren't doing anything for anybody at all—except the government, which should have been *paying* us for doing what we were doing. But we couldn't understand that quite yet.

The July 23rd caper went like this: Skip had apparently arranged a hideout for Pun in the Upper Peninsula of Michigan, and he and Jack Forrest borrowed a van to carry Pun up there with some supplies to hold him for a while. They jumped in the van and drove through the middle of Michigan in the middle of day, stopping along the way to pick up a few beers just as if they were a bunch of college kids on their way to the beach. Their utter lack of discipline and simple common sense cost them their freedom when they were stopped by a state police cruiser after dumping some empty beer cans by the side of the road, and their capture threw the rest of us into a panic. Pun was put under a $100,000 cash bond, and Skip and Jack under $30,000 bonds which were impossible for us to raise. Besides, they had been caught dead in the act and we could see no way to beat their cases, so Skip and Jack pled guilty to one 5-year charge and had two others dropped in return. They were given the maximum sentence—5 flat—and railroaded off to the penitentiary.

The total *senselessness* of what had happened was what hit us the hardest—it began to dawn on all of us that we had just been stumbling along doing whatever popped into our heads without regard for either the personal or political consequences of our actions, and that something had to be done about it *immediately* if we wanted to have any future effectiveness, let alone survive. John as usual heard the news about the capture over the radio in Marquette and he *flipped out,* kicking off what proved to be nine months of intensive discussion of our whole situation with an attack on Pun and

Skip and Jack as crazed individualists who were living in a fantasy world of their own. This was typical of the kind of operation we had at the time, and it started things off on a bad note, but within two months the early antagonisms had cooled down and all of us were finally beginning to discuss our problems and to seek collective solutions to them.

CRITICISM & SELF-CRITICISM

The early antagonism John expressed over the incident made it hard for the real issues to come to the surface. The whole discussion was carried on in terms of personalities rather than issues at first, and it took us a while to see that it wasn't about personalities but about political contradictions that had been building under the surface for a long time. Once we got that straight we were able to start progressing more rapidly toward a solution, but it still took us months to arrive at a harmonious synthesis.

John's imprisonment gave him time to do a lot of studying, primarily of political theory and history, and he was the first of us to realize that we had not been "revolutionaries" at all but merely *rebels* acting more out of our frustration and anger than anything else. John's antagonistic position at the beginning complicated things more than they should've been, but we finally realized that the only way to settle anything was by using the revolutionary principle of "unity-criticism-unity," which means that people have to see that their interests are basically the same even though they may have serious disagreements on specific issues, and work together from a base of unity of purpose to struggle out their opposing views in order to arrive at a new unity. This is what saved us in the end—all the people who really did have the same basic interests made up their minds to stay and struggle out our contradictions scientifically, taking them out of the realm of personalities and emotions and putting the discussion on the level of issues and political policies. This was all new to us, but we kept at it and finally got it all together.

By late fall we were still struggling, and we still couldn't agree on what to do—John had proposed that we change our name to the Woodstock People's Party, and everybody else came to agree that we had to get rid of the name White Panthers because it didn't fit anymore. But we could not all agree on that name, so we decided to postpone the discussion of the name on the 1st of December until the end of the upcoming CIA Conspiracy Trial, and to maintain our unity at least until after the trial, when we would be able to take up the ideological struggle (battle of ideas) again.

RAINBOW PEOPLE'S PARTY

It was just at this time that Pun and Genie came up with the name Rainbow People's Party and laid it on the table for discussion as an alternative to the name Woodstock. Then John was taken to the Wayne County jail to prepare for the CIA Trial, and he and Pun had a chance to rap a few times for the first time in almost two years. They found that they were in almost total agreement, and Pun convinced John that the Rainbow image was even better for describing our culture than the Woodstock myth.

All in all the whole process was really dynamic, and we all learned an incredible amount from it. We worked out a lot of personal contradictions between different individuals in the process, and we managed to bring most of our problems right into the open so we could settle them. Everybody learned from everybody else, and by April we had all come to the same conclusion, which had seemed impossible even two months before. So on May 1 we announced the formation of The Rainbow People's Party, and published the first issue of the *Ann Arbor Sun*. The different ideas that people had were discussed in a lot of detail and were either accepted and developed to a higher level, or rejected in whole or in part. We really learned that we could solve our problems by discussing them openly instead of keeping our disagreements and resentments and shit to ourselves, going around talking behind people's backs, forming cliques and factions, etc. It blew our minds!

Now we still aren't as together as we want to be, and we still have not accomplished most of the goals we set for ourselves, but we've discovered the correct methods of thinking and methods of work and, what's more important, we're *using* them in our daily activity. We know we have a long way to go, but we know from our experience in this heavy ideological struggle that we *can* do it if we work together and follow the correct procedures. A lot of people believe that freeks are incapable of organizing themselves, that our people can't get ourselves together and become a strong revolutionary force so we can have some control over our own destinies in this country, but we know better now. We thought we were going to fall apart ourselves, but we managed to pull ourselves together by a reaffirmation of our faith in each other and in the principles we have come to believe in over the years. We're starting to learn from our mistakes and turn them into advantages, and that's a great step forward.

JULY 23

A year has passed since the July 23rd scene and we feel like we're a whole different people from what we were a year ago. We're still together—in fact we're more together now than we've ever been—and we're doing a lot better work than ever. We don't know what will happen this July 23rd. Since 1967 July 23rd has been a big day for us, which is only natural because we've been relating ourselves to the Sun as our symbol since then, and this day is the first day of Leo (the Sun sign). The Detroit uprising of July 23rd, 1967 brought us out of our hippie bag and helped us better understand the relation of our culture to the black liberation movement; on July 23rd, 1968 John Sinclair and Fred Smith got beat up at a MC-5 job in Oakland County, which made us see how it wasn't

enough just to play the music and hope for the best—that led directly to the founding of the White Panther Party; John was sent to the penitentiary on July 25th, 1969, which made it possible for him to start his study and thus for all of us to come to a better understanding of our political role in the world-wide liberation movement; and Pun, Jack and Skip got captured on July 23rd, 1970, which made us start getting ourselves together through ideological struggle and change our whole approach to the problem of liberating the rainbow colony. Now we're ready to move on—we have come to welcome calamity in its various forms, because it constantly pushes us forward to new levels of understanding and activity. We now understand that our lives progress in cycles just like the Sun, constantly moving, constantly changing, constantly becoming brighter and purer. We can never forget the lessons of July 23rd, and we hope that you can understand us a little better now.

Long live the Spirit of the Sun!

Rainbow Power to the People of the Future!!

—Central Committee,
Rainbow People's Party
John Sinclair, Chairman
Leni Sinclair
Gary Grimshaw
Pun Plamondon
Genie Plamondon
Frank Bach
Peggy Taube
David Fenton
David Sinclair, Chief of Staff
July 23, 1971

RAINBOW READING & LISTING LIST

ROCK & ROLL

KICK OUT THE JAMS —MC5 (Elektra)

CHEAP THRILLS—Big Brother & the Holding Company (Columbia)

ARE YOU EXPERIENCED?—Jimi Hendrix Experience (Reprise)

SMASH HITS—Jimi Hendrix Experience (Reprise)

FREAK OUT!—Mothers of Invention (MGM)

HIGH TIME—MC5 (Atlantic)

DETROIT—Mitch Ryder (Paramount)

OZONE—Commander Cody and His Lost Planet Airmen (Paramount)

STOOGES—Stooges (Elektra)

FUN HOUSE—Stooges (Elektra)

GRIS-GRIS—Dr. John (Atco)

BABYLON—Dr. John (Atco)

SUN MOON & HERBS —Dr. John (Atco)

BRINGING IT ALL BACK HOME—Bob Dylan (Columbia)

HIGHWAY 61 REVISITED—Bob Dylan (Columbia)

BLONDE ON BLONDE —Bob Dylan (Columbia)

JOHN WESLEY HARDING—Bob Dylan (Columbia)

BEGGARS BANQUET —Rolling Stones (London)

LET IT BLEED—Rolling Stones (London)

STICKY FINGERS—Rolling Stones (Rolling Stones)

REVOLVER—Beatles (Capitol)

SGT. PEPPER'S LONELY HEARTS CLUB BAND— Beatles (Capitol)

BOOGIE WITH CANNED HEAT—Canned Heat (Liberty)

SUNSHINE SUPERMAN—Donovan (Epic)

MY GENERATION— The Who (Decca)

SAFE AS MILK—Captain Beefheart & His Magic Band (Buddah)

THE FUGS (2nd album) —Fugs (ESP-Disk')

WHITE LIGHT/WHITE HEAT—Velvet Underground (MGM)

JEFFERSON AIRPLANE TAKES OFF—Jefferson Airplane (RCA)

VOLUNTEERS—Jefferson Airplane (RCA)

THE GRATEFUL DEAD (1st album)—Grateful Dead (Reprise)

ELECTRIC MUSIC FOR THE MIND AND BODY—Country Joe & the Fish (Vanguard)

LOVE (1st album)— Love (Elektra)

DA CAPO—Love (Elektra)

THE DOORS (1st album)—Doors (Elektra)

FRESH CREAM —Cream (Atco)

WHEELS OF FIRE —Cream (Atco)

BLUESBREAKERS —John Mayall (London)

VINCEBUS ERUPTUM —Blue Cheer (Phillips)

SUNSET—The Rationals (Crewe)

TRAVELLER'S TALE
—SRC (Capitol)

RAMBLIN GAMBLING MAN—Bob Seger (Capitol)

MONGREL—Bob Seger (Capitol)

SURVIVAL—Grand Funk Railroad (Capitol)

E PLURIBUS FUNK
—Grand Funk Railroad (Capitol)

CREEDENCE CLEAR-WATER REVIVAL (1st album)—Creedence Clearwater Revival (Fantasy).

BAYOU COUNTRY
—Creedence Clearwater Revival (Fantasy)

SANDERS' TRUCK STOP
—Ed Sanders (Warner)

SPIRITS KNOWN AND UNKNOWN—Leon Thomas (Flying Dutchman)

EDGAR WINTER'S WHITE TRASH—Edgar Winter (Epic)

LIVE—Johnny Winter And (Columbia)

JOHNNY WINTER (1st album)—Johnny Winter (Columbia)

SLY & THE FAMILY STONE'S GREATEST HITS—Sly & the Family Stone (Epic)

RHYTHM & BLUES

HISTORY OF RHYTHM & BLUES (Volumes 1-4)
—(Atlantic)

PAUL BUTTERFIELD BLUES BAND (1st album)—Paul Butterfield (Elektra)

THE RESURRECTION OF PIGBOY CRABSHAW—Paul Butterfield (Elektra)

J. GEILS BAND—(Atlantic)

ELMORE JAMES
—Elmore James (Bell)

CHUCK BERRY'S GOLD-EN DECADE—Chuck Berry (Chess)

16 GREATEST HITS
—Bo Diddley (Chess)

THE BEST OF MUDDY WATERS—Muddy Waters (Chess)

ELECTRIC MUD—Muddy Waters (Chess)

MOANIN' IN THE MOONLIGHT—Howlin' Wolf (Chess)

THE LONDON SESSIONS
—Howlin' Wolf (Chess)

16 GREATEST HITS (1st edition)—B.B. King (Crown)

JAMES BROWN LIVE AT THE APOLLO VOLUME 1—James Brown (King)

BOBBY BLUE BLAND'S GREATEST HITS—Bobby Blue Bland (Duke)

HOUSE OF THE BLUES—John Lee Hooker (Checker)

URBAN BLUES—John Lee Hooker (ABC)

SERVE YOU RIGHT TO SUFFER—John Lee Hooker (Impulse)

I'M JIMMY REED—Jimmy Reed (Veejay)

THE JIMMY REED STORY—Jimmy Reed (Veejay)

OTIS REDDING IN EUROPE—Otis Redding (Atlantic)

ARETHA'S GOLD—Aretha Franklin (Atlantic)

CHICAGO/THE BLUES/TODAY (3 volumes)—(Vanguard)

DETROIT BLUES—(Blues Classics)

GOLDEN GOODIES (Volumes 2, 3, 6, 7, 12)—(Roulette)

LIGHTNIN' IN NEW YORK—Lightning Hopkins (Candid/Barnaby)

WEST SIDE SOUL—Magic Sam (Delmark)

HOODOO MAN BLUES—Junior Wells (Delmark)

OTIS SPANN IS THE BLUES—Otis Spann (Candid/Barnaby)

THE BEST OF SONNY

Sinclair and Dr. John, photo by David Fenton

BOY WILLIAMSON—Sonny Boy Williamson(Chess)

GREATEST HITS—Little Richard (Speciality)

GREAT JUKEBOX HITS—Hank Ballard & the Midnighters (King)

ALL AROUND THE WORLD—Little Willie John (King)

I PUT A SPELL ON YOU—Screamin' Jay Hawkins (Okeh)

THE BEST OF LITTLE WALTER—Little Walter (Chess)

GREATEST HITS FROM THE BEGINNING—The Miracles (Motown)

GREATEST HITS—The Temptations (Motown)

GREATEST HITS—Martha and the Vandellas (Motown)

GREATEST HITS—Four Tops (Motown)

SEIZE THE TIME—Elaine Brown (Vault)

SPOKEN

DIG—Eldridge Cleaver

MESSAGE TO THE GRASS ROOTS—Malcolm X (Afro-American Broadcasting Co.)

BY ANY MEANS NECESSARY—Malcolm X (Douglas)

THE LAST POETS—The Last Poets (Douglas)

THIS IS MADNESS—The Last Poets (Douglas)

THE SICK HUMOR OF LENNY BRUCE—Lenny Bruce (Fantasy)

WHAT I WAS ARRESTED FOR—Lenny Bruce (Douglas)

I AM NOT A NUT, ELECT ME—Lenny Bruce (Fantasy)

LENNY BRUCE AMERICAN—Lenny Bruce (Fantasy)

BERKELEY CONCERT
—Lenny Bruce (Straight)

AIN'T NO AMBULANC-
ES FOR NO NIGGUHS
TONIGHT—Stanley
Crouch (Flying Dutchman)

SOUL & SO LEDAD
—Angela Davis (Flying
Dutchman)

HOWL & OTHER
POEMS—Allen Ginsberg
(Fantasy)

A NIGHT AT SANTA
RITA—Robert Scheer
(Flying Dutchman)

MURDER AT KENT
STATE—Pete Hamill
(Flying Dutchman)

LORD BUCKLEY'S
HITS—Lord Buckley
(World Pacific)

MASSACRE AT MY
LAI—Pete Hamill
(Flying Dutchman)

NEW BLACK MUSIC

NOTHING IS—Sun Ra
(ESP-Disk')

THE HELIOCENTRIC
WORLDS OF SUN RA
(Volumes 1 & 2)—Sun Ra
(ESP-Disk')

THE MAGIC CITY—Sun
Ra (Saturn Research)

ATLANTIS—Sun Ra
(Saturn Research)

STRANGE STRINGS
—Sun Ra (Saturn Research)

A LOVE SUPREME—
John Coltrane (Impulse)

COLTRANE—John
Coltrane (Impulse)

LIVE AT BIRDLAND
—John Coltrane (Impulse)

MEDITATIONS
—John Coltrane (Impulse)

SELFLESSNESS
—John Coltrane (Impulse)

KULU SE MAMA
—John Coltrane (Impulse)

COSMIC MUSIC—John
Coltrane (Impulse)

UNIT STRUCTURES
—Cecil Taylor Unit
(Blue Note)

INTO THE HOT—
Cecil Taylor & Gil Evans
(Impulse)

JAZZ COMPOSERS OR-
CHESTRA—Jazz Compos-
ers Orchestra (JCOA)

TAUHID—Pharoah
Sanders (Impulse)

KARMA—Pharoah
Sanders (Impulse)

THEMBI—Pharoah
Sanders (Impulse)

FIRE MUSIC—
Archie Shepp (Impulse)

MAMA TOO TIGHT—
Archie Shepp (Impulse)

THE MAGIC OF JUJU—
Archie Shepp (Impulse)

ORNETTE COLEMAN
TOWN HALL
CONCERT—Ornette
Coleman (ESP-Disk')

THIS IS OUR MUSIC—
Ornette Coleman (Atlantic)

ORNETTE ON TENOR—
Ornette Coleman (Atlantic)

FRIENDS & NEIGH-
BORS—Ornette Coleman
(Flying Dutchman)

BELLS—Albert Ayler
(ESP-Disk')

NEW GRASS—Albert
Ayler (Impulse)

THE BLACK SAINT &
THE SINNER LADY—
Charles Mingus (Impulse)

MINGUS PRESENTS
MINGUS—Charles Min-
gus (Candid/Barnaby)

EVOLUTION—Grachan
Moncur (Blue Note)

LET FREEDOM RING—
Jackie McLean (Blue Note)

LIFETIME—Tony Williams
(Blue Note)

OUT TO LUNCH
—Eric Dolphy (Blue Note)

OUT THERE
—Eric Dolphy (Prestige)

IRON MAN
—Eric Dolphy (Douglas)

LIBERATION MUSIC
ORCHESTRA—Charlie
Haden (Impulse)

THE THIRD WORLD
—Gato Barbieri (Flying
Dutchman)

THE MARION BROWN
QUINTET—Marion
Brown (ESP-Disk')

SONG FOR—Joseph
Jarman (Delmark)

AS IF IT WERE THE
SEASONS—Joseph Jarman
(Delmark)

SOUND—Roscoe Mitchell
(Delmark)

LEVELS & DECREES OF
LIGHT—Richard Abrams
(Delmark)

HUMILITY IN THE
LIGHT OF THE
CREATOR—Maurice
McIntyre (Delmark)

NUMBERS 1 & 2—Lester Bowie (Nessa)

CONGLIPTIOUS—Roscoe Mitchell (Nessa)

COMPLETE COMMU-NION—Don Cherry (Blue Note)

SKETCHES OF SPAIN—Miles Davis (Columbia)

KIND OF BLUE—Miles Davis (Columbia)

MILESTONES—Miles Davis (Columbia)

BITCHES BREW—Miles Davis (Columbia)

MILES DAVIS AT THE FILLMORE—MWes Davis (Columbia)

"is"—Chick Corea (Solid State)

PATTI WATERS SINGS—Patti Waters (ESP-Disk')

BLACK WOMAN—Sonny Sharrock (Embryo)

EVERYWHERE—Roswell Rudd (Impulse)

COMPULSION—Andrew Hill (Blue Note)

FRANK WRIGHT TRIO—Frank Wright (ESP-Disk')

BURTON GREENE QUARTET—Burton Greene (ESP-Disk')

WHY NOT—Marion Brown (ESP-Disk')

THE GIANT IS AWAK-ENED—Horace Tapscott (Flying Dutchman)

QUARTET—John Carter/Bobby Bradford (Flying Dutchman)

CONTEMPORARY JAZZ QUINTET—Contemporary Jazz Quintet (Blue Note)

MULTIDIRECTION-AL—Contemporary Jazz Quintet (Blue Note)

BOOKS

GUITAR ARMY—John Sinclair

MUSIC & POLITICS—John Sinclair & Robert Levin

SHOTS—David Fenton

TRIAL—Tom Hayden

WEATHERMAN—edited by Harold Jacobs

GETTING BUSTED—edited by Ross Firestone

THE DRUG BUST—John Dominick

FREE MARIJUANA!—Michael Aldrich

FIRE! Writings from the Underground Press—edited by paul, jon & carol

THE CONSPIRACY—Chicago 8

WE ARE EVERY-WHERE—Jerry Rubin

WOODSTOCK NA-TION—Abbie Hoffman

REVOLUTION FOR THE HELL OF IT—Abbie Hoffman

STEAL THIS BOOK—Abbie Hoffman

DO IT!—Jerry Rubin

THE NEW LEFT: A Documentary History—edited by Massimo Teodori

THE MOVEMENT TOWARD A NEW AMERICA—edited by Mitchell Goodman

WHOLE EARTH CATA-LOG PSYCHEDELIC PRAYERS—Timothy Leary

JAIL NOTES—Timothy Leary

REVOLUTIONARY LETTERS—Diane DiPrima

HOWL & OTHER POEMS—Allen Ginsberg

PLANET NEWS—Allen Ginsberg

NAKED LUNCH—William Burroughs

THE SOFT MACH/NE—William Burroughs

NOVA EXPRESS—William Burroughs

THE JOB—William Burroughs

HUMAN UNIVERSE—Charles Olson

MEAT SCIENCE ES-SAYS—Michael McClure

DARK BROWN—Michael McClure

THE MAXIMUS POEMS—Charles Olson

FOR LOVE—Robert Creeley

THE NEW AMERICAN POETRY 1945-1960—Edited by Donald Allen

PEACE EYE—Ed Sanders

REBELLION & REPRES-SION—Tom Hayden

POT: A HANDBOOK OF MARIJUANA—John Rosevear

ON THE ROAD—Jack Kerouac

THE DHARMA BUMS—Jack Kerouac

John Coltrane and Sinclair, photo by Leni Sinclair

MOUNTAINS & RIVERS WITHOUT END
—Gary Snyder

EARTH HOUSE HOLD
—Gary Snyder

POISONED WHEAT
—Michael McClure

BEEN DOWN SO LONG IT LOOKS LIKE UP TO ME—Richard Farina

V. —Thomas Pynchon

TROUT FISHING IN AMERICA—Richard Brautigan

THE STRANGE ODYSSEY OF HOWARD POW!
—Bill Hutton

A HISTORY OF AMERIKA—Bill Hutton

THE SUN—Jim Semark

ONE FLEW OVER THE CUCKOO'S NEST
—Ken Kesey

THE ELECTRIC KOOL-AID ACID TEST—Tom Wolfe

REALLY THE BLUES
—Mezz Mezzrow

THE AIR-CONDITIONED NIGHTMARE—Henry Miller

THE JOURNAL OF ALBION MOONLIGHT
—Kenneth Patchen

RED FLAG/BLACK FLAG—Patrick Seale & Maureen McConville

SEIZE THE TIME
—Bobby Seale

THE GENIUS OF HUEY P. NEWTON—Huey P. Newton

ESSAYS FROM THE MINISTER OF DEFENSE
—Huey P. Newton

SOUL ON ICE
—Eldridge Cleaver

POST-PRISON WRIT-INGS AND SPEECHES
—Eldridge Cleaver

CONVERSATION WITH ELDRIDGE CLEAVER

PALANTE—Michael Abramson and the Young Lords Party

OUR THING IS DRUM
—Kenny Cockrel & Mike Hamlin

THE POLITICAL THOUGHT OF JAMES FORMAN—James Forman

MALCOLM X SPEAKS

THE AUTOBIOGRAPHY OF MALCOLM X

DIE NIGGER DIE
—H. Rap Brown

STOKELY SPEAKS: BLACK POWER BACK TO PAN-AFRICANISM
—Stokely Carmichael

SOLEDAD BROTHER
—George Jackson

IF THEY COME IN THE MORNING—Angela Davis

THE SPOOK WHO SAT BY THE DOOR—Sam Greenlee

BLUES PEOPLE
—LeRoi Jones

BLACK MUSIC
—LeRoi Jones

FOUR LIVES IN THE BEBOP BUSINESS
—A.B. Spellman

SISTERHOOD IS POWERFUL—Edited by Robin Morgan

THE FEMALE EUNUCH
—Germaine Greer

THE DIALECTIC OF SEX—Shulamith Firestone

THE EMANCIPATION OF WOMEN—V.I. Lenin

DANCE THE EAGLE TO SLEEP—Marge Piercy

WOMEN IN SEXIST SOCIETY—edited by Vivian Gornick & Barbara K. Moran

THE WRETCHED OF THE EARTH
—Frantz Fanon

A DYING COLONIAL-ISM—Frantz Fanon

HANDBOOK OF REVO-LUTIONARY WAR-FARE—Kwame Nkrumah

QUOTATIONS FROM CHAIRMAN MAO TSE-TUNG

LONG LIVE THE VICTORY OF PEOPLE'S WAR—Lin Piao

SELECTED WORKS OF MAO TSE-TUNG (Volumes 1-4)

ON PRACTICE
—Mao Tse-tung

ON CONTRADICTION
—Mao Tse-tung

MAO TSE-TUNG ON LITERATURE & ART

ESSENTIAL WORKS OF LENIN—edited by Henry M. Christman

LEFT-WING COMMU-NISM, AN INFANTILE DISORDER—V.I. Lenin

THE COMMUNIST MANIFESTO—Karl Marx & Frederick Engels

THE ORIGIN OF THE FAMILY, PRIVATE PROPERTY & THE STATE—Frederick Engels

RED STAR OVER CHINA—Edgar Snow

HO CHI MINH ON REVOLUTION—Edited by Bernard B. Fall

PRISON DIARY
—Ho Chi Minh

SELECTED POEMS
—Mao Tse-tung

PEOPLE'S WAR PEOPLE'S ARMY—Vo Nguyen Giap

GUERRILLA WARFARE
—Che Guevara

REMINISCENCES OF THE CUBAN REVOLU-TIONARY WAR
—Che Guevara

VENCEREMOS! SPEECH-ES AND WRITINGS OF CHE GUEVARA—Edited by John Gerassi

FIDEL CASTRO SPEAKS—Edited by Martin Kenner

CASTRO'S CUBA, CUBA'S FIDEL—Lee Lockwood

LISTEN YANKEE!
—C. Wright Mills

THE POWER ELITE
—C. Wright Mills

TEN DAYS THAT SHOOK THE WORLD—John Reed

POLITICAL AND PHILOSOPHIC WORK OF MARX & ENGELS
—Edited by Lewis Feuer

FANSHEN
—William Hinton

THE OTHER SIDE OF THE RIVER—Edgar Snow

REVOLUTION IN THE REVOLUTION
—Regis Debray

DYNAMITE: THE HISTORY OF CLASS VIOLENCE IN AMERICA
—Louis Adamic

THE NEW EMPIRE
—Brooks Adams

THE GREAT FRONTIER—Walter Prescott Webb

THE GUTENBERG GAL-AXY—Marshall McLuhan

UNDERSTANDING ME-DIA—Marshall McLuhan

THE GREENING OF AMERICA—Charles Reich

FUTURE SHOCK
—Alvin Toffler

AN ESSAY ON LIBERA-TION—Herbert Marcuse

THE INDIAN HERITAGE OF AMERICA
—Alvin M. Josephy, Jr.

THE NEW INDIANS
—Stan Steiner

CUSTER DIED FOR YOUR SINS
—Vine Deloria, Jr.

WE SPEAK YOU LIS-TEN—Vine Deloria, Jr.

BURY MY HEART AT WOUNDED KNEE
—Dee Brown

BLACK ELK SPEAKS

THE INVISIBLE GOVERNMENT—David Wise & Thomas B. Ross

THE NARRATIVE OF NAT TURNER

JOHN BROWN
—Frederick Douglass

THE NEW MANDA-RINS—Noam Chomsky

THE RISE AND FALL OF THE 3rd REICH
—William Shirer

THE MASS PSYCHOL-OGY OF FASCISM
—Wilhelm Reich

THE RICH AND THE SUPER-RICH—Frederick Lundberg and

THE TEACHINGS OF DON JUAN—Carlos Castaneda

Guitar Army ©1972, 2007 by John Sinclair
A Process Media Book with Attached CD
Guitar Army CD ©2007 under the names of all participants
ISBN: 978-1-934170-00-7
10 9 8 7 6 5 4 3 2 1

The original 1972 edition of Guitar Army was published by Douglas Book Corporation and was "conceived and coordinated by Leni Sinclair, designed & produced by Gary Grimshaw and released through Rainbow Energies. The title is from the song 'Guitar Army' by Scott Morgan / the Rationals. Most of the writings first appeared in the people's newspapers of Detroit and Ann Arbor: the Fifth Estate, Ann Arbor Sun, Ann Arbor Argus, White Panther News Service, Big Fat / Dance, Creem, University Review, and Music & Politics, a Jazz Press Book, 1971."

"Special thanks to all the people who have helped make this book possible, particularly to Peter Werbe, Ken Kelley, Dave Marsh, Barry Kramer, Peter Steinberger, and W. Rexford Benoit; to the Central Committee and the Central Staff of the Rainbow People's Party (Leni Sinclair, Gary Grimshaw, Pun Plamondon, Genie Plamondon, Frank Bach, Peggy Taube, David Fenton, David Sinclair, Bob & Gary Rasmussen, Ane LaVasseur, Hiawatha Bailey, John Collins, Kathy Kelley, Ann Hoover, Sam Smith, Mike Minnich, Jeannie Walsh and Craig Blazier); to my attorneys, Chuck Ravitz, Arthur Kinoy, Bill Kunstler, Lenny Weinglass, Neal Bush, Marc Stickgold, Randy Karfonta, Kenneth V. Cockrel, Ken Mogul, Gerry Schwartzbach, and especially to comrade Buck Davis; to my editor and co-conspirator Ross Firestone; to my mother and father; to Jerry Lubin & Barbara Holliday on the radio; to Ed Sanders, who invented the language; to John & Yoko; and especially to my rainbow sisters in Syracuse, Liz Gaynes & Marion Roth—thank you!"

The Process Media publishers wish to thank Al Campbell for turning us on to John Sinclair's world. And to Michael Simmons, Wayne and Margaret Kramer, Leni Sinclair, Lely Constantinople, Kevin Coogan, David Fenton, James Semark, and most of all, John Sinclair for enabling us to do this new edition of a classic book.

Process Media
PO Box 39910
Los Angeles, CA 90039
www.processmediainc.com   Designed by Bill Smith

CD CREDITS

[01] Allen Ginsberg: "Prayer For John Sinclair" (Rainbow Records 45) Produced by Allen Ginsberg. Recorded in New York City, Fall 1971.

[02] MC5: "Motor City Is Burning" (Ice Pick Slim, Alive/Total Energy NRCD 0008) Produced by John Sinclair. Recorded at the Grande Ballroom, Detroit, October 30-31, 1968.

[03] John Sinclair: "Homage to John Coltrane" (Detroit Artists Workshop 40th Anniversary Collection) Produced by James Semark, Cary Loren & John Sinclair. Recorded at the Detroit Artists Workshop, November 22, 1964.

[04] Artists Workshop Music Ensemble: "The Pimp's Vision" (previously unissued) Produced by John Sinclair. Recorded at Lower Deroy Auditorium, WSU, Detroit, November 20, 1965.

[05] Gary Grimshaw: "Learning the Language" (Music Is Revolution) Produced by Cary Loren. Recorded at White Panther Party Central Committee Meeting, Ann Arbor, circa 1968-69.

[06] Rationals: "Guitar Army" (Genesis Records 45) Produced by The Rationals. Recorded in Detroit, 1969.

[07] White Panther Party Central Committee: "Music Is a Revolutionary Force" (Music Is Revolution) Produced by Cary Loren. Recorded at WPP Central Committee Meeting, Ann Arbor, circa 1968-69.

[08] Up: "Just Like an Aborigine" (SunDance Records 45) Produced by David Sinclair & The Up. Recorded in Ypsilanti, MI, 1969.

[09] White Panther Party Central Committee: "Black Panthers & White Panthers" (Music Is Revolution) Produced by Cary Loren. Recorded at WPP Central Committee Meeting, Ann Arbor, circa 1968-69.

[10] John Sinclair: "The Poem for Warner Stringfellow" (excerpt) (Music Is Revolution) Produced by Cary Loren. (Place and date of recording unknown)

[11] MC5: "Looking at You" (A-Square 45 #333) Produced by John Sinclair. Recorded at United Sound Studio, Detroit, January 1968.

[12] Bobby Seale: "Prison Interview" (Music Is Revolution) Produced by Cary Loren. (Place and date of recording unknown.)

[13] Uprising: "Long Hard Road" (45 rpm single issued on Motor City's Burnin, Alive/Total Energy NRCD 3014). (Additional information unknown.)

[14] James Semark: "John Coltrane Rhythm Ballad for All" (Detroit Artists Workshop 40th Anniversary Collection). Produced by James Semark, Cary Loren & John Sinclair. Recorded at the Detroit Artists Workshop, November 22, 1964

[15] John Sinclair: "I Wanna Freakize 'Em" (Music Is Revolution) Produced by Cary Loren. Recorded at WPP Central Committee Meeting, Ann Arbor, circa 1968-69.

[16] Up: "Free John Now" (Rainbow Records 45) Produced by David Sinclair & The Up. Recorded in Ann Arbor, November 1971.

[17] John Sinclair & Wayne Kramer: "friday the 13th" (Alive Records 10" LP) Produced by Wayne Kramer & John Sinclair. Recorded in Nashville & New Orleans, 1994.

Note: The Music Is Revolution CD was produced by Cary Loren from recorded materials in the John & Leni Sinclair Collection at the Bentley Historical Library, University of Michigan, Ann Arbor, Michigan.

Mastered by Michael Belfer at David Bianco Recorders, North Hollywood, CA.

GUITAR ARMY [CD]

[01] **Allen Ginsberg:** Prayer for John Sinclair 3:22

[02] **MC5:** Motor City is Burning 4:23

[03] **John Sinclair:** Homage to John Coltrane 3:56

[04] **Artists Workshop Music Ensemble:** The Pimp's Vision 6:07

[05] **Gary Grimshaw:** Learning the Language 0:27

[06] **Rationals:** Guitar Army 2:47

[07] **WPP Central Committee:** Music is a Revolutionary Force 3:39

[08] **UP!:** Just Like an Aborigine 4:08

[09] **WPP Central Committee:** Black Panthers & White Panthers 2:59

[10] **John Sinclair:** Poem for Warner Stringfellow 6:27

[11] **MC5:** Looking at You 2:49

[12] **Bobby Seale:** Prison Interview 5:49

[13] **Uprising:** Long Hard Road 5:54

[14] **James Semark:** John Coltrane Rhythm Ballad for All 8:55

[15] **John Sinclair:** I Wanna Freakize 'Em 1:05

[16] **UP!:** Free John Now 4:02

[17] **John Sinclair & Wayne Kramer:** Friday the 13th 3:46